GEAR UP, MISHAPS DOWN

GEAR UP, MISHAPS DOWN
THE EVOLUTION OF NAVAL AVIATION SAFETY, 1950–2000

Vice Adm. Robert F. Dunn, USN (Ret.)

Naval Institute Press
Annapolis, Maryland

This book was brought to publication with the generous assistance of the Naval Historical Foundation.

Naval Institute Press
291 Wood Road
Annapolis, MD 21402

© 2017 by Robert F. Dunn

All rights reserved. No part of this book may be reproduced or utilized in any form or by any means, electronic or mechanical, including photocopying and recording, or by any information storage and retrieval system, without permission in writing from the publisher.

First Naval Institute Press paperback edition published in 2024.
ISBN: 978-1-68247-947-6 (paperback)

The Library of Congress has cataloged the hardcover edition as follows:
Names: Dunn, Robert F., 1928- author.
Title: Gear up, mishaps down : the evolution of naval aviation safety, 1950-2000 / Robert F. Dunn, Vice Admiral, U.S. Navy (Retired).
Other titles: Evolution of naval aviation safety, 1950-2000
Description: Annapolis, MD : Naval Institute Press, [2017] | Includes bibliographical references and index.
Identifiers: LCCN 2016040838 (print) | LCCN 2016043875 (ebook) | ISBN 9781682470053 (hardcover : alk. paper) | ISBN 9781682470220 (epub) | ISBN 9781682470220 (ePDF) | ISBN 9781682470220 (mobi)
Subjects: LCSH: United States. Navy—Aviation—Safety measures. | United States. Navy—Aviation—History—20th century.
Classification: LCC VG93 .A79 2017 (print) | LCC VG93 (ebook) | DDC 363.11/935994097309045—dc23
LC record available at https://lccn.loc.gov/2016040838

♾ Print editions meet the requirements of ANSI/NISO z39.48-1992 (Permanence of Paper).
Printed in the United States of America.

9 8 7 6 5 4 3 2 1

Contents

	List of Illustrations	VII
	Foreword by David M. North	IX
PREFACE	A Most Remarkable Story	XI
CHAPTER 1	Black as Midnight	1
CHAPTER 2	Difficult Days: A Soaring Mishap Rate	5
CHAPTER 3	The Competition: American Aviation Overall	15
CHAPTER 4	Beginning to Get It Right	20
CHAPTER 5	Naval Aviation's Transition to Jets	29
CHAPTER 6	Aircraft Carriers: Changes and Modifications	33
CHAPTER 7	Beyond Jets and Aircraft Carriers	43
CHAPTER 8	The Catalyst for Improvement: The Naval Safety Center	46
CHAPTER 9	Six Amazing Years: RAGs, NATOPS, and More	58
CHAPTER 10	The Doc: Aerospace Medicine—Flight Surgeons and More	70
CHAPTER 11	Discovering Human Factors	84
CHAPTER 12	Maintenance and Supply	91
CHAPTER 13	The Underappreciated: Aircraft, Aircraft Systems, and Design Safety	103
CHAPTER 14	Making Believe: Simulators and Synthetic Trainers	113
CHAPTER 15	On to the Twenty-First Century: ORM, CRM, and Culture Workshops	125
CHAPTER 16	Success: Summary and Conclusions	133
AFTERWORD		137
APPENDIX 1	Marine Aviation	139
APPENDIX 2	Naval Safety Center Yearly Major Mishap Statistics	141
APPENDIX 3	Navy and Marine Accident Reporting Classifications	145
APPENDIX 4	Aviation-Oriented Safety Center Publications	147
APPENDIX 5	Principal Carrier Alterations	149
APPENDIX 6	Typical Straight-Deck Carrier Landing Pattern	151
	Chronology	153
	Notes	163
	Glossary	179
	Bibliography	185
	Index	195

Illustrations

Photos

F2H Phantoms	1
LSO at night	2
Deck crash	3
"Dilbert," "Grampaw Pettibone," and "Anymouse" cartoons	7
Korean close air support (aerial view)	10
Korean close air support	11
P2V carrier launch	21
HU-2 carrier landing	22
Fairchild R4Q Flying Boxcar	23
AJ Savage air-refueling an F7U Cutlass	31
Angle-of-attack indicator	32
Cutlass launching on a steam cat	38
Mirror landing	39
James H. Flatley	50
Mishap investigators working in the field	52
Vice Admiral Pirie	67
Flight physical exam	72
Dr. Ashton Graybiel	75
Ejection-seat trainer	76
Capt. Frank Austin	80
Captain Mitchell and Joe Foss	82
Flight surgeon wings	83
Vice Adm. Eugene Grinstead	95
Link Trainer	115
Rear Adm. Luis de Florez poses for Wheeler Williams	116
NCLT pilot view	118

Figures

Figure 3-1	Navy and Air Force mishap rates	15
Figure 3-2	FAA Part 121 mishap rate	16
Figure 3-3	Naval aviation Class A mishap rate	18
Figure 11-1	Swiss-Cheese Model	88
Figure 13-1	Graphic major mishaps vs. first flight	103
Figure 15-1	ORM Process Model	131
Figure A6-1	Straight-deck landing pattern	151

Tables

Table 6-1	Carrier Mishap Comparison	35
Table 15-1	CRM Skills	127
Table 15-2	New and Old Ways Comparison	130

Foreword

My first direct involvement with a major aircraft mishap occurred during a Mediterranean cruise in the USS *Saratoga* in 1959. While on the flight deck during night operations, I watched our squadron executive officer get too low in the approach and hit the end of the ship. He then careened up the flight deck and crashed into the water. There was no chance of recovery. It was a stark reminder of the dangers involved in carrier aviation for a young junior-grade lieutenant.

Unfortunately, my experience was all too common. In 1950, some 481 aircraft were destroyed and 227 people killed in naval aviation, both at sea and ashore. In today's terms, that would mean that more than four air wings had been wiped out during the year. It was a nadir; things did get better, as evidenced by the amazing safety performance in more recent years, but not without a great deal of dedicated effort and the development of a new mind-set.

Vice Admiral Dunn details the decades-long process of that effort to improve safety, including refinement of aircraft procurement practices, the embracing of technological improvements, and development of new cockpit-management techniques.

There are not many naval aviators who could equal Dunn's dedication or his experience as a champion of aviation safety throughout the Navy. His long flying experience began in the 1950s with the Douglas AD Skyraider and culminated in 1988 in the F/A-18 strike-fighter. His safety experience includes attendance at the University of Southern California School of Aviation Safety. Throughout his career—as a squadron commander, a carrier skipper, and finally Deputy Chief of Naval Operations for Air Warfare—he put into practice his ever-growing knowledge of the subject covered in this book: naval aviation safety.

The book does a first-rate job of describing the unacceptable rate of mishaps in the early 1950s, then moving through what transpired over more than fifty years so that today's naval aviation mishap rate is as good as or better than that of any other flying organization. While no mishap is acceptable, we now much better understand how a mishap may happen and what needs to be done in the way of prevention. By recounting this impressive record of accomplishment, this book provides a great service to the Navy and to naval aviation safety. It is also a testament to professional achievement and a model for future safety improvement endeavors in other professions.

David M. North
Naval Aviator
Former Editor in Chief, *Aviation Week & Space Technology*

Preface
A Most Remarkable Story

For the better part of a century naval aviation[1] has been at the forefront in defense of the United States. Of all the armed forces it has been the first on scene and the first into action. It is a forward-deployed force of sailors and Marines operating from aircraft carriers, amphibious forces, and other ships, small and large, and land-based patrol aircraft on station around the world. That force is ever ready to carry out the orders of the president, whether for humanitarian relief, mere presence, or even combat.

The downside of this story is that all of this capability began with terrible peacetime losses of people and aircraft. In the 1950s the mishap rate for naval aviation was far higher than that of the Air Force and far higher than it should ever have been. The upside of the story is that by the end of the twentieth century that had been corrected, and this book describes how it was done. Today naval aviation is at least as safe as Air Force aviation, safer than general aviation, and approaches even commercial aviation in terms of mishaps per given time period. Despite the need to maintain high readiness for combat and in the face of continued high-tempo operations prompted by various crises around the world, including those in the Middle East and around the Persian Gulf, saber rattling by North Korea and China, and increasing tensions with Russia, naval aviation has never been safer.

Figures tell the story: while those involved will be quick to declare that improvement must continue, from 1954, when naval aviation lost 536 people and 776 aircraft in 2,213 major mishaps, there has been remarkable improvement, until in 2014 naval aviation suffered only twenty major mishaps. "Still too many," one might conclude, but what a far cry from six decades before! Today naval aviation takes a backseat to no other enterprise in either flying safety or readiness to meet all missions. The following narrative describes how that improvement was wrought. It's a remarkable story.

GEAR UP, MISHAPS DOWN

1

Black as Midnight

Lord guard and guide those who fly,
Through the great spaces of the sky.

"Navy Hymn," second verse

It was a dark night at sea. The overcast shut out any possible moonlight or starlight. All was pitch-black; there was no horizon. The only things to be seen in the darkness were a pair of closely spaced red lights, "truck lights,"[1] at the top of the carrier's mast, and two more pairs atop two nearby destroyers. All around it was black as midnight.

Only a handful of aircraft were airborne, and it was time to bring them home. The carrier increased speed and turned slowly into the wind, its four screws churning up a phosphorescent wake giving the airborne pilots just a hint of the

F2H Banshees in the break by the ship. *NHHC*

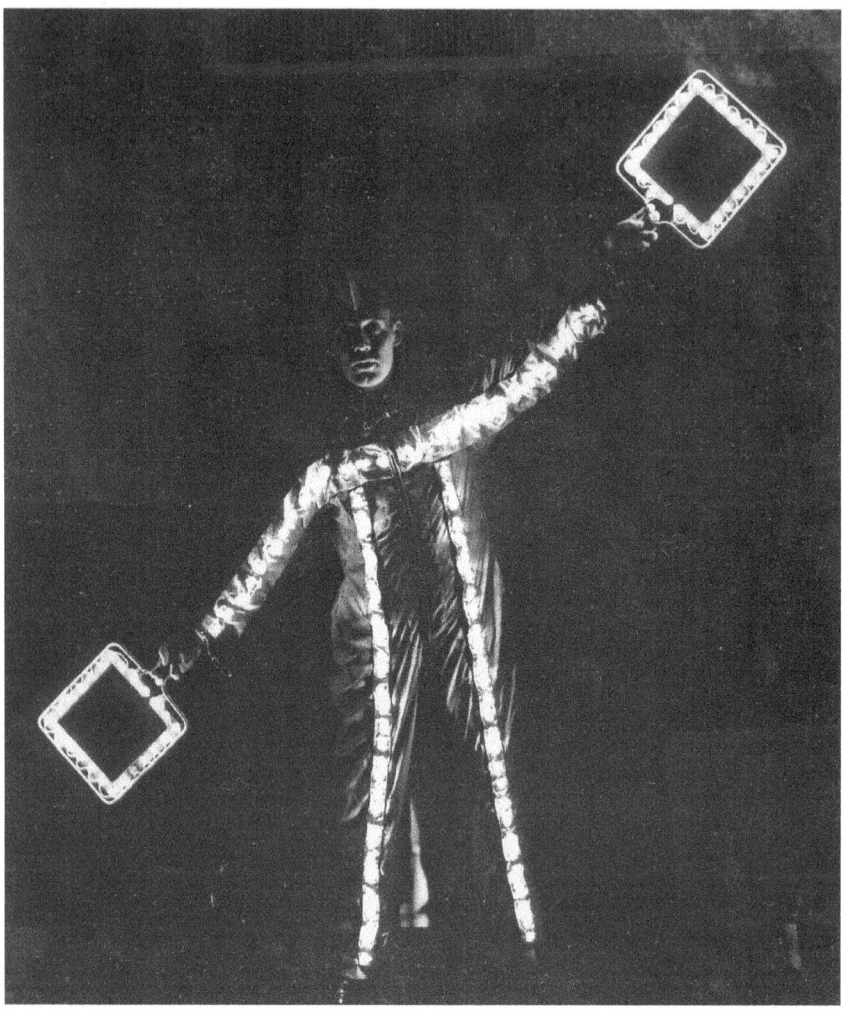

LSO AT NIGHT. *NHHC*

recovery course, the course they would need to fly to land aboard. The destroyers took positions matching the carrier's course, one half-mile abeam the carrier, the other aft and slightly to the starboard of the carrier's wake.

A flight of four McDonnell F2H-2 Banshees appeared out of the gloom and flew by the carrier's starboard side, parallel to its course, at three hundred feet and three hundred knots, tailhooks down. Once ahead of the ship, the leader signaled with his lights and made a sharp left turn, a "break," away from the other three aircraft, turning until he was on a heading reciprocal to the ship's course, "downwind."[2] Simultaneously he descended gradually to 125 feet over the water, extended his speedbrakes and lowered his landing gear and flaps, all the while slowing to 125 knots. The other three aircraft followed in timed succession and landed without incident.

When the fourth aircraft was abeam the carrier, he began a slow descending 180-degree left turn to arrive with about ninety degrees more to turn at ninety feet over the water. Simultaneously slowing the aircraft to the optimum landing speed that he had mentally calculated for his weight (usually about 105 knots), he continued his turn to the same heading as the ship and slightly slowed his descent until he sighted the glow of the landing signal officer's (LSO's) lighted wands. At the same time, he saw the landing-area centerline lights and the "dustpan" lights illuminating the outboard edges of the landing area. Otherwise, the ship was completely dark.

Fellow pilots gathered in "vultures' row" in the carrier's island, and personnel on the flight deck sighted the aircraft as it came out of its descending turn and lined up with the flight deck. The approach seemed steady when, unexpectedly, there was an excited call on the radio from the LSO, "Power. Power!! Power!!!" The approaching aircraft was settling more than it should. Despite the darkness of the night the nose of the aircraft seemed to be moving higher, the taillight going ever lower, and the aircraft sinking below the glide path. Then, over the radio, "Wave off! Wave off!! *Wave off!!!*," followed by a flash, a burst of light, a screeching flight-deck-crash alarm, and a call on

DECK CRASH. *NHHC*

the shipwide announcing system, "Fire on the flight deck! Fire on the flight deck!" The Banshee had hit the ramp, the rounded end of the flight deck at the stern of the ship. There was no ejection, no chute. The fuselage broke apart and exploded. Part of it fell into the sea. The rest skidded up the flight deck in a fireball, killing and injuring deck crewmen as it went, coming to rest against aircraft parked forward.

An experienced pilot was dead. A family and a squadron despaired. A shipmate lost, an aircraft lost, another statistic to add to the horrendous safety record of naval aviation in the 1950s.

It was not only carrier accidents, and not all accidents were at night. In the Naval Air Training Command, midair collisions and spins into the ground were all too common. Patrol squadrons chalked up numerous disappearances over the water. Weapons deliveries by all sorts of aircraft were plagued with pulling out too low from their dives and flying through their own bomb blasts or flying into the ground. Transports had their share of mishaps. In July 1953, a twin-engine R4Q transport crashed on takeoff from Whiting Field in northwest Florida. Forty-five people were lost. In 1954, one of the worst years in naval aviation, 536 people died in aircraft accidents and 776 aircraft were destroyed. The accident rate grew to the point that three people were killed every two days, and more than two major accidents happened every day of the year. The senior leadership was at a loss as to what to do to reduce the cost. Personal correspondence between aviation flag officers of the period often lamented the frequency of "crashes," but mentioned or suggested no new ways of doing business. One admiral probably expressed a widespread sentiment when he wrote in a personal letter, "We continue to have airplane accidents that I am afraid will always be with us. We continue to crack 'em up."[3]

Fortunately, many refused to accept that accidents "will always be with us," and they sought ways to save lives, conserve treasure, and increase readiness. As a result of their efforts and the efforts of so many others through the years, we find that in the first three months of calendar year 2011, the all-Navy/Marine accident rate was less than one accident per hundred thousand flight hours. More recently, the F/A-18 Hornet, one of the most demanding aircraft in the Navy/Marine inventory, completed fiscal year (FY) 2013 with no major mishaps; an amazing feat. Even more amazing, the principal concern of the Naval Safety Center today is no longer aircraft accidents (although there is still a vigorous accident-prevention and analysis program) but motorcycle mishaps.

This book tells how it came to pass.

2

Difficult Days
A Soaring Mishap Rate

Naval aviation's first recorded fatal accident occurred near Annapolis on 20 June 1913. A thunderstorm upset the hydroaeroplane flown by Lt. John Towers and Ens. William Billingsley. Ensign Billingsley was tossed out and fell to his death. There were other accidents after that, not all fatal, but all adding to lessons learned at the cost of people, aircraft, and reputations. In the early years all aviation, not just naval aviation, was recognized as a dangerous, even daredevil, business. In 2014, in an unpublished paper, Professor Roger Bohn of the University of California, San Diego, termed these years the "heroic era" of aviation.[1] Although the total number of flying hours was low, between 1913 and 1917 nineteen pilots and crewmen died in naval aviation aircraft mishaps. Then, as naval aviation entered World War I, the numbers of flying hours and deaths rose. In 1918 alone, nineteen deaths were recorded, only four due to combat.

Following the war, mishaps, including deaths, closely paralleled flying hours. They seemed to have had little to do with whether the flying was from carriers, other ships, afloat, or ashore, although, as one might expect, the accident rate while training was somewhat higher than it was in the fleet. Flight into bad weather, sometimes purposeful, sometimes inadvertent, was a leading cause of accidents.

Before World War II, accidents resulting in the loss of life, injury to personnel, damage to material, or the loss of aircraft were investigated by a board of inquiry, which was often made up of local senior personnel assigned to the naval command or the naval district in which the event occurred. Other than that, mishap investigation was informal. Beyond boards of inquiry, a written report may or may not have been required by the unit commander, and determination of facts was most often limited to how not to make the same mistake again or making a particular component more reliable or safer. For example, seat belts resulted from the Billingsley accident, and instrumentation was developed to address lessons learned during flights at night and in bad weather. In addition, engineers and flight surgeons often participated in accident investigations, which contributed much to the knowledge of the effects of the flight environment on humans and of the resultant need for safety equipment. While that approach may not have been particularly scientific or all-encompassing, it began to pay off. At the same time, the Bureau of Aeronautics (BuAer) and the Naval Aircraft Factory in Philadelphia also attempted to learn lessons from each accident. Thus, naval aviation, along with the rest of aviation, moved gradually into what Bohn calls the "rules plus instruments" era.

Increasing involvement of flight surgeons in selection of flight candidates and systems improvements, better weather forecasting, simulators (such as Link Trainers), standardization of the various flight instruction schools, and more also played important roles. Nevertheless, the safety record during World War II was hardly a model. In the four war years of 1942–45, there were 8,836 deaths and 25,678 major accidents, not counting combat losses.

Though money was less of a constraint than in peacetime, leadership could not and did not ignore the dramatic rise of costs in terms of lives and money. Increased emphasis was put on safety education, but more importantly, the "system" reacted too. In August 1943, the Chief of Naval Air Intermediate Training directed that an aviation safety board be established at each training center under his command. A few months later, the Chief of Naval Operations (CNO) took up the idea and issued a similar directive to all primary and operational commands. Next, in early 1944, the Deputy Chief of Naval Operations for Air Warfare (DCNO [Air]) and Chief BuAer announced jointly their intention to issue consecutively numbered bulletins concerning the safe operation of naval aircraft. These bulletins turned out to be forerunners of *Approach,* the now long-running Naval Safety Center publication. That June, DCNO (Air) directed the establishment of Aviation Safety Boards in all commands and the appointment of a flight safety officer in each squadron. Safety boards were in fact established in most major aviation commands, but aviation safety officers, when assigned, were mostly on the basis of collateral duty within the operations department. Finally, in July 1944, a Flight Safety Section was established in the office of the DCNO (Air) in the Pentagon, and it was assigned the responsibility for the direction and supervision of the aviation safety program.

While it took some time to devise and promulgate safety programs, others in other offices and in the fleet were designing their own programs. Among the first to be heard from were cartoonists who gave birth to "Dilbert" (and his companion "Spoiler" the mechanic), "Grampaw Pettibone,"[2] and "Anymouse,"[3] all with us to this day.

Supplementing and expanding on the cartoons were a series of *Sense* pamphlets, humorously written and illustrated and filled with important information like gunnery, recognition, ditching, Aleutian weather, parachute operation and survival, and warnings about such things as flat-hatting and flying through clouds without a clearance. A favorite of the latter genre centered on a cartoon picturing two vultures perched on a mountain top, surrounded by clouds beneath them and

"Dilbert" was created by then-captain Arthur Doyle and Lt. Cdr. Bob Osborn in early 1942. Doyle had seen the carton gremlin characters used by the RAF to train its pilots and mechanics to become more safety conscious. "Dilbert" became the fat, dumb, and happy pilot, and Spoiler became his mechanic. They appeared on posters and flyers throughout the fleet in ready rooms and in hangars, each one conveying a succinct message of how not to do something. Even though lighthearted, they carried lessons that invariably struck home. To this day, pilots who flew in the 1940s and 1950s remember clearly "Dilbert's" lessons. Closely associated with "Dilbert," "Spoiler the Mechanic" posters were equally effective.

"DILBERT" CARTOON
Naval Aviation Museum Library, with permission

"Grampaw Pettibone" was created and written by Lt. Cdr. Spencer "Seth" Warner, a naval aviator who headed the Office of Safety Counselor in the Bureau of Aeronautics Training Division. His idea was to develop a character who would impart his wisdom about flying, thus helping in the safety effort. In January 1943 he teamed with Bob Osborn, creator of "Dilbert," to produce a column in the *BuAer Newsletter* (later named *Naval Aviation News*) featuring "Gramps." Following a description of a mishap, "Grampaw Pettibone" railed at young fliers for making stupid mistakes. It was a hit from the beginning, and accidents lessened as pilots took "Gramps'" advice to use the checklist, buckle safety belts, and more. "Gramps," with his sage advice, still appears today as one of the most popular features in *Naval Aviation News*.

"GRAMPAW PETTIBONE" CARTOON
Naval Aviation News

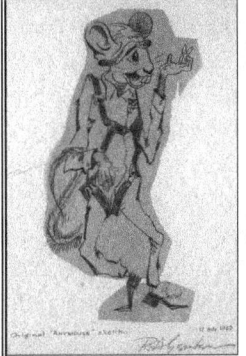

"ANYMOUSE" CARTOON
Approach, *Naval Safety Center magazine*

"Anymouse" was brought into naval aviation in 1945 by Lt. Cdr. Trgve Holl, the VR-31 squadron safety officer. He provided a form to squadron personnel, pilots, and maintenance troops alike, encouraging them to make anonymous reports of near-accidents, incidents, mistakes, or even hairy tales, tales told either on themselves or others. In this way nameless, and therefore blameless, pilots and crewmen could gain valuable knowledge from the experience of others.

The concept was highly successful, and from the time "Anymouse" reported to the Naval Aviation Safety Center in 1953, many of his exploits were published in *Approach* for all naval aviation to read and learn from.

Since then the "Anymouse" concept has been adopted by the U.S. Air Force, several foreign air forces, and several commercial airlines as well.

watching Dilbert about to head into the clouds. The caption read, "Here comes our hot lunch on a VFR [visual flight rules] flight plan." One would think several times about flying into the clouds without a flight plan once having seen that poster. *Sense* pamphlets covering over a hundred different subjects and providing commonsense safety rules for each were issued between 1943 and 1970s, updated to cover such subjects as "Jet Sense." All aviation ships, squadrons, and shore stations received liberal distribution of *Sense* pamphlets and the posters that replicated many of the cartoons carried in the pamphlets themselves. These safety gems were liberally displayed in hangars and on board ships during World War II and into the 1950s. Beyond safety reports and publications safety, movies became staples of both flight training and as leads before the evening movie in ready rooms. Despite these efforts, high loss rates continued through the end of the war.

Less than five years after the end of World War II, with massive demobilization and huge defense cutbacks, the Navy and the Marines were barely hanging on. Popular opinion, encouraged by the leadership of the newly established U.S. Air Force, held that never again would there be a conventional war. The idea was that land-based intercontinental bombers capable of delivering nuclear weapons would keep the peace, and the Air Force moved to consolidate all aircraft under their aegis. The chairman of the Joint Chiefs of Staff declared that the Marine Corps was redundant, as there would never again be a need for an amphibious assault. The Navy Department budget was in shambles, and the "revolt of the admirals"[4] did little in the short run to remedy the situation. Secretary of Defense Louis Johnson only grudgingly allowed the deployment of two aircraft carriers to the Mediterranean and one to the western Pacific. Almost the final blow came in 1949 when he canceled without warning the construction of the USS *United States,* scheduled to be the first truly post–World War II aircraft carrier, and one that might well have enhanced not only capability but also naval aviation safety.

Meanwhile, Navy ships and people were laid up, and force levels reached new lows. From a total of twenty large aircraft carriers at the end of World War II, the nation was down to four.[5] The number of light carriers (CVLs) was reduced from eight to four, and the number of escort carriers (CVEs) went from seventy to four. Air stations were closed, flying hours were cut, and recruiting was severely restricted. In 1945, there had been 49,380 Navy pilots and 10,229 Marines. By 1950, there were only 9,481 Navy pilots and 1,922 Marines.[6] To make matters worse, the naval services were losing pilots and aircraft to accidents at an alarming rate. In the first four postwar years, 1946–49, over seven thousand Navy and Marine aircraft were destroyed in accidents and almost a thousand people were killed. Morale was low, and by today's standards the record was horrific. In 1953 the Naval Aviation Safety Activity reported reviewing an average of twenty-five aircraft accident reports per day.[7] In March 1954, Commander Air Force Atlantic Fleet saw fit to write to the Commander Fleet Air Mediterranean expressing concern over the four accidents suffered by Fleet Aircraft Support Squadron 77 in just six months.[8]

Despite the awful mishap rate, Navy/Marine leadership swallowed hard and began to pursue remedies toward reducing mishaps. They saw the future of the Navy as centered on naval aviation and insisted that the Navy had a role to play in any sort of war, especially a nuclear war, a conflict that would be largely dependent on a carrier-based nuclear delivery capability. Thus, aircraft large enough to carry the huge nuclear weapons of the day but that could be operated from carriers were developed.[9] At the same time, Navy leadership reasoned that conventional war was not passé and that the future of naval aviation depended on ambitious development and acquisition of carrier-suitable jet fighter and attack aircraft, antisubmarine warfare (ASW) aircraft, and capable, long-range, high-endurance, land-based patrol and transport aircraft. Although helicopters were new, difficult to fly, and not always reliable, it was clear that their integration into fleet operations, both Navy and Marine, was imperative. Hand in hand with that development had to be the capability to operate at night and in bad weather conditions. Thus, at the beginning of the 1950s all Navy pilots became instrument qualified, and not too many years later night operations at sea were not unusual.

None of this did anything to reduce the awful number of naval aviation mishaps or the terrible loss of lives and aircraft. In 1950, 227 people were killed, and 481 aircraft were destroyed. It would get worse as jets began replacing the largely World War II prop aircraft in the carrier force and naval aviation began once more to fly combat missions—this time, over Korea.

In June 1950, the North Koreans caught the world by surprise when they invaded South Korea. Republic of Korea (ROK) troops, together with the few American occupation troops available from Japan, were unable to stem the tide. Air Force air support based in Japan was marginal, given the range, but an American aircraft carrier, *Valley Forge,* the only one in the western Pacific at the time, was soon on the scene with the first real tactical air support for badly mauled American and allied ground forces. The *"Valley"* was soon joined by HMS *Triumph,* and for a considerable time was the only air available to support the troops.

That sudden onset of war prompted swift growth in the Navy Department budget, rapid recommissioning of mothballed ships and squadrons, the raising of recruiting quotas, and the recall of thousands of reservists, many of them for aviation assignments. It thrust relatively junior and inexperienced pilots into combat with jet aircraft, after only a minimum amount of jet experience and using procedures developed for prop aircraft on straight-deck carriers. The Chief of Naval Air Reserve Training reported that 38 percent of the officers reporting to him for further assignment to fleet squadrons had not flown since 1945 or 1946.[10] The maintenance crews were hardly any better off, learning on the job about jet maintenance from newly printed manuals and circulars. It was little wonder that during the

KOREAN CLOSE AIR SUPPORT (AERIAL VIEW). *NHHC*

Korean War years the Navy/Marine accident rate soared and nearly two thousand people were killed in noncombat mishaps.

While the crews on station in the Far East and those training to go there did the best they could, based on the experience and equipment they had, the entire shore-based naval aviation establishment struggled to support the fighting forces. It started with a structure developed during World War II and now still recovering from the ravages of rapid demobilization and inadequate postwar funding. Procurement, supply and maintenance, personnel management, training, and safety were among the major areas of responsibilities falling to the staffs of the CNO, the Bureau of Aeronautics, the "type commanders" (the commanders of Naval Air Forces Atlantic and Pacific) and others even closer to the fleet. There was also the matter of service-wide attitudes—not a trivial matter, as it turned out.

For more than 150 years, the Navy had operated with what some came to term an "executive leadership" philosophy.[11] That is, naval officers had, both in training and by experience, largely been subject only to decentralized authority, with

KOREAN CLOSE AIR SUPPORT. *NHHC*

decision making left to officers on the scene. They are taught to take the initiative, act independently, and exercise authority. This has been manifested in many ways throughout the history of the U.S. Navy and Marine Corps, and naval aviation is no exception. In fact, in naval aviation it is more the rule than the exception. This has given U.S. naval aviators an outstanding reputation as air-combat fliers second to none, but it has also led to a less than stellar mishap record.

Meanwhile, it became increasingly obvious that the Air Force mishap experience was far better than that of the Navy and Marine Corps. (See chapter 3.) Some opined that the reason may have been a truth underlying the oft-quoted apocryphal statement, "In the Air Force you can't do anything unless it's specifically permitted. The Navy and Marines lay out everything you can't do and the rest is allowed."[12] Thus, in this era before widespread standardization, the commanding officer set the priorities and established his own "right way" to do things. One result was inconsistent, mainly awful, mishap performance.

Exacerbating that "right way or the highway" attitude was the personnel assignment policy. Until 1957, when it shifted to the Bureau of Naval Personnel (BuPers), the responsibility for detailing aviation personnel resided within the staff of the DCNO (Air).[13] In actual practice, the assignments of junior officers and enlisted people were made by the type commanders, AirLant and AirPac, but there was a lot of room for favoritism, especially for those ordered to command, who were assigned from an office on the CNO staff. Far too many got their assignments because they had friends in the right places, whether they had the requisite aviation and leadership skills to command or not. Certainly there were many good commanding officers (COs),[14] but there were enough not so good as to affect the accident rate. Stories are legion, but a CO leading a four-plane division of Panthers into a mountain in the clouds is one. A CO trying to lead a twelve-plane formation in a tail-chase loop over San Francisco Bay is another. In the former case, four pilots died, and four aircraft were stricken. Airplanes scattered throughout the sky over the bay and—it was nothing short of miraculous that no one was hurt. Unfortunately, since pilots (and others) grow up watching what their squadron commanding officers do, problems continued. Sans an effective safety program, things could only get worse.

Before the early 1950s, there was only a minimally defined safety program in naval aviation. The job of the squadron safety officer was still a collateral duty. Safety briefs consisted of a review of recent accidents, of which there were many, and the admonition to "Fly safe." Flight operations were standardized only within squadrons, perhaps on rare occasion within air groups. When a squadron commanding officer or operations officer changed, very often so did the standard operating procedures. Professionalism among the leadership at the squadron level was apt to be hit or miss. New-aircraft checkouts were problematic. For example, the following are quotes from 1948: "Training consisted of looking at the handbook, cockpit checkout, then go"; or else: "This is the low pressure fuel cock; this is the high pressure fuel cock; it flies real easy"; another: "Checkout consisted of reading the handbook and watching a movie." There was a widespread notion that naval aviation was not in the safety business but in the business of accomplishing the missions assigned. Because some of those missions were very dangerous, many aviators did in fact cast safety aside, simply accepting all risks.

Mishap investigation was rudimentary, and minimal effort was made to codify lessons learned from mishaps or near mishaps. What data there were consisted largely of a record of the number of accidents any one pilot had. Mishap causes were not always identified, and when all else failed the reason most often listed was "pilot error."

Maintenance and supply too were rudimentary by today's standards, built on experiences in the simpler and more plentifully supplied World War II era. It was before the era of automation, of course, and almost everything centered on the maintenance chief's "wheelbook." The most-used spare parts were stored in the chief's cruise box, and what he didn't have there he would "cumshaw" from a colleague.

Design and test also deserve some of the blame for the high mishap rates of the fifties. New aircraft capable of meeting and defeating the Soviet threat were often

> The "wheelbook" was a small notebook, usually with a green cover, that fit in the maintenance chief's hip pocket. Everything worth knowing about the status and maintenance of squadron aircraft was recorded by the chief in this booklet. Capt. Rosario "Zip" Rausa, USN (Ret.), has described a wheelbook as follows.
>
>> In VA-85 we had a CPO [chief petty officer] named "Krupsky," a barrel-chested, stoop-shouldered, muscular and unusually energetic and dedicated man with a well-worn green book he kept in his rear pocket and retrieved with frequency throughout the day as he ranged from the flight deck to hangar deck and Ready Five. If something had happened to him, or he lost that book, we'd be in deep trouble. Thankfully, he never lost it.

pushed into the fleet without proper design or testing. Examples are rife, but leading among them is the F7U Cutlass, far ahead of its time, with twin afterburning engines and three hydraulic systems. One Cutlass squadron deployed on board ship in 1956 with twelve aircraft and returned home with but two, the rest having crashed and taken five pilots with them. An even worse record was compiled by an AF Guardian propeller-driven squadron of ASW aircraft that lost twenty-two out of twenty-two aircraft on one cruise.

Gradually, with the recognition that something had to be done, things began to get better. After a brief rise in 1951 and 1952, the naval aviation mishap rate—the number of major aircraft accidents per hundred thousand flight hours in the Navy and Marine Corps—began to drop from a horrendous high to the present, when an accident is a rare event.[15] Over those same years' attitudes, policies, and procedures were changed; organizations were adjusted for more efficiency; equipment was improved and made more reliable; training became more focused; and leadership exerted more positive influence.

Today, not only squadrons but air wings, air stations, and aviation ships have safety officers.[16] Indeed, almost all safety officers have completed courses of study at naval aviation safety schools. Operations are standardized through NATOPS. (See chapter 9.) Every aircrewman and maintenance person reporting to a fleet unit must first undergo intensive training at a replacement training squadron. Commanding officers are screened by a board of more senior officers, hosted in the Bureau of Naval Personnel. Then, once approved by the board, the standard is for the screened officer to serve first as executive officer of a squadron, then "fleet up" to command it. Every mishap or near-mishap is investigated by trained investigators. All aviation personnel are encouraged to report problems—anonymously, if they prefer.

It's now universally recognized that simply to call a mishap "pilot error" does not do anything to prevent similar mishaps in the future or generate help for any one person or for the overall system. The questions "how?" and "why?" must be answered. Human factors (see chapters 10 and 11), once the sole province of the flight surgeon, are now addressed in briefings and in investigations. Maintenance and supply have graduated from the primitive wheelbook system and a separate supply system managed by a largely disassociated corps to a computer-assisted, integrated team of dedicated supply and maintenance professionals, trained and oriented to provide the best support and best safety available. Quality assurance, once the sole province of the maintenance officer, now belongs to the safety officer. Technological improvements in both aircraft and facilities, on board ship and ashore, have been numerous. Flight surgeons have begun to be assigned to individual squadrons, and because of their expertise in two demanding professions, medicine and flight, they have often made major contributions to safety. Finally, and more recently, the concepts of Crew Resource Management (CRM) and Operational Risk Management (ORM) and Culture Workshops have been brought into the effort. (See chapter 15.) From these beginnings, naval aviation safety performance has improved dramatically, an improvement described in more detail in the pages that follow. More importantly, there is no diminution in the overall effort to continue to improve naval aviation safety.

3

The Competition
American Aviation Overall

Naval Aviation was not alone in facing new challenges in the 1950s. Commercial and general aviation, the U.S. Air Force, and foreign air forces had similar challenges. The transition to jets, progress in aircraft, engine and systems designs, and instrumentation, and the search for reliability were fairly common in post–World War II aviation. Also common was the need to operate safely and effectively at night, in all weather and in conformance with rules set by various regulatory bodies. Despite political difficulties between the senior leaderships of the Navy and the Air Force, the Navy's Bureau of Aeronautics and the Air Force's Air Development Center cooperated extensively. There was also extensive cooperation with the civil sector; lessons learned were quickly shared. Although some vendors were oriented toward only one major customer, all learned from the others, and basic differences in requirements between services and the commercial world were few. Everyone flew in the same airspace and followed the same

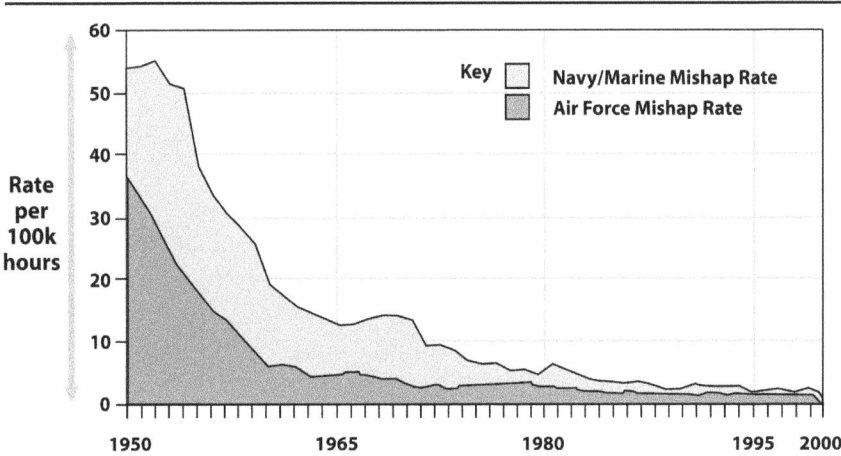

Figure 3-1 Navy and Air Force mishap rates
Naval Safety Center and Air Force Safety Center data, created by Guy Arceneaux

air-traffic-control rules and procedures. Everyone depended on reliable controls, engines, and flight instruments, especially when flying at night or in the clouds. These circumstances tended to build commonality in both equipment and operations, thus the similarity, or "look alike" shapes, of the curves of the various mishap experiences, depicted in the following figures.

Note that Navy/Marine, Air Force, and general aviation mishap rates are calculated per hundred thousand flight hours but the commercial Part 121[1] rates per million flight hours. Yet, the similarity in the slopes of improvement over the years studied is noteworthy. This reflects the many common improvements and enhancements in training, procedures, and equipment, all discussed below and in subsequent chapters.

There was also international cooperation. Even before World War II, civil aviation in Europe and the United States had sought ways to overcome such common problems as navigating at night and landing and taking off in reduced visibility. In the postwar world, especially with the advent of regular transoceanic operations, solving these problems became imperative on the commercial side. As a result, such innovations as the VHF omnidirectional radio range (VOR), distance-measuring equipment (DME), and other navigation systems became operational in the civilian world long before similar systems were made available to most military aircraft.

Likewise, development of new and more reliable aircraft instrumentation came largely in response to the demands of commercial aviation. The electrical attitude indicator, the horizontal situation indicator, instrument landing systems, and more all got their starts in commercial aircraft.[2] While airborne radar was

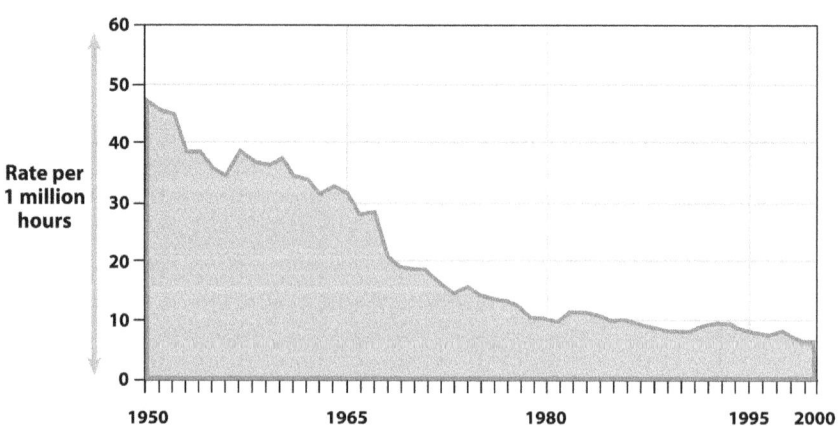

Figure 3-2 FAA Part 121 mishap rate
FAA data, created by Guy Arceneaux

developed to meet the needs of war, it quickly proved essential to safe commercial travel. That technology proved to be extremely important in particular for long-range navigation and approaches under instrument conditions. Because of the weight of early installations, radar first made its mark in mishap avoidance in multiengine aircraft, sometimes even facilitating landings in poor visibility with inadequate ground control, a forerunner to ground-controlled approach (GCA) and Navy carrier-controlled approach (CCA). Such equipment and systems contributed markedly to a universal improvement in safety during the 1950s.

That isn't to say there weren't rivalries among the several camps, but these tended to play out most visibly in Congress, the Pentagon, and the media, where the issues were mostly about roles, missions, and money. In the fleet and in Air Force squadrons, and in the cockpits of commercial airliners, it was a different story. There, it was a question of how best to get the job done in the safest possible manner. Getting to know one another better helped.

Most commercial pilots in the 1950s started flying in the Air Force, the Navy or the Marines. There were also exchange programs wherein Air Force pilots were assigned tours of duty in Navy squadrons and vice versa. Navy pilots went to the U.S. Air Force Test Pilot School at Edwards Air Force Base, in California, and Air Force pilots went to the Navy Test Pilot School at Patuxent River, Maryland. Even though differences in outlook and ways of doing business persisted, such exchanges resulted in better understanding. This may well be a principal reason why Navy and Air Force mishap curves so closely resemble one another in shape, albeit differing in dimensions.

Finally, there was special outreach throughout the aviation world, through participation in frequent Flight Safety Foundation conferences and seminars and close communication with such agencies as the National Advisory Committee on Aeronautics (NACA)[3] and the National Transportation Safety Board (NTSB).[4]

Thus, the fact that the several mishap curves have similar shapes is reflective of progress in American aviation as a whole. Most of what separated naval aviation from the rest lay in differences stemming from institutional culture and operations at sea: the latter a uniquely Navy-Marine (and Coast Guard) realm. Yet, today, neither culture nor operations at sea make for significant differences on the ever-diminishing curve of aircraft mishaps—a remarkable achievement.

While such considerations go far toward explaining the similarity in shapes of the figures in this chapter, when it comes to Naval Aviation, where the starting point in 1950 is so much higher, amplification is needed. That is depicted in figure 3-3, a chart updated and published frequently by the Naval Safety Center.

As will be seen in subsequent chapters, figure 3-3 is only an overview of the subject and as such is apt to be misleading. While the curve itself is accurate and based on real mishap data, several of the annotations are either in error or misplaced, and important events and changes are omitted. For example, from the

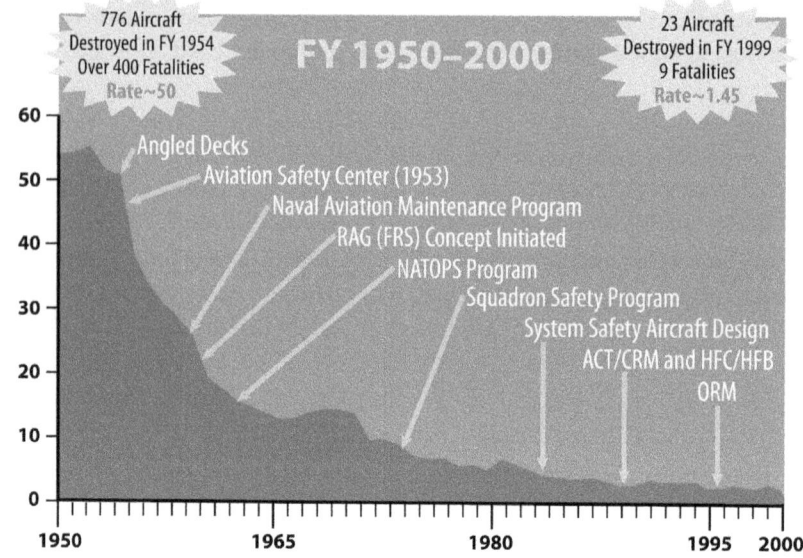

Figure 3-3 Naval aviation Class A mishap rate
Naval Safety Center data, created by Guy Arceneaux

annotations one might conclude that it was the advent of angled decks on carriers that led to the long and steady decline in the mishap rate. Such a conclusion overlooks the fact that the driving force behind angled decks (and steam catapults) was not safety but the search for a way to operate the newer jets and heavy, nuclear-delivery-capable bombers from the carriers and, in general, to operate all aircraft more efficiently. Safety was a by-product of that effort. At the same time, not all aircraft carriers were converted to the angled deck simultaneously; also, a large percentage of naval aviation flight hours and accidents were accrued when not embarked in a carrier. In addition, missing at even first glance is the impact of such things as improved leadership, the coming of age of the Naval Safety Center, the establishment of aviation safety schools, improved maintenance and supply, advances in aircraft, engines, and avionics, and the positive influence of the aerospace medical community, all discussed in subsequent chapters.

Moreover, not recognized at all are the constant effort and the many small steps taken by a variety of commands, offices, and individuals that led to such dramatic improvement in the Navy and Marine mishap record, even while new and higher-performance aircraft joined the fleet and increased night and all-weather flying was required. On top of all that were the almost continuous demands of the Cold War and combat in several hot wars. These omissions from figure 3-3, along with the annotations on figure 3-3, are discussed in later chapters.[5]

It was a combination of experiences in commercial aviation, the Air Force, the naval services, and a number of nondefense government agencies that influenced the tremendous changes depicted in the figures of this chapter. These changes, in turn, led to conservation of lives and resources and enhancement of the operational readiness and effectiveness of naval aviation in the last half of the twentieth century. The following pages focus on naval aviation, but the backdrop is the progress in American aviation as a whole.

In naval aviation, beyond the many planes and crews lost to enemy fire in Korea and Vietnam, the vast majority of aircraft losses were due to mishaps associated with procedural, technical, and organizational problems, and not a few to poor leadership or training. Simultaneously, and thus exacerbating the situation, most of the airplanes that populated the flight decks of aircraft carriers from the introduction of the FH-1 Phantom through the retirement of the F-14 Tomcat required extensive training and were, with few exceptions, hard to maintain and could kill an undertrained or unwary crew. Nor was it much different for other sea-based and shore-based elements of naval aviation, including those that flew and maintained the increasing numbers of helicopters flown from all sorts of platforms in often difficult circumstances. Many men and a few women gave their lives trying to operate these machines in the challenging environment of the sea.[6]

Today the story of naval aviation safety is one of success, but it cannot be fully appreciated if what went before is not known and understood—a story will be told in the following chapters.

4

Beginning to Get It Right

As the 1950s began, the Navy and Marine Corps were still suffering from the effects of rapid post–World War II demobilization and shrinking budgets, along with the simultaneous challenge of being ready to meet the Soviet and Chinese threats. At the same time, and hard to ignore, there was determination in powerful circles that the Air Force should be in charge of all military aviation. To survive, naval aviation had to measure up and overcome.

A major challenge that had to be dealt with was the question of nuclear delivery. Nuclear bombs were big, and the Air Force had big bombers. The Navy did not. Early on, the Navy overcame this problem by using twin-engine propeller patrol planes (P2Vs) launched from a *Midway*-class carrier. Later, it developed a large, carrier-capable, multiengine aircraft, the AJ Savage. When smaller nuclear weapons were built, they were adapted to selected fighter and attack aircraft. At first, this capability was assigned to specially trained units, but it quickly spread to entire squadrons.

Concurrently, naval aviation had to be ready for myriad types of missions, whether nuclear or conventional, day or night, or in bad weather. During World War II specially trained individuals and squadrons had been dedicated to night and all-weather flying. Now, all pilots had to be so trained and continuously qualified. At the same time antisubmarine warfare, both land based and sea based, grew in importance as awareness of the growing Soviet submarine fleet came to the fore. Even while these and other newer, ever-growing, and ever-more-demanding operational requirements had to be met, jets began replacing props. All this dictated different kinds of training and organization, both of which had to be developed and implemented. In the process, airplanes and aircrews were too often lost, and, sadly, in some circles that was accepted as "the cost of doing business."

With the advent of the Korean War it was suddenly back to conventional combat, conducting strikes from carriers on preplanned targets, close air support, and armed reconnaissance. While these were missions not too different from those of the closing stages of World War II, they would now be at night and in bad weather, including jets from carriers designed for slower and more forgiving prop aircraft.

P2V CARRIER LAUNCH. *NHHC*

The war also demanded more pilots on short notice, so the reserves, some with only minimal recent flight time, were called up and the pilot training rate was increased. In the Pacific Fleet, carrier-based ASW tended to be put aside, but the Atlantic Fleet continued to train and prepare for the possibility of a Soviet attack, requiring it to train for and be proficient in not only long-range strike, at night and in all types of weather, but for ASW as well. The times were dynamic, and the Navy-Marine accident rate showed it. Some of the highest postwar mishap rates and numbers of aircrew killed came in the first years of the decade. The reasons were many, but among them was the continued use of practices and procedures developed during World War II, despite the new requirements of the Cold War and Korea. Flying the new jets and higher-performance props and long-range patrol aircraft at night in all-weather conditions using techniques and often flight and navigation systems from World War II was a recipe for serious problems. Eventually, the ability to fly and fight effectively at night and in bad weather became a hallmark of the Navy and Marines, but not without cost.

Once the Korean War began, the operational requirements laid on the Navy and Marines in general and naval aviation in particular was unprecedented, especially by pre–World War II standards. From 1950 through 1959, carrier task forces responded not only to Korea but to crises surrounding the Tachen Islands, the Suez, Jordan, Lebanon, Quemoy/Matsu, and Laos. "Regular" cruises were long, eight and nine months, and frequent. People and equipment began to wear out, and most of the cruise books of the period carried long lists of people lost in aircraft mishaps. It wasn't uncommon for carrier squadrons to lose over half their aircraft in one cruise.

HU-2 CARRIER LANDING. *NHHC*

Meanwhile, the helicopter came into its own, first from carriers for search and rescue then in an increasingly important role in ASW, by day and night and in all weather, and for inserting Marines ashore as well. Unfortunately, their mishap experience was atypical for the day.

Nor were shore-based operations immune to the rising mishap rate. In 1954 there were four land-based TBM accidents in one squadron in a year, including a fatal spin with a load of passengers approaching the Capodichino Airport at Naples, Italy. In other accidents too, large transport aircraft were lost with full passenger loads. Short of money, the Reserves transitioned to jets, with little or no purposeful training.[1]

The Naval Air Training Command too saw an increase in the number of mishaps as the pilot training rate burgeoned to meet the needs of the Korean War. Across the spectrum of naval aviation, new missions and new demands caused new problems, and the accident rate soared. Against that background of seemingly ever-increasing number of accidents and the need to be ready to meet an enemy threat ranging from nuclear war to submarine warfare to sustained combat in support of allies in all sorts of circumstances, innovation became the order of the day. Many of those innovations eventually led to the steep downturn in the all-Navy accident rate, from its high then to where it is today.

Fairchild R4Q Flying Boxcar. *NHHC*

While not generally realized at the time, the first big step in understanding why the accident rate was as high as it was and then in figuring out how to reduce it was taken with the establishment of the Naval Aviation Safety Activity in 1951, followed closely by the Flatley Report in 1953.[2] The details of both these events are described in chapter 8, but at this point their significance has to be acknowledged. The report itself was prompted by the crash of a Marine R4Q transport carrying forty Naval Reserve Officer Training Corps midshipmen and a crew of six on a night takeoff from Whiting Field; forty-four people died.[3] The ensuing report concluded that one of the major factors in the crash was lack of aircrew proficiency at night, not an uncommon situation in the early 1950s.

Unless absolutely required, most pilots prefer not to fly at night. Daytime flying is fun—especially out at sea, away from controlled airspace, where puffy cumulus clouds become pylons, as one darts close by with seeming abandon. The world is good, and for a carrier-type aviator, few things can be more exhilarating than a tail chase among white clouds under a blue, sunlit sky over the water. Let night descend, however, with those same clouds hiding whatever moon or starlight there may be, and over the water, the dark sky merging with the blackness of the sea, and it's another story.

Likewise, flying in clouds for long periods, subject to the subtle vagaries of night vision and the urges of vertigo, dependent on instruments that could tumble out of control and on radios of uncertain dependability, was not on many pilots' list of fun things to do. Checking in with Air Traffic Control was bothersome, especially with the cranky radios of the day; unauthorized "self-cleared penetrations" were too often used to descend through cloud layers.[4]

Not to say that either night or instrument flying were new—they were not. For years, airmen had been flying at night or on instrument flight plans, although mostly only when they had to. No naval aviator was unfamiliar with night or instrument flying. Everyone got a taste of it in the Naval Air Training Command, and there was a long-standing requirement that each pilot log a specified minimum number of flight hours at night and on instruments. But too often the former requirement was met only when the moon was full and the latter only when the air was smooth. In particular, night requirements were almost certain to be satisfied from an airfield, not from a carrier. Before the Korean War, there were specialized squadrons that trained to fly and fight at night and in clouds—composite squadrons, three on each coast[5]—and several of those units had had tremendous success in World War II. But they were the exception, hardly the rule. After the war that expertise was allowed to atrophy and the carrier navy returned to its fair weather roots.[6]

It didn't help either that air station commanding officers disliked night flying because it caused complaints from neighbors. Carrier commanding officers disliked it because it kept the crews from the nightly movies in the hangar bays. Composite squadrons supplied detachments to each deploying ship to provide night-attack and fighter capability, but their skills tended to atrophy as the cruise went on, because captains and admirals had those other priorities. The record compiled by a Composite Squadron 4 (VC-4) detachment of five planes on one deployment is not atypical: twelve accidents, three of them fatal during night VFR, eight resulting in "strike damage" to (that is, equivalent to total loss) the aircraft.[7] Even when they did fly, it was hardly easy. "The division between day and night operations soon changed," again explains Captain O'Rourke, in the Fall 1998 issue of *Hook*. "That all began to shift when Soviet submarines that didn't care about the weather above them, enemy fighters and bombers that flew at night, and North Korean supply and troop movements that used the cover of darkness."[8]

Such operations prompted aircraft systems and training to change too. The advent of jet aircraft only exacerbated the problems, since they flew faster and burned fuel at a greater rate. Jets couldn't afford to waste time and gas trying to orient themselves on a low-frequency navigation range or fly a cumbersome approach pattern. Cockpit instruments and radios weren't built for high speed or sustained operations, either. Beyond certain angles of bank or degrees of pitch, the gyro horizon could tumble. At such times, to keep wings level or to maintain a certain level of bank, the pilot would have to revert to the "needle/ball," first used in the 1920s, and only the airspeed and a vertical speed indicator were available for clues as to nose position.[9] Communications often depended on a radio with a limited number of frequencies. Moreover, many pilots considered flying at night or in bad weather not flying at all, but survival. Such opinion was probably prompted by such records as that compiled by VC-4. In one year that squadron had fifty-two major accidents, involving eighteen fatalities. On the other hand, only a small percentage of accidents was, in fact, directly attributable to night or flying in reduced visibility. Aviators who could not abide the limited instrument flying requirements of the day either avoided them or asked to be relieved from flight status. In any case, because of both operational and safety imperatives, those attitudes and that training and equipment began to change.

Given the prospects of nuclear war, fleet air defense, search and rescue, troop support, and new equipment, top leadership recognized both the fleetwide problems and the potential of across-the-board proficiency in night and instrument flight. This prompted the CNO in October 1950 to direct the establishment of a permanent Instrument Flight Board at each station, air group, and squadron. All Group I naval aviators[10] were henceforth required to maintain a valid instrument rating. About that same time, the course at the All Weather Flight School in Corpus Christi, Texas, was made mandatory for all flight students prior to getting their wings. Simultaneously, a dedicated shore establishment and industry worked the problems and adapted commercial equipment to make things better. These efforts proved to be major contributions to a downturn in the number of mishaps throughout carrier- and land-based naval aviation, and in the Air Force and commercial aviation as well. Although the following paragraphs are focused on naval aviation, these near-universal improvements could well explain the similarity in the slopes of the curves in figures 3-1, 3-2, and 3-3.

Again, it's not that naval aviators were totally unfamiliar with instrument flying before the CNO's 1951 edict; all had long been trained in the rudiments. Flying under a hood with an instructor safety pilot and spending time in the Link Trainer were parts of the undergraduate flight syllabus. Unfortunately, that was often the end of it—thus frequent "self-cleared penetrations" and (thankfully, less often) spins out of the overcast into the ground.

In August 1948, VCN-1 and VCN-2, the home squadrons for night-fighter and night-attack detachments, were redesignated as Fleet All Weather Training Unit Pacific (FAWTUPAC)[11] and Fleet All Weather Training Unit Atlantic (FAWTULANT),[12] respectively. While continuing to train and provide night detachments to deploying carriers, they took on the added missions of instrument training for daytime air group pilots and final qualification training for all-weather air controllers. Not all pilots received this training, however.

At the start of the 1950s, most of the instruments available in the cockpit for navigation and flight reference were air driven—that is, operated by air from the pitot-static system. Exceptions were the magnetic compass, generally used as a backup to the gyrocompass, the turn needle, a radio altimeter, and in certain land-based aircraft or seaplanes, the bubble octant. Such instruments had been satisfactory in earlier and slower-moving aircraft, but now, with the advent of high-performance jets operating in all-weather conditions, they fell short. Whether owing to mechanical malfunction or inadequate pilot performance, they often led to accidents. The air-driven artificial horizon would tumble beyond certain angles of bank and nose attitudes; the gyro compass would continually precess; and the magnetic compass would lag or lead headings in a turn. The octant, of course, was not feasible in a single-place aircraft.

Flying in weather or at night on only a magnetic compass and airspeed, turn-and-bank, and rate-of-climb indicators was difficult at best, and the radio altimeter was frequently unreliable. A new suite of flight instruments was needed, and fortunately for fleet readiness and for the accident record, they soon came into the inventory.

By the late 1950s, all aircraft were equipped with much more reliable and easier-to-read electric-driven attitude indicators and compasses. Some aircraft were equipped so that on just one, nontumbling instrument the pilot could now read pitch, bank, and rate of climb, thus making instrument scanning at night or in weather very much easier. One of the most effective of such indicators, installed as early as 1954, was the "Lear remote-reference pictorial vertical gyro attitude indicator." That instrument displayed a miniature airplane against a moving background sphere painted to simulate sky, horizon, and Earth and inscribed in such a way that a pilot could read exact angles of climb, dive, and turn. At the time it seemed an incredible advance in the technology of flight instruments, and undoubtedly it saved more than one tactical aircraft from a fatal end. Sophisticated digital displays and inertial and satellite-based systems were far in the future.

Hand-in-hand with continuously improving flight instruments were improved external sources of help to aircrews faced with "blind flying." Not being able to see landmarks because of clouds or because they were over the faceless expanse of the oceans was once one of the most vexing problems that faced aviators. It was even worse when communications were spotty or nonexistent. Prior to the 1950s, most aircraft radios operated largely in the VHF band, and in most carrier aircraft only a few, preset channels were available. To change any of the preset frequencies, a crystal in the radio set had to be replaced by ground technicians. This was cumbersome, at the minimum, and at the extreme it could mean mishaps if the aircrew didn't have the right frequency to contact ground or shipboard controllers when flying on instruments. A major breakthrough occurred in the early-1950s when carrier aircraft began to be equipped with multichannel ultra-high-frequency (UHF) radios.

For overland navigation, pilots used the Civil Aeronautics Administration's low-frequency ranges and nondirectional (NDB) and marker beacons, although not all aircraft had an automatic direction finder (ADF) capable of receiving the

NDB. Nor was it always easy in a single-place aircraft to turn the "coffee grinder" handle on the low-frequency radio to tune in a range, especially when in the clouds. Ashore, the location of the fixed-in-place air station was not that much of a problem, but in the early 1950s aircraft operating from carriers outside visual range could not depend on ship's radar, which had an effective range for issuing vectors of no more than twenty miles. Aircraft had to rely on the YE/YG[13] or in later years the ship's own ADF with dead reckoning (DR) overwater as the only fallback. Beyond chart-board estimates based on DR and visual estimates of wind by observing wave patterns, there was no way to measure distance from the transmitting station. In those circumstances, the chances for loss were obvious and in practice intolerable.

One equipment innovation, actually a mechanical computer, briefly saw service in the fleet. That was the AN/ASN-6 Ground Position Indicator. The pilot would crank in the latitude and longitude of his launch point, set wind direction and force in accordance with predictions from the weather officer (or read the drift himself from the waves if close enough to the water) and do away with the constant course and speed updates required for a maneuvering board. This was never a very popular device; it was eventually replaced by inertial navigation, but first it was overtaken by radar and TACAN.

When TACAN, a line-of-sight air navigation aid that showed bearing and distance to a selected station, came along, such dubious maneuvers as holding on a marker beacon or at the intersection of two low-frequency ranges listening for aural tones or depending on a maneuvering board or even the Ground Position Indicator became things of the past. For those who had relied for years on DR, low-frequency ranges, beacons, and homers, this was a phenomenal improvement. It started with air stations, but beginning as early as 1955, all aircraft carriers began to be equipped with TACAN. Pilots now knew continuously the range, bearing, and distance of the home base. With TACAN jets were now able to make a "jet penetration," an instrument approach to the carrier in a teardrop pattern from a high-altitude holding pattern, thus conserving fuel. Once beneath the clouds the aircraft could enter the normal carrier landing pattern or, in bad weather, make the penetration to a carrier-controlled approach, a shipboard version of the long-established ground-controlled approach, the GCA.[14]

The first GCAs grew directly from World War II developments of precision radar used in combat-air-patrol fighter direction and antiaircraft-gunfire control. Navy air controlmen were trained as early as 1943, and in that same year the CNO approved GCA as the Navy's standard "talkdown" to visual conditions air-control system. GCA soon thereafter proved itself ashore. To afford the option of an instrument landing aboard a ship at sea, the CCA was developed. An early system was used aboard the USS *Philippine Sea* in October 1948, and once fully developed and installed in other carriers it enhanced markedly their readiness to conduct sustained flight operations in all kinds of weather. The system undoubtedly saved many aircraft, but because records weren't kept the actual numbers of those saves cannot be ascertained. In any case, if the forecast weather indicated the need for a CCA on return, the flight just did not go. This was especially so when the initial approach relied on a ship's low-frequency homing signal, but things got better when CCA became more acceptable and reliable and when TACAN became available to feed the CCA pattern.

Radar had long been used by night fighters and night-attack aircraft, so it was a relatively easy to envision use of radar as a navigation device and for assistance in instrument approaches by other aircraft types. It took awhile for the use of such equipment to become standard, but once widely available it was readily accepted. Reports in *Naval Aviation News* like one describing how a transport aircraft narrowly avoided crashing into a cliff on an instrument approach by using radar did much to further its acceptance in the fleet.

There are no statistics on how many aircraft or how many lives have been saved by radar or GCA/CCA because chances are that without those facilities approaches to low ceilings in poor visibility would not have begun in the first place, but the confidence instilled in aircrews just from knowing that such capabilities were available most certainly enhanced combat readiness and most probably did save lives. The data are buried in the general downslope of the mishap experiences shown in figures 3-1, 3-2, and 3-3. Nevertheless, it is a certainty that much of the improvement in mishap performance between 1950 and 1960 can be attributed to the employment of better flight instruments and better navigation facilities, as well as better-performing aircraft.

5

Naval Aviation's Transition to Jets

The Navy and Marines began their transitions to jet aircraft in the years immediately after World War II.[1] A number of different aircraft types were built and tried out, and by the start of the Korean War in 1950 every carrier air group had been equipped with at least two squadrons of jets, usually the Grumman F9F Panther or the McDonnell F2H Banshee, and some had a detachment of all-weather F3D Skyknights.[2] All three aircraft types operated to the limits of their operational endurance, and the maintenance record and accident rate showed it. It didn't help at all that these jets burned fuel at an unprecedented rate and were operated from carriers using procedures and shipboard equipment (catapults and arresting gear) modified only slightly from those developed for their propeller-driven predecessors. They flew from straight-deck carriers, launched from hydraulic catapults, and flew the traditional "flat pattern" in their approaches to the ship for landing. (See chapter 1 and appendix 6.) The Banshees and Skyknights did the same thing at night. In retrospect, it's a wonder the accident rate operating from ships was no worse than it was; many opined, "It's just another airplane."

The trouble was that jets were not "just another airplane." Not only did things happen faster, requiring faster pilot responses, but stalls and spins were less forgiving and fuel burned at a faster rate. As fuel was consumed the aircraft's weight and balance changed, much more so than was usual with "props." (The optimum airspeed on approach varies with the aircraft's weight. It does with props too, but because a higher fraction of a jet's weight is fuel, that weight varies much more.) The jet cockpit was much simpler: no prop control, no carburetor heat control, no mixture control, and no supercharger control, all of which led to an attitude that "It's just another airplane, only easier." That was soon discovered to be a faulty concept, one that, along with "Show me how to start it and I'll fly it," overlooked the fact that too often the new jet pilot didn't understand aerodynamics at the higher airspeeds and found himself in unexpected trouble. Engines had not attained nearly the service life or reliability they reached in later years, and their acceleration took seemingly ages longer than the tried, true, and reliable "recips" (reciprocating—i.e., piston—engines).

When newer jets came into the inventory, they did no better. In some cases they did worse. For example, in FY 1954 the F7U Cutlass compiled a whopping 191 accidents per hundred thousand flight hours. The FJ Fury, a much less demanding aircraft, logged 177 accidents per hundred thousand hours and the F2H Banshee 145 per hundred thousand hours. Rates such as these explain in large measure the upswing in the mishap curve between 1950 and 1954.

Other reasons for the upswing undoubtedly lie among the facts that while the Navy grappled with the question of which jets would be best fitted for all the missions expected of it, its leaders were competing with the Air Force for missions and attempting to keep up with what was known of the Soviets. As one result, manufacturers conducted fifteen first flights of new jets in the decade of the fifties. (See chapter 13, figure 13-1.) Add to that the seven first flights of earlier jets made in the late 1940s, and the fact that it was a period of unprecedented development is obvious. While there is rarely a mishap on the first flight of a new aircraft, other early flight mishap experience is often less than stellar. Reliance on what was for all intents and purposes trial and error resulted in the fielding and rapid obsolescence of a succession of different jets, each reflecting solutions to the defects discovered in earlier models. In types that see long service, "bugs" can be worked out, crews get ever more accustomed to the aircraft, and all hands move up the learning curve—all this contributing to a good safety record.

Despite a few aircraft that eventually rendered long service, naval aviation's transition to jets was agonizingly slow. Both the Air Force and commercial aviation completed their transitions significantly earlier than did the Navy and Marines. The one naval jet that flew first in the 1950s and had a long service life was the A-4 Skyhawk; none of the other 1950s first-flyers had nearly so long a life.[3] On the other hand, the years after 1960 saw several jets with reasonably long service—the F-4 Phantom, the A-6 Intruder, and the F/A-18 Hornet in its various configurations among them. Indeed, such long service contributed in no small measure to the steadily improving mishap rate from 1960 onward. At the same time, innovations external to the aircraft themselves contributed to improvements in flight safety.

A major innovation that helped the jets immeasurably was in-flight refueling.[4] Like so many things to do with carrier aviation, it was a British development imported and used by all three American services. While initially adopted to extend range, it soon proved itself in the safety arena. During carrier operations, the capability saved many an aircraft when for whatever reason a flight deck became "fouled" (blocked or otherwise unavailable for landing). Unfortunately, there is no record of the number of aircraft "saved" because of in-flight refueling. The number must be quite high, considering the frequency of sudden onsets of "zero-zero weather" (zero visibility, zero ceiling), crashes on the flight deck, and arresting-gear or engineering malfunctions in the ship.

Among the first aircraft to be equipped to receive fuel from a tanker were the F9F-8 Cougar, the F7U-3 Cutlass, and, only slightly later, the FJ-3 Fury. The first tankers were modified AJ Savages, a small fleet of which had been built to carry

AJ Savage air-refueling an F7U Cutlass. *NHHC*

the enormous nuclear weapons of the 1940s. They were good, solid aircraft for in-flight refueling but nearing the end of their service lives and of commensurately uncertain reliability by the time they were put into service as refuelers. It was thus quite a scene when AJs refueled F7Us. The preference was always to do the refueling overhead the ship, so that if it didn't work the Cutlass could land immediately, the matchup being so unreliable. Things did improve after that, and today in-flight refueling from a "buddy store"[5] or dedicated Air Force or allied tanker is routine.

As for flight instruments, one of the most effective was the angle-of-attack indicator, installed first in carrier aircraft, starting in 1954, and then extended to all the fleet.[6] Its effectiveness stemmed from the fact that landing approach speeds, especially when landing aboard an aircraft carrier, are critical. Too fast, and the aircraft will probably not touch down in the desired area and may break the tailhook or an arresting cable or even, in earlier days, crash into the barrier (a fence raised during landings to prevent such aircraft from crashing into planes parked forward). Too slow, and the aircraft may stall and fall into the water or hit the stern of the ship. At the minimum, too slow or too fast will prompt a wave-off from the LSO.

ANGLE-OF-ATTACK INDICATOR. Approach, *Naval Safety Center*

Prior to the installation of angle-of-attack indicators, the pilot was required to calculate his approach speed according to the weight of the aircraft and its configuration and external load: flaps up or down or partial, speed brakes in or out. Also, the heavier the plane and its stores the more approach speed was required, but at the same angle of attack. The optimum airspeed could vary by as much as nine or ten knots. Trying to remember and maintain the indicated airspeed by looking down to the instrument panel while at the same time looking out to line up on the ship's centerline and trying to fly the proper glide slope as indicated by either the LSO or "the mirror" (we'll get to that) was often a serious, sometimes a deadly, problem. Add to the mix the fact that in the earlier jets there wasn't much margin between stall and approach speeds in the first place. A bomb that wouldn't drop when released, or unused fuel, could make a significant change in the optimum airspeed. The angle-of-attack indicator solved all those shortcomings.

As time went on, jet engines became more reliable, and irreversible control systems with artificial "feel" were installed. Stability augmentation, ejection seats, air conditioning, and other modifications followed.[7] All in all, as the decade of the fifties progressed, so did the safety of operating Navy and Marine aircraft. The evidence is the reduction by more than half of naval aviation's major mishap rate between 1950 and 1959[8] and the corresponding saving of lives and aircraft and the improvement of readiness throughout the fleet. A considerable factor in that achievement was the transition to jets. No longer did many leaders continue to believe "airplane accidents will always be with us."

6

Aircraft Carriers
Changes and Modifications

During World War II, the aircraft carrier replaced the battleship as queen of the fleet. Time after time it demonstrated its utility, its importance, and the critical need for its capabilities. Soon after the war, and despite struggles with naysayers, it proved its continuing importance, this time as a component of the nation's nuclear deterrent, while not compromising its other utilities. Of even more importance was its new role of being on station, on call, and ever ready for a long string of crises from Korea to Lebanon to Cuba and more.

Yet after the war returning aviation leaders were not completely satisfied with the carriers that had won the war. They sought to apply the lessons they had learned to build the naval aviation of the future. Ideas and concepts were plentiful, but the scenario that was most agreed on was that airplanes would be bigger, they would be jet propelled, and that operating such aircraft from a ship would require a ship that was larger and lacked the impediments of an island structure or any other sort of topside interference. The objections of the engineers, who saw the need for stacks to facilitate boiler draft, and of navigators and communicators, who needed elevated ship-control stations and antennas, were disregarded.[1] Thus the first postwar carrier, the USS *United States,* was laid down with a flush deck, with no island, topside antennas, or weapons. The retelling of the cancellation of *United States* and the subsequent "Revolt of the Admirals"[2] is not in itself particularly relevant to a history of naval aviation safety, but it did serendipitously delay the construction of the first post–World War II carrier until the British concepts of the angled deck,[3] steam catapults, and mirror landing systems came along. All these led to a much safer, let alone more efficient, way to operate aircraft from a ship.

Until the advent of those British-developed systems, aircraft would land aboard carriers much as described in chapter 1. Besides the always-present possibility of a ramp strike, it was not uncommon for an aircraft to miss all the wires and hit the barrier. The angled deck precluded the need for such a barrier except in the rare instance of inability to lower the landing gear or loss of the tailhook. Thus arose the conventional wisdom among many, especially carrier aviators, that the installation of angled decks on American aircraft carriers was the single change that underlay the dramatic improvements in naval aviation safety as a whole from 1955 onward. Without doubt, the angled deck was a breakthrough in carrier landing safety and efficiency, but it wasn't just angled decks. Not only was the carrier fleet not converted to the angled deck all at once, but the mirror landing system and steam catapult, to be discussed later, were introduced about the same time.[4] Also, when the large-deck *Forrestal* class began entering the fleet in 1955, operations became even safer and more efficient. Simultaneously, throughout naval aviation better airplanes, better cockpit instrumentation, better navigation aids, better control and even better personnel management were arriving. Thus, as important as it was, citing "angled deck" as the single enabler of increasingly safe aircraft carrier operations is, at best, misleading. It's also of some note that the angled deck came about not because the leaders of naval aviation looked to it as a giant leap in aviation safety but because they wanted more capability to operate larger new aircraft.

The U.S. Navy's first evaluation of the angled deck, initially termed the "canted deck," was in May 1952. An angled deck was painted on the straight deck of *Midway*, one of the three largest carriers at the time. Based on the success of those tests, *Antietam*, an *Essex*-class ship, was converted to an actual angled deck in the late fall of that same year.[5]

Two years later, in February 1955, after successful *Antietam* evaluations, plans for further conversions were approved by the Ships Characteristics Board (SCB) and issued as SCBs 27C and 125—the term "27 Charlie," used as a catchall for the many alterations introduced into a number of ships to follow.[6] *Shangri-la* was the first in a five-year-long stream of eighteen ships to be converted to angled deck, steam catapults, and improved arresting gear, finishing with *Coral Sea* in March 1960.[7] The first postwar carrier, *Forrestal*, had been laid down as a flush-deck ship but was changed to an angled deck even as she was being built, incorporating lessons learned from other fleet carriers earlier modified. *Saratoga, Ranger,* and *Independence* followed *Forrestal*, all commissioned with steam "cats" and the mirror landing system—or, later, the Fresnel Lens Optical Landing System (FLOLS) or, still later, the Improved FLOLS (IFLOLS).

The angled deck received universal acclaim from carrier pilots. That enthusiasm is probably best expressed by Capt. Jerry O'Rourke, slightly paraphrased as,

> It's hard to describe the remarkably different feelings for a pilot in those last few seconds of a straight deck landing as opposed to an angled deck approach. There's always room for a little error on the angle; there was essentially no margin for mistake on the straight deck. A bolter [missing all arresting wires and having to get instantly back in the air] off the angle might be embarrassing, but you get a sort of "born again" exuberance when you add full power and apply a little back stick and hurtle

back aloft. On a straight deck, even if you were in good shape at the cut[8] there was an infinitesimal instant of horrible pending doom as you slashed toward the barriers.[9]

As described by Captain O'Rourke from the pilot's point of view, the biggest advantage of the angled deck was that if for some reason the aircraft's hook failed to engage an arresting wire the pilot merely added power, took off down the angle, and reentered the landing pattern to try again.

Intuitively, it would seem that the carrier landing safety record should have improved over those same years. The data in table 6-1, extracted from an undated CNO report, shows that it did improve but only slightly. Except for FY 1956, the accident records of the converted ships were not much different than those of the straight decks. Complicating the data a bit is that in 1956 there was one angled-deck CVL [light carrier] and a CVE [escort carrier] in the mix, and in 1957 there was one CVL that did not operate jets. Also, not all mishaps can be attributed to jets. Carriers of all types also operated various prop aircraft and helicopters.

Improved mishap rate or not, angled-deck conversions were accepted in the fleet with enthusiasm by all, from junior pilots to flag officers, whose feelings were similar to those of Captain O'Rourke. More importantly, as the need to accommodate increased numbers of higher-performance aircraft rose and as night and all-weather flying became the norms, those who were there could hardly believe they had ever flown onto straight decks and were still around to tell about it. Such an emotional response may be difficult to pin down with statistics, and in any case, one must not conclude that it was only the angled deck and associated improvements that led to the steep reduction in aircraft mishaps. After all, aside from carrier mishaps there were numerous other mishaps as well. As shown in table 6-1,

Table 6-1 Carrier Mishap Comparison

	FY 1956	FY 1957	FY 1958
Total all Navy mishaps	1,456	1,298	1,106
Total CV landings	138,344	160,797	145,719
Total CV mishaps	245	211	148
Total CV mishap rate	0.18	0.13	0.10
Angled-deck landings	38,357	104,783	123,846
Angled-deck mishaps	50	146	124
Angled mishap rate	0.13	0.14	0.10
Axial-deck landings	99,987	56,014	21,873
Axial-deck mishaps	195	65	24
Axial mishap rate	0.20	0.11	0.11

carrier mishaps were just 16 percent of the total, hardly a preponderance on which to draw conclusions. Note also that on both angled- and straight-deck ships, not all mishaps occurred on landing. Crashes after failed catapult launches and major "crunches"[10] are also included but are not broken out in the data. It's rather obvious, then, that there were other factors contributing to making Navy and Marine skies safer.[10a] In fact, while angled decks did indeed enhance safety on the margin, their adoption did more for operational effectiveness than it did for safety.

Catapults too are part of the aircraft-carrier safety story, Navy aircraft having been first catapulted in 1912.[11] Motive power for catapults had included gravity (sliding down steel cables), compressed air, gunpowder, and hydraulic fluid. In more modern times, the needed energy source was almost always gunpowder on cruisers and battleships and hydraulics in aircraft carriers. During World War II, deck launches—that is, free-running, solely under the aircraft's own power—were the norm off the larger carriers. On the smaller carriers, because of lack of space for a deck run, the first aircraft to be launched would sometimes be catapulted, but as soon as there was enough space and wind over the deck was sufficient, deck runs were preferred. Toward the end of the war, as the aircraft got heavier, more and more of them were catapulted, but the deck run was still preferred.

The very early Navy jets, such as the FH-1 Phantom, were launched with a deck run, but it took pretty much the whole length of the deck of a CVB, as heavy carriers were then known, of the *Midway* class. To achieve a more efficient launch, the existing hydraulic cats were beefed up as much as they could be, and the first jet-blast deflectors were installed as well. Even as new jets, especially large new jets, were on the drawing boards, a more capable catapult had to be devised. Considering that hydraulic cats with enough capacity to launch the newer and heavier jets (up to and including the Douglas A-3 Skywarrior) were growing too large for even the CVBs, the designers briefly considered steam. But, and belying later experience, it was thought that drawing steam for the catapults would fatally compromise the ship's steam-driven propulsion plant. Later, electricity was considered and electromagnetic catapults too, briefly, but they were rejected early on for reasons of ships' electrical capacity.[12] Finally, it was decided to use gunpowder. In fact, the ill-fated USS *United States* was designed with gunpowder cats in mind. This approach was not without its shortcomings, however. Not only was gunpowder more hazardous than hydraulic fluid, but storing enough charges to last a full cruise would have exceeded the magazine capacity of the most optimistic design and would have been a logistics problem of the first order.

Thus, the jet fighters used in Korea, largely the F9F Panther and the F2H Banshee, were launched from hydraulic catapults very similar to those used by carriers at the end of World War II, only slightly modified and upgraded. The jolt delivered to the aircraft and the pilot as the catapult fired was always expected, but even so it took one's breath away. Once airborne, the first thing a pilot would do after raising his landing gear was "uncage his eyeballs."[13]

There were indeed catapult malfunctions, up to and including "cold shots," putting plane and pilot in the water. This quote from a letter to BuAer from ComAirLant is instructive:

> The newer aircraft now being received are putting greater and greater load on both ships and catapults. We are being forced to operate closer to maximum limits and with lower factors of safety with each new jet aircraft. The source of the troubles is thus readily explainable. However, the catapults must work, and successfully, since carriers with modern air groups are helpless without them. I do not say this is right, but it is a fact. It is essential, therefore, that all catapult troubles be closely followed and corrective measures taken at the first sign of trouble.[14]

Not said, but even more important in the long run, is that the existing catapults were only marginally capable of launching the larger aircraft, such as the A-3, even then in testing.

Once again, the Royal Navy came to the rescue, and by May 1954 an American carrier, *Hancock,* had for the first time been fitted with the British-developed steam catapults. Operations in *Hancock* were so successful that by May 1957 steam catapults had been installed in *Franklin D. Roosevelt* and in six additional *Essex*-class carriers. *Midway, Oriskany,* and *Coral Sea* followed, while *Forrestal* and all subsequent new carriers were built with steam cats. So by March 1960, all fourteen attack carriers—four *Forrestal*s, three *Midway*s, and seven modernized *Essex*es—and ten antisubmarine warfare carriers (CVSs) had steam catapults.

This did not solve completely the lingering problems of catapulting aircraft, especially jet aircraft, but it went a long way. Such problems persisted into the 1960s and beyond, but rarely was the problem the catapult itself. More often, it was inappropriate rigging of the "bridle" attaching the aircraft to the catapult shuttle or mismanagement of fuel, such as unbalanced or less-than-full drop tanks.[15] Any contribution there might have been from steam catapults themselves was negligible.

Then, about the same time as the angled deck and steam catapults, came the mirror landing system, another British development. Prior to the adoption of the mirror, approaches to carriers were made at a relatively low altitude with a final, curving, descending, approach turn to a "cut" signaled by the LSO just ten or fifteen feet above the flight deck at the very end of the ship. (See chapter 1.) If the pilot failed to use the proper technique after the cut, dropping the nose a bit and then flaring to a landing attitude he might either hit the ramp (the aft-most, blunt

38 Chapter 6

Cutlass launching on a steam cat. *NHHC*

end of the flight deck) or float into the barrier. With a mirror landing system installed, the landing approach was started from a significantly higher altitude, eight hundred feet as opposed to 125 feet, and the turn to the landing heading was a steady descent to just four hundred feet astern of the ship, followed by a straight-in, constant descent at a constant angle of attack. Using the light image, "the ball," in the mirror for glide-slope guidance instead of flag signals from an LSO, the pilot kept the power on until the aircraft touched down, at which time full throttle was added in case of bolter.

This was especially advantageous to the earlier jets, with their slow engine acceleration. Keeping some power on until touchdown and then adding full throttle significantly reduced the engine "spool up" time, thus minimizing any problems with takeoff from the angled deck if necessary. In addition, the increase

MIRROR LANDING. *NHHC*

in hook-to-ramp distance using the mirror, with a higher starting altitude and a slightly steeper angle of descent, was an even more significant advantage. "Hook to ramp" is the vertical distance between the trailing tip of the tailhook and the flight deck as the landing aircraft passes over the very end of the deck—the greater the distance the more margin in event of close-in glide-slope error. It varies somewhat from aircraft type to aircraft type and even between classes of aircraft carriers, the CVBs and *Forrestals* affording greater hook-to-ramp clearance than the 27Cs. In any case, higher hook-to-ramp distances made ramp strikes, crashing into the end of the flight deck, increasingly unlikely. While the gentler approach itself improved boarding rates (that is, fewer wave-offs), especially at night, there is little hard evidence (although there is some folklore extant) that mishap rates were improved accordingly.

Interestingly, when the mirror was first introduced to the fleet there was considerable lack of confidence in the system. In fact, early on pilots were required to qualify first on paddles (that is, LSO guidance),and only later were they permitted to qualify on the mirror. On some ships, only paddle passes were permitted at night or with a pitching deck. That attitude soon disappeared, especially with the advent of a stabilized mirror or Fresnel lens.

Lighting at night was another issue. According to one who was there, "The whole ship lighting setup at the beginning was pretty awful . . . [the lighting system] having been designed more to confuse World War II submarines than to help aircraft get aboard." Among other things, the centerline lights of the early 1950s were notoriously unreliable. The conventional wisdom was that showing lights had to be held to a minimum, for two reasons: to avoid visual detection by an enemy and to protect night vision. Consequently, from ready rooms to passages leading to the flight deck and onto the flight deck itself, only red lights could be used, and those only sparingly. Preflight inspection of an aircraft spotted on the flight deck at night was a hazard with only flashlights with red lenses. Aircrew, plane captains, and flight directors were all affected. Then, as commanders realized that any enemy would detect the force first with radar or sonar, things began to relax a bit. First came "dustpan" lights and eventually white floodlights. "Heresy!" cried the old-timers. Yet according to a Naval Safety Center survey, there was "no statistical difference in night aircraft accident/performance (bolter) rates in the 'before' and 'after' white lighting period. . . . It was agreed that other important needs are being met by using the lighting; namely, comfort and efficiency of operations [pilots, deck handling crews and others]." Another way to put it is that flight crews, flight-deck crews, and maintainers were all a lot happier and more efficient when the lights came on.

In addition to lighting, increased use of photography also helped. Both stills and 16 mm movies of carrier landings had long been used in accident investigations and in pilot and LSO debriefs of landings to improve performance. Such photography had limitations, however. Handheld photography on a windy and busy flight deck was difficult and at night virtually useless. To improve the capability, cameras with gun-camera-type film cartridges were mounted on the starboard side aft of the island, so as to include the aircraft, LSO, and deck. Filming started when the landing aircraft was at the ninety-degree position on the approach and continued until it "trapped" (caught a wire and was safely halted on deck) or was waved off. The system had its limitations, but a filmed debrief helped both the pilot and the LSO.

When the mirror came along, the camera was moved to the top of the mirror, which worked extremely well with the longer straight-in path of the mirror approach. Then, television arrived aboard ship, and a Pilot Landing Aid Television (PLAT)[16] was developed and installed, in a three-camera configuration: one embedded in the centerline of the landing area, one mounted on the island, and one set to record SPN-12 (relative speed), wind over the deck, and other data. The first PLAT was installed in *Coral Sea* in late 1961, and was rapidly implemented in all other active carriers as well. Not only was there now a record of every landing for use in mishap or near-mishap investigations and for LSO debriefs, but the

PLAT was soon piped to every ready room, Carrier Air Traffic Control, and even the bridge, so everyone could watch each plane's and pilot's landing progress.

Subsequent modifications and alterations to the mirror landing system brought a Fresnel lens in place of a mirror, a source light, and a stabilized system working off the ship's stable element to mitigate the apparent effect of the ship's pitch and heave in heavy weather. But once again, these evolutionary modifications did more for operational effectiveness than they did for safety.

With all that done, there was yet another system with seeming potential for carrier-landing improvement—the automatic approach. For many years there had been attempts to design an on-board-the-aircraft system that would guide the pilot through an approach to a landing, sometimes without the pilot having to touch the controls. In the early 1950s, a "coupler" that held the plane on glide path was indeed developed and used in transport aircraft. Then, after a period of concentrated development by BuAer engineers, an F3D Skyknight completed a Mode I (completely automatic) landing on USS *Antietam*. Subsequently, the system that supported automatic landings, the SPN-10, was installed on carriers and at selected naval air stations.[17] The Automated Carrier Landing System (ACLS), with the SPN-10 and its successor systems, had and has three modes: Mode I (automatic, tied into the aircraft autopilot), Mode II (semiautomatic, with cockpit signal displays but aircraft controlled by the pilot), and Mode III (manual or precision talkdown).

One would think that ACLS, particularly in Modes I and II, would have reduced the carrier-landing mishap rate significantly. Yet, there is general reluctance to use it, based on the argument that pilots must retain their hands-on carrier landing skills, and an automatic system doesn't allow that. There also was, and is, an argument that reliance on an automated system means atrophy of fine motor skills for lack of practice. Interestingly, that same argument seldom arises with regard to the automatic throttle. Nevertheless, with such attitudes prevalent the system's potential for more efficient recoveries (that is, fewer wave-offs) is not realized. On the other hand, the mere availability of ACLS on a cloudy day or a stormy night does do something, even if it is small, intangible, and mostly psychological, for the safety of the operation.

It thus appears that the several changes in aircraft-carrier configuration in the 1950s may not have done much for safety but did do a lot for operating efficiency. While the safety aspects of the changes were not trivial, the data apparently do not support the argument that they brought about dramatic improvements in safety. Rather, one could reasonably conclude that it was the advent of the larger *Forrestal* and subsequent classes of carriers that had more to do with safety than did the angled deck and so on. At the same time the advent of large and higher-performing jet aircraft posed operating problems for the *Essex* class and their modified kin, but those operating problems seem to have been solved more by operational adjustments than by modifications to the ships. What the modifications did do was to enhance operational capabilities at night and in all types of weather, in all but the most severe sea states, and with the heaviest and highest-performing jets.

The result of these efforts is seen today less in enhanced safety as in readiness to meet challenges of all dimensions in support of the United States and its allies around the world. It's a story worth retelling, time and time again.

7

Beyond Jets and Aircraft Carriers

The advent of jets is often cited as the principal reason for the high mishap rates of the early 1950s, but it should be noted that other communities had their share of mishaps as well. Consider that the land-based P2V Neptune did not achieve a mishap rate below ten per hundred thousand hours of flying until 1958. The accident rate for the S2 Tracker hovered in the high thirties per hundred thousand flight hours, and the T28 Trojan, the principal basic trainer for the Navy and Marine Corps, never got below forty-six.[1] Other aircraft, both carrier and noncarrier, also had their share of mishaps, beyond the 17 July 1953 R4Q Flying Boxcar crash on takeoff from Whiting Field discussed in more detail in chapter 8.[2] On 22 March 1955, an R6D Liftmaster crashed into the Pali on Oahu, with sixty-three killed, and on 11 October 1956, another R6D disappeared over the Atlantic, with fifty-nine lost. Then, on 25 February 1960, still another R6D collided in the air with an Argentine DC-3 close to Sugarloaf Mountain in Rio de Janeiro. Thirty-eight occupants of the American aircraft perished, as well as twenty-six passengers and crew of the Brazilian aircraft. As helicopters came into the inventory in increasing numbers, they too contributed to the high mishap rate.[3] Thus, it was not only jets. Such high numbers of mishaps were not easily reduced, but by the end of the decade several significant steps had been taken, and mishap numbers had begun to fall.

One of the more subtle changes, but one that wrought a huge impact, occurred in April 1957, when the responsibility for the assignment ("detailing") of all aviation officers in the grade of commander and above was shifted from the staff of the DCNO (Air) to the Chief of Naval Personnel.[4] On the large staff of the DCNO there had been room for politicking by aspiring commanding officers and for "cousin detailing," assignment based on whom one knew. These practices too often led to inadequate, or even bad, leadership in the fleet, leading in turn to far too many mishaps. Upon assuming responsibility, the Bureau of Naval Personnel established semiformal screening boards to identify potential commanding officers. This initiative minimized the chances that less-qualified individuals would be assigned as COs. Instead, officers with appropriate experience and proven leadership capabilities were selected for these all-important frontline assignments. It wasn't long before the mishap record began to reflect the change.

In addition to proven leaders, there was also a need for more thoroughly trained pilots, aircrew, and maintainers as more-sophisticated and more-demanding aircraft began to enter the fleet. The attitude of "If you show me how to start it I can fly it," coupled with maintenance conducted out of the chief's hip pocket and spare parts out of a cruise box, just wouldn't do anymore. This began to be corrected by creating replacement air groups on each coast—a story covered in detail in chapter 9.

Adding to the changes for the better were the ever-increasing efforts of the Naval Aviation Safety Center, aeromedical and human-factor sciences, more orderly and scientific maintenance and logistics programs, and steady improvements in aircraft systems, including engines. The positive effect of those efforts is best evidenced by the steady decline in the mishap rate: from over fifty-three accidents per hundred thousand flying hours in 1950, peaking at almost fifty-five in 1952, to twenty-five at the end of the decade in 1959 (see appendix 2), all with commensurate savings of lives and conservation of dollars. The major reasons for the change are the several important innovations described above, despite the fact that along the way not only did demands of the service increase but the operating environment changed significantly as well.

The Cold War, the Korean War, and several crises for which naval forces were marshaled called for an increase in both numbers and capability, thereby prompting a sustained high rate of pilot training and high operational tempo around the world. Across the board, naval aviation was able to deliver offensive capability with a variety of weapons, both conventional and nuclear, and was able to do that in all types of weather and at night, the mishap rate notwithstanding. Meanwhile, technology continued to advance, as reflected in increasing numbers of newly developed aircraft. Between 1950 and 1959, no less than nineteen new designs achieved first flight. By way of comparison, in the 1990s only three new aircraft reached first flight. Adapting to so many new aircraft in so short a time did not help the mishap rate. (See chapter 13.)

The aircraft carrier, thanks to a continuous infusion of new technologies, maintained its place as the centerpiece of the Navy and remained crucial to the nation's defense and because of these technologies became less conspicuous in the mishap rate. At the same time, maritime air surveillance and ASW remained crucial to the nation's defense, especially as the Soviet Union began deploying more and more ballistic-missile submarines.

Concurrently, naval aviation transitioned from a largely daytime and clear weather force to one that could operate effectively regardless of environmental circumstances, while accommodating to the age of jets, heavier aircraft, and increasingly capable helicopters. Yet, as it did all this it managed to reduce the number of major mishaps by half and to become a more capable force. While the advent of such carrier improvements as the angled deck, the mirror landing system, and more reliable steam catapults played roles in both operational capability and safety (see chapter 6), it must be noted that those advances were phased in over a period of years, not all at once, and even so, not all of naval aviation consisted of carrier flying. What was really significant was the introduction of better training, steadily improving and "easier to fly" (though more capable) aircraft, improved facilities afloat and ashore, learning from accident investigations, and importing lessons learned from the Air Force and from commercial aviation.

Foremost among the reasons why, as we've seen, the mishap rate was reduced by half between the early 1950s and the early 1960s (see appendix 2) was a focused leadership, determined to do whatever had to be done to save lives, equipment, and treasure while maintaining and even improving readiness to meet commitments to the nation. In this, leaders were assisted by better personnel management and ever-improving technologies—airborne, afloat, and ashore, many of them borrowed from or developed in cooperation with allies, commercial aviation, or the Air Force. Most important, all of this laid the groundwork for even more improvement in the years to come, a story to be told in the chapters that follow.

8

The Catalyst for Improvement
The Naval Safety Center

> Our product is safety, our process is education and our profit is measured in the preservation of lives and equipment and increased mission readiness.
>
> Naval Aviation Safety Center command history, 1966

Of all the events that marked naval aviation safety between 1951 and 1958, none were more significant than the establishment and growth in importance of the Naval Aviation Safety Center.[1] Only the adoption of Naval Air Training and Operating Procedures Standardization (NATOPS) and the establishment of the replacement-air-group (RAG) system, both of which came later, had similar significance. What came to be the Safety Center as it is known today did not arise all at once. It took dedicated effort and dedicated people, as well as help from outsiders, to effect what is today an outstanding naval aviation safety record. The center was also built on what went before.

In the years before and into World War II, the Bureau of Aeronautics endeavored to investigate problems and mishaps to learn from them and, where appropriate, pass on lessons learned to the fleet. BuAer also issued a weekly summary of mishaps, and in 1917 it initiated *Naval Aviation News,* in newsletter format, dedicated in large part to aviation safety education.[2]

By the start of World War II, all major commands had safety offices; that of the Naval Air Training Command was the largest, but Commander Air Forces Pacific (ComAirPac) and Commander Air Forces Atlantic (ComAirLant)[3] also included offices that recorded mishaps and issued directives. Then in 1943, shortly after the Office of the Deputy Chief of Naval Operations (Air) was established on the CNO staff, the new DCNO teamed up with the chief of BuAer and began to issue consecutively numbered safety bulletins; these constituted the forerunner of *Approach,* the now widely acclaimed Navy and Marine Corps aviation safety magazine. Shortly thereafter, the DCNO (Air), OP-05, directed the establishment of aviation safety boards in all commands and the appointment of a flight safety officer in each squadron. He also established a Flight Safety Branch in his office consisting of six line officers, one civilian, and a flight surgeon who reported directly to the Bureau of Medicine and Surgery, with additional duty with OP-05. To this small office was assigned the responsibility for the direction and supervision of an aviation safety program. Then, in October 1950, the CNO, recognizing that instrument training and qualification had both operational and safety implications, directed that aviation commands establish permanent instrument flight boards and further required that all Group I naval aviators[4] maintain valid instrument ratings.

Still, more was needed, however; in large measure, the safety effort in the fleet had fallen off from what it had been during World War II. During the war, every operating naval aviation unit had had a safety officer, most often the flight officer, then the third-ranking officer in the squadron. There were assistants for material safety and flight safety, and a flight surgeon was available. There was a manual of instructions for conducting a safety program and for initiating an accident investigation when necessary. Given the turmoil of the times that sort of organization worked well, and it carried over to the postwar years. But with postwar personnel shortages, the place of the safety officer in the organization was apt to shift with the whims of the individual squadron commanding officer. By the mid-1950s, the safety officer was most often a collateral duty for an assistant operations officer (or the LSO in a carrier squadron); his duties were little more than hanging safety posters, briefing accidents involving similar-type aircraft, and putting together accident reports as needed.

In Washington, the major tasks of the Flight Safety section of OP-05 were to review all aircraft accidents and discern whether any one accident or a pattern of accidents called for changes in training or procedures or modifications to equipment. They also kept files on pilots involved in accidents. There was also close association with BuAer with regard to design and materiel matters. Publications were the section's real strength, however. "Grampaw Pettibone" operated from the offices of Flight Safety Branch and was published in *Naval Aviation News*.[5] As such, he was an integral part of the flight-safety page written by that branch, along with Flight Safety Bulletins, "Dilbert," and *WRECKord* posters. The branch also made inputs to BuAer for various technical orders.

Despite the efforts of these dedicated few, the individual safety efforts of OPNAV, BuAer, the Training Command, and Commanders AirLant and AirPac continued to need some sort of coordination, if not consolidation. It was obvious that the all-Navy mishap rate was unacceptable and growing. In fiscal year 1951, for example, 675 Navy and Marine aircraft were lost and 391 people were killed. The all-Navy mishap rate was fifty-four accidents per hundred thousand flight hours.[6] Neither fleet readiness nor the budget nor the Navy-Marine image could continue to tolerate such losses.

Recognizing this, the CNO convened an ad hoc committee to review the situation and make recommendations that might ameliorate it. The committee made five recommendations, of which only one was implemented: the establishment of a CNO Aviation Safety Council. Sadly, in practice, the council does not seem to have contributed much to aviation safety. Still needing some sort of action, naval aviation next, as large organizations so often do when frustrated, consolidated and reorganized—and this time it worked to the good. On 1 December 1951, with the aim of creating an entity that would work with the entire aviation establishment and the fleet, most of the many responsibilities and the majority of the people in the Flight Safety Branch were transferred to a new Naval Aviation Safety Activity, on board Naval Air Station Norfolk, Virginia. It would be a single activity coordinating all naval aviation safety.

Coordination, yes, but authority, no—from the beginning, the Naval Aviation Safety Activity had no authority to dictate changes. Mishaps, incidents, and mistakes were shared with the fleet in various media, but since safety was (and is) a command responsibility, it was up to the line commanders and the individual pilots and maintainers to learn from those mistakes. In the event of mishap or incident, the activity would rely on analysis and, perhaps, a follow-up with suggestions on how to avoid a similar problem the next time. Some took the suggestions, some did not, but that sharing of experiences and development of corrective actions helped establish a steadily improving mishap record.

In the beginning, that effort built on much of the good work done and procedures developed previously in OP-05's Flight Safety Branch. Even though now in Norfolk, its successor continued to function as an adjunct to OP-05. On the other hand, it also began with a number of problems not having much to do with safety. First and foremost, it was not a command; the senior officer, a commander, was an officer-in-charge and did not have the authority or image of a commanding officer. Second, the activity was housed in a distant corner of the naval air station. With a Naval Air Station (NAS) Norfolk mailing address, it was looked upon by much of the naval aviation establishment as just another East Coast/Norfolk activity. Units on the West Coast and overseas tended to give it short shrift. Lastly, its staff was quite small, just twenty-nine persons total: twelve officers, eleven enlisted, and six civilian. However, as a CNO activity, it operated with the authority of the DCNO (Air). It was also a foretaste of things to come. Except for size, that early Naval Aviation Safety Activity was remarkably similar to today's naval aviation directorate of the Naval Safety Center. There were departments for accident records, safety literature, and medical safety (headed by a flight surgeon), departments all clearly reflecting a transfer of function from BuAer and the OPNAV staffs.

At first there was no accident-investigation section; the activity made do instead with its Analysis and Research Department, using punched cards sorted by long pins through their borders. Using this method, which now seems so antiquated, trends were noted and problem areas were identified. Of perhaps greater importance, there was also an Air Force captain assigned, the USAF Flight Safety Liaison Officer.

The Air Force had compiled a mishap record much better than that of the Navy and Marines, and that record was improving. Perhaps there was something to learn from those colleagues in light blue. There were problems swallowing that concept, however. First, few Navy leaders thought the Air Force could teach them much. In fact, there was widespread concern, especially among senior Navy leadership, that too much interaction would lead to absorption of naval aviation by the Air Force. Second, there was also the age-old Navy tradition of an "executive leadership philosophy," a concept of not interfering with the way a commanding officer did his job (which included safety). Yet there were glimmers of change of attitude. A few Navy pilots had flown with the Air Force and there was a handful of Air Force pilots flying with the Navy. Most importantly, when it came to aviation safety, it was hard to ignore the fact that the Air Force mishap record was far better than the Navy's. It was better even allowing for the different flying regimes, such as no carrier operations in the Air Force and in the Navy/Marines little of the long-range straight-and-level flight that Air Force bombers and transports were used to.

The key principle in the Air Force system was tough investigation under the auspices of an inspector-general group at Norton Air Force Base (AFB), often followed by discipline when fault and culpability could be assigned.[7] The naval services found it hard to buy into investigations from outside the chain of command, let alone discipline stemming from that, and so never took up the Air Force system. They did, however, buy into thorough investigation as a vehicle for finding and correcting causes of accidents and then use of results as the basis for remedy. It was also hard to miss that the Air Force Directorate of Flight Safety Research at Norton AFB was headed by a major general and staffed with nearly 190 officers, 154 enlisted, and 155 civilians. Clearly, the Air Force was putting an emphasis on aviation safety far beyond that given it by the Navy and Marines.

In recognition of that simple observation, in July 1953 a Navy commander joined the Norton staff, and the flow of information between the two agencies increased, to the advantage of Navy/Marine Corps aviation. Next, in July and August, came a sequence of two closely spaced and related events that changed then and for years to come the Naval Aviation Safety Program. The first was when on 17 July 1953 a Marine R4Q Flying Boxcar twin-engine transport crashed on a night takeoff from Whiting Field, killing five of the six aircrew and forty of forty-two Naval Reserve Officer Training Corps midshipmen on board. The second was the advent on scene, even as the accident report was working its way through the chain of command, of a new officer-in-charge at the Naval Safety Activity: a hard-charging World War II combat fighter pilot who brooked no nonsense, Capt.(later Vice Adm.) James H. Flatley.[8]

JAMES H. FLATLEY. *NHHC*

The accident report arrived on Flatley's desk shortly after he took over. He could hardly believe what he read. The accident board's overall conclusion was that the cause of the accident was "undetermined."⁹ Yet, when one reads the report, the pilots' lack of night flying experience is glaringly obvious. In fact, there was good reason for wondering whether the crew should have been assigned the mission at all.

The midshipmen had finished their summer aviation training at NAS Corpus Christi, Texas, and were on their way to their next phase in Norfolk. Marine Air Group 35 supplied the aircraft and the crew. The flight from Corpus to Whiting

Field, just northeast of Pensacola, was uneventful. At Whiting it was a clear July night, some isolated low fog, the field operating under visual flight rules. After refueling and filing a flight plan the aircraft started, taxied, performed the required engine checks, and positioned itself on runway 31. The less-experienced first pilot was in the left seat, in charge of takeoff. The plane commander occupied the right seat and assisted. Cleared for takeoff, the aircraft made what seemed to tower personnel a normal departure until, suddenly, just after it became airborne, there was a flash of fire and the aircraft dropped and disappeared into a small copse of trees in a shower of flames. The crash crew and local firefighters arrived on the scene to find only three persons still alive: two midshipmen and the navigator, a Marine corporal. In accordance with instructions, an accident board was formed and an investigation conducted.

Flatley immediately dug into the details and drew the conclusion that the pilots had been unqualified for their mission and therefore the fault lay largely in a serious lack of supervision. When one reviews the accident report almost sixty years after the mishap, chain of command is impossible to quarrel with Flatley's subsequent course of action. He marshaled what facts he could and launched a sixty-four-page official letter to the CNO, "Review of Naval Aviation Accident Prevention Methods," later to become known as the "Flatley Report."[10]

His letter painted a bleak picture of the state of naval aviation safety. In fiscal year 1953, more than one out of every four aircraft had been involved in an accident; 423 people had been killed in mishaps. The letter described some typical mishaps. A pilot had misjudged his altitude and flew into the water while making an unauthorized low pass. Another had led a flight of five aircraft into clouds and had flown into a mountain. Yet another had run out of fuel at night over water, with no lifejacket or raft. Of 2,226 major accidents, experts deemed that 22 percent had been avoidable. (Later analysis shows it was worse than that.) In its nine separate conclusions the letter made a convincing case for sweeping improvements in the way naval aviation worked to prevent accidents. For a litany of reasons there were too many avoidable mishaps. Not only carelessness or negligence but also poor leadership, poor or incomplete training, lack of technical knowledge, and poorly designed equipment and procedures were frequent factors. To begin to correct these deficiencies, Flatley recommended that all aspects of the Naval Aviation Safety Program be reviewed by a board, headed by a flag officer, "for the purpose of informing DCNO (Air) as to what courses of actions appear necessary to improve the Navy's system of reducing and preventing aviation accidents." This was heady stuff for a four-stripe captain, but it got results. Later reviews of this report and the follow-up actions have declared that Flatley's efforts saved naval aviation.[11] They are not far off the mark.

Among Flatley's observations was that the system for reporting and then correcting errors was unwieldy. Another was that handbook corrections were slow to

MISHAP INVESTIGATORS WORKING IN THE FIELD. Foundation, *Naval Aviation Museum Foundation Quarterly*, with permission

implement and sometimes in error themselves. Experienced supervisors were in short supply, and inspections were often inadequate. Crash investigations were apt to be grossly incomplete. Last, but not least, one of the report's most far-reaching observations was the need to get useful information to the squadrons more effectively. The Navy was then getting some publications from the Air Force, but Navy squadrons needed their own—publications that dealt with the problems they faced every day. Thus a recommendation followed that the quantity and quality of aviation-safety print media be increased.[12]

Improvements in the activity's prestige, organization, and efforts began almost immediately. The Assistant Secretary of the Navy (Air) and OP-05 were among the first to act. The activity was almost immediately authorized to grow to fifty-six people, then to eighty-eight. Top Navy leadership increased the emphasis on the flow of information to and from the field and among the Safety Center, OP-05, and BuAer. It also mandated better investigations of mishaps and more meaningful analyses of causes and recognition of trends.

In 1954, primary billets for safety officers in every fleet and Training Command squadron and on major air staffs were established, and prospective safety officers began to be sent to the eight-week aviation safety course at the University of Southern California.[13] Graduates were detailed as safety officers in squadrons and on stations throughout the fleet, where they formed a nucleus for the center's accident investigation teams.[14]

In the beginning, those teams were activated only upon invitation from a command, usually a major command. As time went on and their expertise and reputation grew, they were launched on every accident where there was large loss of life, substantial collateral damage, or spectacular events that garnered widespread media coverage. Today, with so few aircraft accidents anywhere in naval aviation, the Safety Center's accident investigation teams are apt to deploy on almost every major mishap.

Liaison with the Air Force continued and was expanded to include participation in USAF-Industry Safety Conferences, regular presentations highlighting the special nature of naval air operations, and requests for industry and Air Force help in solving problems. Meanwhile, successive commanders, along with OPNAV and BuAer representatives, reached out to other aviation organizations, such as the Flight Safety Foundation, regularly hosting and participating in seminars and conducting regular Safety Council meetings.

The importance of the Flatley Report can hardly be overemphasized. Captain Flatley's long letter is the genesis of much of what the Naval Safety Center and, indeed, naval aviation itself is today. It took a courageous and outspoken fighter pilot, "stuck" in what he thought was not much of a job, to get the facts and lay them before the CNO. From Flatley's report stemmed directly the establishment of trained and professional accident investigation teams, more definitive and accurate determinations of the causes of mishaps, augmentation of the Safety Center staff, the establishment of an Aviation Safety Literature Department at the activity, and more. Only six months later, the activity traded its officer-in-charge for a flag officer and a year after that was redesignated as the Naval Aviation Safety Center.

Publications grew in importance. Specifically, as stated in a command report of the time, "The publications department provides the major 'voice' of the Navy's aviation safety program"; *Approach* magazine, published first in July 1955, was the "primary Navy-wide published media" for aviation safety. *Approach* "is written in an easy reading style in order to present technical information and official directives in a manner that will interest as well as educate the reader."[15]

Credit too, of course, should go to those nameless staff officers in the office of the DCNO (Air) who recognized the worth of the Flatley Report and presented it to the critical decision makers of the day. Unfortunately, Vice Admiral Flatley died early, and the Navy never realized the potential he might have had in store. Nevertheless, his influence is felt throughout naval aviation to this day.[16]

Succeeding generations of officers-in-charge, commanding officers and staffs saw to it that safety improvements did not end with the Flatley Report. The center's expertise and purview grew steadily. By 1956 there were six departments: including publications, crash investigation, maintenance and material, records and statistics, aeromedical, and analysis and research. Each department took seriously its job of passing on what was learned from crash investigations, maintenance, material and statistical analyses, and research of all types. Contributions to improved aircrew and maintenance-personnel training, aircraft systems, equipment and procedures became legion. More and more throughout the fleet was heard the question, "What does the Safety Center say?"

That growing importance of the Safety Center is reflected in the fact that since 1957 all its commanders have been flag officers, save for brief, intermittent periods. The center's importance has been further underscored by the major contributions of its dedicated people to Navy/Marine Corps operational readiness and safety. The thousands of "lessons learned" from mishap investigations, trend analyses, on-site visits to examine the details of squadron safety programs and deficiencies, and, for many years, "Anymouse" reports[17] got collated at the Safety Center and published on its website and in its various print media. These products were also reported to manufacturers, maintenance and supply organizations, and operators, by which means they contributed to ever-safer operations. Thus, Safety Center personnel have made and continue to make major contributions to almost every aspect of this success story. Among them are the Naval Aviation Maintenance Program, the replacement air group/fleet readiness squadron concept, NATOPS, the Squadron Safety Program, and the introduction of system safety into design.

The importance of aviation medicine was recognized in January 1968, when the Naval Aviation Safety Center was designated by BuMed as a training site for the Aerospace Residency Program: a six-month period out of the three-year residency administered by the Naval Aerospace Medical Institute in Pensacola.[18]

Outreach to other safety organizations increased and received more emphasis. Regular liaison was established with the Air Force, the Army, the National Transportation Safety Board, the Federal Aviation Agency (FAA), the National Aeronautics and Space Administration (NASA), and the Flight Safety Foundation. Some of the more valuable exchanges occurred at periodic seminars and conferences, many originated by the Naval Aviation Safety Center. Lessons learned were shared also through the several Safety Center publications and applied to naval aviation safety training and regulations.

When NATOPS (see chapter 9) came along, it wasn't long before safety and that program were married and the naval aviation safety experience improved even more. All this, in large measure, was due to the wisdom so long ago of taking up formal safety education. From the beginning, the philosophy of the Safety Center was that the best way to avoid mishaps was through education—thus publications, seminar outreach, and message traffic where appropriate. The basis for these outputs was a system of review and analysis of a variety of reports and requests as well as of unsatisfactory-equipment reports, surveys, and personal contact. However, some of the most valuable lessons were learned from thorough investigation and analysis of mishaps.

From the earliest days, the responsibility for mishap investigations belonged to the reporting custodian of the aircraft. It remains so today; however, the Safety Center has long maintained a "Go-team" of accident investigator experts who are ready to join any investigation on short notice, either at the request of the reporting custodian or automatically in the event of a particularly significant event (such as a large loss of life, the loss of a new aircraft, or case involving multiple custodians, such as Air Force or civilian aircraft or property). Normally, Safety Center experts are not part of, but work closely with, the reporting custodian's mishap board. From participation in these investigations, and from review and analysis of the Aircraft Accident Report once processed through the chain of command to the Safety Center, lessons are learned, flight or maintenance procedures may be modified, and feedback is afforded the manufacturer. It's a system that has worked exceedingly well for years.

There are two basic reasons why the system works so well. First, it is widely understood that the purpose of the accident investigation is not to assess blame but to gain factual knowledge in order that similar occurrences may be prevented. A second reason is that the mishap investigation is conducted outside the Navy Department's judicial system. In particular, witness statements are "privileged"— that is, none of the results of a mishap investigation, conclusions, evidence, or statements can be used in any sort of judicial process. This is clearly spelled out in the September 1959 *Judge Advocate Journal*:

> The privileged status of mishap investigations is rooted in now long-standing Navy Regulations, instructions and law. The mishap investigators, the witnesses and persons involved in any mishap are protected in law from any sort of prosecution or recrimination for what they may have done or said in connection with an aircraft mishap. Investigators and the chain of command can thereby derive from all available evidence the causes of any particular mishap and commence corrective actions based on that evidence. On the other hand, it's recognized that there may well have been actions leading up to or during the mishap for which legal or disciplinary actions are appropriate. It's not the aircraft mishap report or investigators that determine this, however. Instead, where circumstances warrant there is a separate legal investigation convened in accordance with the Manual for Courts Martial. In this legal investigation witnesses are advised of their rights, sworn statements may be taken and punishments may be awarded. In many ways, this dual path arrangement is key to learning all possible lessons from any given aircraft mishap thus pointing the way toward

remedial measures, whether with regard to personnel training, procedures or equipment thus facilitating improvement in the Navy and Marine aviation mishap rates.[19]

This affords witnesses and investigators alike the opportunity to be free and open as to the causes of any mishap, so corrective action can be taken without fear of reprisal or punishment. Thus, lessons are learned and fed back to the people and offices that can profit most.[20]

Feedback has consisted, of course, of a host of things other than aviation safety schools, publication of lessons learned from mishap investigations and a wide range of media. Early on, it was realized that these would not be enough. Outreach by way of conferences would and did help. Another way was to take the message, whatever it happened to be, directly to the fleet, whether major commands or squadrons. Initially there was the perception that much of the outreach amounted to coercion. That was overcome when it was understood that the Safety Center was about not coercion but education. One prime method of education was the Safety Survey.

The Safety Survey was at first an outlier with regard to the way the Navy did business. It was and is a "white hat" visit, requested by the unit, a review by peers for which one doesn't have to prepare. The reporting senior doesn't even hear about the results of a Safety Survey visit unless the commanding officer chooses to share them. It's an honest-to-goodness "We're here to help" effort, with no strings attached—no recriminations expected or allowed. After a somewhat shaky start, the Safety Survey has proven to be one of the most popular and effective accident-prevention stratagems yet devised, and it is a tool much used and appreciated by commanding officers.

In May 1968, the command was assigned responsibility for surface-ship and submarine safety programs, concurrently dropping the word "aviation" from its title and becoming the Naval Safety Center. The staff grew to nearly three hundred people, roughly half military and half government civilian. The Aviation Investigation and Aeromedical Divisions continued as part of the Aviation Directorate, but the erstwhile Media and Statistics Divisions were made parts of the larger Safety Center effort. One result has been that vastly increased data-gathering and data-analysis techniques have been applied to such areas as motor vehicles, off-duty and recreation, and system and industrial safety. Publications, now the products of the Media and Marketing Directorate, continue to be the center's real strength. In August 1969, the center reported that it published and automatically distributed to the fleet and the shore establishment nine different magazines, newsletters, and summaries. In keeping with the times, there is less print media today, and several publications familiar to old hands have disappeared, the *Weekly Summary* prominent among them. There is no less communication, however;

whatever has been lost from print media has been more than made up with electronics, the medium of choice of today's sailors and Marines.

Despite the reorganization and the expanding scope of the Safety Center, the traditional efforts of the Naval Aviation Safety Center continue, but now with the addition of divisions dealing with Operational Risk Management (ORM), Culture Workshops, bird and animal strike hazards (BASH), and more. Improvements in capability, efficiency, and service to the fleet continue. Aviation mishaps have become the exception instead of the rule; the reductions in mishap rates and loss of equipment and people have been little less than startling when one compares today with 1950. The Safety Center's contributions to fleet readiness are manifold. Those who conceived of such a center and those who have worked with it have indeed helped to save lives and equipment and have made major contributions to mission readiness. Today, the Naval Safety Center enjoys a respect and has an influence only dreamed of by those who first saw the need. Their product is indeed *safety:* "The process is education and the profit is measured in the preservation of lives and equipment and increased mission readiness."[21]

9

Six Amazing Years

RAGs, NATOPS, and More

Between the start of 1958 and the end of 1963, the Navy and Marines logged an especially remarkable achievement in aviation safety.[1] In a period of only six years, six years that included intensive operations of some of the most difficult aircraft in the fleet—the Crusader, the Demon, the Skyray, Tiger, Phantom, Vigilante, and Skywarrior—the all-Navy major mishap rate was reduced by more than half and was launched on a downward trajectory that continued to the end of the century. In that five years were established replacement-air-group training, a system known as "Level Readiness," a Naval Air Training and Operations Standardization program, an improved system for selection and assignment of personnel, a more responsive system for maintenance and supply support, and more. Some of these concepts go hand in glove and need to be discussed together.

As seen in earlier chapters, the number of naval aviation mishaps was set on a gradually improving trajectory in the mid-1950s. Training, safety awareness, and equipment and procedural changes had been, for the most part, institutionalized, but an even bigger correction was needed. The seeds for that bigger correction lay in the Naval Air Training Command and a couple of other pockets of excellence around the fleet. Unlike so many institutional improvements that begin with the rank and file, it was Navy leadership at the highest levels that recognized the possibilities; thus the RAG concept, NATOPS, and more were born.

Replacement training was the first to be developed, but once adopted, it led to others; it led especially to Level Readiness and NATOPS. Formerly, newly designated aviators or those being reassigned from other duty reported directly to fleet squadrons, usually while the squadrons were in between-deployment regroup and workup status. It was up to the squadron to checkout the "nugget" in whatever aircraft the squadron happened to be flying. For those who had flown similar aircraft—say the F6F Hellcat, the AD Skyraider, the TBM, or the P5M—in the Training Command or at previous duty stations it was no big deal, but for those who had never before flown a jet, checking out in one was a big deal indeed. In some ways, it was even harder for more senior pilots coming from shipboard or shore duty where they had flown little but the twin-engined SNB four hours each month and were now expected not only to master a new airplane but to lead as well.

A related issue particularly pertinent to carrier squadrons manifested itself later in the training cycle when it was time to work in air group–sized operations. Normally, there was no more than casual exchange with other squadrons in the air group, and if they happened to be based at distant naval air stations, as many were, it was worse. This was a special problem with the air task groups left over from the Korean War and with the various detachments that were needed to flesh out air-group capabilities. Leaders didn't know one another, and junior pilots didn't know the more senior leadership in other squadrons or on the air group staff.[2] They knew little about working with other-type aircraft, as they would have to once air group–scale air operations began, usually on first embarkation or "workup" at Guantanamo Bay, Cuba, or NAS Fallon, in Nevada, or in the assigned carrier.

A third group of issues for carrier air groups had to do with specialty training, maintenance, and supply. While Marines had fewer problems, given that they were based primarily at Marine Corps Air Station (MCAS) Cherry Point (in North Carolina) and El Toro (California), squadrons in a Navy air group tended to be based at the same naval air station, in order to facilitate air-group command and control, but the practice exacerbated problems of training, maintenance, and supply, owing to the need to distribute goods and services among several air stations. For example: if each group had a squadron of Cougars, a squadron of Panthers, another of Furies, and one of Skyraiders, the host naval air station had to maintain the required aircraft simulators and a fleet air support squadron (FASRON) with intermediate-maintenance capability (that is, beyond the scope of a squadron but not requiring "rework," or overhaul) for each type of aircraft. The same applied to the aviation supply office at each naval air station; in both cases the result was duplication of efforts and lack of standardization up and down each coast. For instrument training, squadron pilots very often had to be sent to other stations on temporary duty, at great expense and loss of time. Thus, for carrier squadrons on the West Coast, services were duplicated at Alameda, Moffett, Miramar, and North Island (all in California), and on the East Coast at Oceana, Norfolk, Cecil Field, Jacksonville, and Key West (the latter three in Florida). Such a system not only placed unneeded demands on test equipment and highly trained maintainers and stretch the spare parts inventories in the supply system but was expensive and terribly wasteful of manpower, all the while doing little to enhance either readiness or safety. That system cried out for some sort of consolidation.

The Navy found models in its own backyard and in a bit of history. In World War II, a pilot ordered to an air group would first go through an Advanced Carrier Training Group, where he mastered the plane he would fly before he reached the carrier. In other words, he was combat ready when he reported to his squadron. That process was dropped soon after the war ended, but the idea was still in institutional memory. Another factor was that in May 1952, ComNavAirPac had established the Fleet Air Gunnery Unit (FAGU) at Naval Air Facility El Centro, California. This was a six-week course for Navy and Marine fighter and attack squadrons, designed to establish a cadre of excellence in ordnance and gunnery in each. Established initially for West Coast squadrons, it expanded later to offer training to the East Coast as well. Thus, in effect, a fleetwide system of standardization for gunnery, bombing, and ordnance-system maintenance was established. Other specialized courses were conducted at various locations teaching all-weather instruments, tactics, and jet transition. A built-in problem with almost all these courses was that they were apt to occur at different times during a pilot's first tour, so some pilots profited therefrom, others not.

There were other models, however. In the Naval Air Training Command, instructors were standardized in a special instructors' school before ever taking on students; one was the Instructors' Basic Training Unit (IBTU) in Pensacola. Another was in April 1955, when the Jet Transition Training Unit (JTTU) was established at Olathe, Kansas, in order to orient erstwhile deskbound pilots to jets.[3]

Even earlier, with the arrival of more demanding jet aircraft into the fleet, Commander Naval Air Pacific Fleet, Vice Admiral William Martin, directed that Cdr. "Jig Dog" Ramage, commanding officer (CO) of VC-3 at Moffett Field, establish a transitional training unit to train pilots and maintenance personnel in standardized procedures for operating and maintaining them. Ramage's squadron had actually operated as a transitional training unit since 1954. Initially, it had been a small unit at Moffett Field operating under the aegis of the Naval Air Test Center, as an adjunct to a fleet indoctrination program for new aircraft. At first, four pilots from each transitioning squadron completed a forty-hour flight syllabus. Later, a cadre of enlisted maintenance people was added to the list of those under instruction, the idea being that these four pilots and the small group of maintainers would form the cores of squadron training efforts. This all began in 1955, just as the squadron began training with the Cutlass. Shortly thereafter Project Checkout, known colloquially as "Cougar College," was organized to train to the swept-wing F9F-6 and later the FJ-4 Fury. This was combined later with Cutlass training.[4] Training for the Skyhawk, Demon, and Skyray followed.[5]

At least partly on the basis of these experiences, a CNO-sponsored conference was called to investigate how to reduce the fleet's accident rate and increase combat readiness of carrier squadrons. The conference was chaired by Rear Adm. James Flatley, the same Flatley who as a captain had issued the now-famed Flatley Report (see chapter 8) and was now in charge of the Aviation Plans Division on the CNO staff. The recommendations of "the Flatley Board" were far-reaching and equal in importance to the Flatley Report, even if somewhat overshadowed in history by it. Among the many recommendations was a BuPers Aviation Career

Plan, establishment of an Aviation Officer Ground Corps (which eventually became part of the initial Naval Aviation Observer program in 1960), implementation of a high-performance-aircraft aerodynamics course in the course of pre-flight training, and establishment of standardized transition-training squadrons for all fleet aircraft.

A further catalyst for a replacement training program may have been an 18 December 1957 letter from Vice Adm. Robert Goldthwaite, then Chief of Naval Air Training (CNATRA), to the Deputy Chief of Naval operations (Air Warfare), OP-05, then Vice Adm. William V. Davis Jr. The letter compared the Air Force's experience with introduction of its Century-series fighters and its program of carefully supervised training with the Navy's much worse experience with relatively unsupervised checkouts in the new jets. Goldthwaite went on to suggest that the CNATRA-supervised training at the Olathe JTTU might be a model for the Navy. Further, he suggested that the issue be put on the agenda for a General Aviation Training Conference to be held the following February.

In light of the Flatley Board's report, Vice Admiral Goldthwaite's recommendation, and experience at Moffett Field, it was easy to visualize the establishment of replacement training squadrons and the establishment of replacement training air groups, or "RAGs" (Air Replacement Groups). That is exactly what happened, and on 10 March 1958 the Chief of Naval Operations approved what is known to this day as the "RAG system": "A reorganization of carrier aviation that would create uniform air groups, provide a more permanent group assignment to ships, and permit a reduction of assigned units and aircraft without also reducing combat readiness."[6] The new organization also provided for a permanent replacement air group to be established on each coast and made responsible for the indoctrination of maintenance personnel, the tactical training of aviators, and the special programs required for the introduction of new models of combat aircraft.

Hand in hand with establishing the RAG system, the Navy instituted what was then known as "base loading." Basically, all aircraft of similar type were consolidated at one station on each coast, colocated with the associated RAG, thereby facilitating checkout, instrument training, simulator training, maintenance training, intermediate maintenance, and supply. It also did wonders for tactics, as pilots met, passed the word, and discussed with others the best way to carry out missions—sometimes in semiformal classrooms, sometimes at officers' club "happy hours."[7]

Early in 1958, two regular carrier air groups were designated as RAGs, with new missions, one on each coast. CVG-4, or "CAG-4," was renamed Readiness Carrier Air Group 4 (RCVG-4) and based at NAS Cecil Field for East Coast carrier squadrons, and CVG-12, or "CAG-12," at NAS Miramar was renamed as the West Coast training group. The mission of the readiness carrier air groups was stated as the indoctrination, familiarization, and training of replacement naval aviators; the indoctrination and on-the-job training of replacement maintenance personnel; and the establishment of fleet introduction programs for new models of carrier combat aircraft.

Later, in April 1962, to bring their title in line with their functions, replacement air groups (RAGs) were redesignated combat readiness air groups (CRAGs). A majority of the squadrons assigned to the former CVGs retained their original names and numbers, but the RCVGs eventually absorbed a mixture of squadrons and aircraft types, each with new training missions. RAG squadrons dedicated to instrument training were also established, to train and refresh pilots in instrument work in two-place aircraft and to administer the required written examinations. Early on, FAGU was also absorbed into the RAGs.

At the outset, RCVG squadrons were spread over Oceana, Jacksonville, Cecil Field, and Key West on the East Coast and Alameda, Moffett, and Miramar on the West. On the Marine side, VMT-1 was established at Cherry Point in July 1958, with a three-element curriculum: the Swept-Wing Jet Transitional and Refresher Course and two instrument courses. There was a similar organization at El Toro for West Coast Marines. Later, replacement patrol air wings were established for maritime patrol (VP) pilots and crews, especially important as they began their transition to the P-3 aircraft. Sometime later, RAGs were established on both coasts for heavy attack and reconnaissance attack aircraft, airborne-early-warning aircraft (E-1s and E-2s), and helicopters. Still later, the two RCVG commanders and staffs were seen as redundant, and in their places were established other supervisory organizations. Today, we have RAGs for each major type of aircraft and mission in the inventory.

RAGs not only familiarized and trained newly reported pilots, and soon naval flight officers (NFOs), in the systems and flight characteristics of their new aircraft but also trained enlisted maintenance personnel in the particulars of their aircraft. Formerly recent graduates of "A" schools (technical training schools of varying lengths, depending upon the rating for which students are being prepared, such as Aviation Ordnanceman) were ordered directly to line squadrons with little or no specific training in maintaining the types of aircraft they were expected to service; there they relied on on-the-job training and the not-always-gentle, often impatient instruction of the "old hands." Now, just like aircrew, all enlisted maintainers were sent to the appropriate RAG to learn the systems and test equipment they were expected to maintain and use. When they reported to their squadrons they could "hit the deck running," without needing lengthy indoctrination, thus simultaneously improving maintenance readiness and reducing costs. An added bonus was that because the RAG squadron and the fleet squadrons that flew the same type aircraft were colocated, a ready reservoir of training and problem-solving talent was always available.

Most importantly, the RAGs had a tremendously positive influence on accident prevention:

> July 1959 marked the end of the first year of Replacement Carrier Air Group operation. RCVG-trained pilots represented 28 percent of the average number of fleet pilots flying A4D, F4D, F11F, F3H, FJ-4 and F8U aircraft during FY '59. A study of their safety record as opposed to squadron trained pilots showed only one in twenty-four RCVG trained pilots was involved in a pilot factor accident as contrasted to one in nine for squadron trained pilots. The RCVG program was estimated to have saved the Navy approximately forty million dollars to date.[8]

RAGs also facilitated readiness, and in that connection they paved the way for what became the "Level Readiness" concept. Prior to the RAG system, as previously noted, squadrons would reconstitute between deployments. The more experienced pilots would depart for other duty soon after a cruise, to be replaced by a combination of pilots from shore duty and nuggets directly from the Training Command. It was then up to the squadron leadership to mold this new group into a cohesive and talented fighting unit. As might be expected, results were mixed, almost solely dependent on the leadership (or lack of it) of the commanding officer, executive officer, and operations officer. The theory behind Level Readiness was that the RAG would train the replacement crews to be talented fighters, ready to blend in with any similar squadron without any further indoctrination. Squadrons would not be totally reconstituted between cruises; aircrews would rotate in and out in accordance with optimum career planning and the needs of the service. The idea was that regardless of where it might be in a deployment cycle, every two months each fleet squadron would lose one full-tour pilot/NFO and gain a replacement of equivalent rank. In this way, the squadron would maintain a constant level of combat readiness.[9]

Interestingly, while the Atlantic Fleet adopted the practice, the Pacific Fleet did not, and even in the Atlantic Fleet not everyone was happy with the arrangement. Among other things, there was suspicion that it was a scheme concocted by the Bureau of Naval Personnel to stretch limited personnel resources. Squadron commanders objected to losing experienced pilots in the middle of a deployment, only to be replaced by unknown quantities—nuggets.[10] Some years later, the Level Readiness concept was modified to enable squadrons preparing to deploy to work up as units with all personnel on board, at least by time of the deployment. Level Readiness paid off any number of times, even in the Pacific Fleet; when a loss in an accident or combat had to be replaced on short notice, the RAG system was able to do that.

As the RAGS got started, the old question about the best way to do certain things reemerged. At first, just like in the pre-RAG individual squadrons, the operations officer or the CO dictated what he thought best. Soon, after a few exchanges between coasts, it became obvious that there must be one best way. Thus came the first glimmers of standardization. Eventually this trend produced what today we know as NATOPS, the Naval Air Training and Operating Procedures Standardization program; however, before getting into that, a slight excursion is appropriate.

In the Spring 2010 issue of the Naval Aviation Museum Foundation's journal, *Foundation,* Col. William T. Hewes, USMC (Ret.), published an article on how it was before NATOPS—in 1956, in his case. Here is what he had to say:

> What the flying did not include in those days was a fully-fledged standardization program and a mature Naval Aviation Safety program. The result, predictably obvious by today's standards, was a horrific accident rate. You see, the folks who led us back then were all wily, steely-eyed veterans of World War II and Korea and knew no fear. They trained us the same way they had been trained—by launching us into the hostile sky largely unsupervised with the hope that the more promising among us would return alive. Surprisingly, some of us did. It was a training system Charles Darwin would have been proud of.[11]

While the remark about merely hoping nuggets would stay alive might be a bit of an exaggeration, it was true that there was little supervision. Orientation to fleet aircraft often consisted of a read of the handbook, a blindfolded cockpit check, a brief on how to start the engine, good wishes, and a pat on the back. More than one nugget was told something like, "Meet me over the field at ten thousand feet," only to find that that rendezvous was the starting point for an air-to-air hassle to test the new guy's skill and mettle.

Not all was completely chaotic before NATOPS, however. If standardization was not the rule in all parts of naval aviation, it was in many. In the Training Command, students preflighted, started, taxied, and operated their training aircraft in standard ways. Takeoff procedures and patterns and flight procedures for a variety of maneuvers, both acrobatic and nonacrobatic, were performed according to strict standards. Flight grades were predicated on those standards. As we saw, instructors were standardized in a special school before ever taking on students.

Then there was instrument flight training. Before 1950, not all naval aviators were qualified to fly on instruments, only those with special training. Everyone else flew according to visual flight rules. With increased emphasis on flying at night and increased requirements for flying near high-traffic metropolitan areas and in airways, as previously discussed (see chapter 4), the CNO directed that by the middle of 1952 all naval aviators would maintain valid instrument ratings. That, of course, required increased training in instrument flying and airways procedures, and that in itself was a kind of standardization. Much of that learning and subsequent practice was codified in an *All-Weather Flight Manual,* a sort of precursor to NATOPS for flying at night and in weather, on instruments.

Meanwhile, in the Training Command and in the fleet, takeoff and landing patterns had long been standardized. The Air Force, Navy, and Marine Corps flew similar patterns at airfields, and all aircraft carriers had the same launch and landing patterns. (In fact, there was a manual in the United States Fleet [USF] and later Naval Warfare Publication [NWP] series that stipulated the patterns.) Also, in the fleet, each organization had a written Standard Operating Procedure, an SOP. The SOP was important if for no other reason that it was on the checklist for every administrative inspection. The problem was that even if the squadron followed its SOP, it changed every time the commanding officer or the operations officer changed. At the same time, lurking in the background was the question, "Why standardize and shut down initiative?" The attitude was summed up like this: "Some people view the idea of everyone in naval aviation doing everything 'the one best way' with some misgivings. They fear that general use of standardized procedures, while it may reduce the accident rate, will result in a reduction of a pilot's ability to 'think on his feet' and deal flexibly with emergencies and combat situations."

Standardization, then, was not necessarily looked upon as a safety factor. After all, propeller-driven aircraft were so similar in cockpit configuration that an experienced pilot could easily step from one type to another without any special training, and many did so. Even going from single-engine to multiengine was not that hard. Every cockpit had a stick (or a yoke), a throttle (or two or four), prop and mixture control(s), magneto switches, perhaps a supercharger lever, and flaps and landing gear controls. They were located in similar positions in every aircraft, and the only thing an experienced pilot needed to fly a new airplane was to know how to start it and the recommended airspeeds for maneuvers and landing. Tactics varied from fighters to bombers to patrol and transport, but that didn't matter if all you wanted to do was to takeoff, cruise, and land. But then came the jets.

The first jets weren't too much different from the props. Sure, the takeoff roll was longer, engine response to throttle movement was quite a bit more sluggish, fuel was used up a lot quicker, and there was less time to correct a bad landing approach. But then, you didn't have that messy throttle quadrant (with mixture, prop, supercharger levers, and carburetor heat), and there were no magnetos. Problems began to develop only when older prop pilots tried flying the jets with habits they had picked up in props. It got worse when the jets began going aboard ship and worse than that when even-higher-performance jets with new capabilities came along. It was then that leadership recognized that something had to be done.

With fleet accident rates at a new high, it was natural to look to examples already established: JTTU, Cougar College, FAGU, and others. Thus, even before NATOPS there was a framework for establishing a methodology for exposing newly indoctrinated pilots to the best possible training and procedures, training and procedures that would improve the mishap performance, and therefore readiness, of all fleet aircraft. Still, the Pacific Fleet, the Atlantic Fleet, and the Naval Air Training Command all had different ideas as to what the best system might be. One example, perhaps apocryphal, was that A-4 pilots from one fleet made approaches with speed brakes out, those from the other with speed brakes in. Yet another problem was the difference of opinion as to the best way to recover from a post-stall gyration in a F7U Cutlass. Still other differences abounded. That's when Vice Adm. Robert Pirie, USN, Deputy Chief of Naval Operations (Air Warfare), OP-05, stepped in. Sources vary as to just what caused him to act, but the fact is that act he did.[12] He took a two-step action that set the tone for what NATOPS is today: a manual for users.

First, he made the basic decision that there must be one best way to make an approach in an A-4, or to recover from a Cutlass post-stall gyration, and other such matters. Therefore, he reasoned, let's get a team together and find that one best way. The next question was whether to take the advice of the members of his staff, all experienced aviators, to let them decide the best way in each case, or to ask the fleet, the current users, to make those decisions. He came down on the side of the current users. The fleet users would write what became NATOPS, and they continue to write and modify it to this day. Those fleet users were the subject-matter experts. Using as a guide a June 1961 Naval Training Device Center publication, *Improvement of Flight Handbooks,* naval aviators—lieutenants and lieutenant commanders, captains and majors—who were actually flying the aircraft in the fleet wrote the books. Agreement had to be reached from squadron to squadron, fleet to fleet, and up the chain of command before any NATOPS manual was approved. Approval came via wing commanders and type commanders to the DCNO (Air). Only after that entire command chain approved did Admiral Pirie and his successors put their signatures on each volume. The end result was that NATOPS stipulated the best method of performing every function in a given aircraft, a giant step toward safe and efficient flight operations.

All NATOPS manuals were similar in organization. There were eight chapters: "Indoctrination," "Shore-Based Procedures," "Carrier-Based Procedures," "Flight Procedures," "Emergency Procedures," "Communications," "Special Mission," and "Miscellaneous." The introduction, however, was probably most important. That's where every reader and every user was invited to make recommendations for changes and modifications. All such inputs were reviewed, and all were considered (and they still are). Thus, through an iterative process the best procedures and practices were (and are) distilled, and combat readiness and operational

> Vice Adm. Robert B. Pirie, a Class of 1926 graduate of the Naval Academy and a naval aviator from June 1929, had early squadron duty then staff duty at the beginning of World War II. He served on Rear Adm. Gerry Bogan's staff as part of Vice Adm. Marc Mitscher's Task Force 58 during the battles of the Marianas, Palau, Leyte Gulf, and Okinawa. After the war, he was commanding officer of the aircraft carriers *Sicily* and *Coral Sea*. Selected by Admiral Arleigh Burke to be the Deputy Chief of Naval Operations, he served in that capacity for a then-unprecedented four and a half years, during which time he made a number of important and long-standing decisions with regard to carrier and aircraft procurement, aviation readiness, and training. He should be particularly remembered as a champion of NATOPS.

VICE ADMIRAL PIRIE
U.S. Naval Institute Photo Archive

effectiveness enhanced, all with a significant reduction in the aircraft accident rate. After it was all done, one very experienced naval aviator wrote, "[NATOPS] is designed as a means of providing the best and safest aircraft training and operating procedures in an easy to use manual for each type of plane we fly, to enable such a manual to be attentive to the needs of the operating forces, and to provide a training tool for Squadron Commanders' use in determining areas of weakness in his training program or in an individual."[13]

In May 1961, the NATOPS program was officially adopted by the Navy and Marine Corps with the promulgation of OPNAV Instruction 3510.9 (the series that governs today). However, there remained a lot of work and coordination to make even one publication happen. As it turned out, it was the helicopter community, with its HSS-1N (later the SH-34) NATOPS, that was first out of the chocks, in that very same May 1961. Other aircraft types soon followed, and within the year NATOPS manuals for forty-seven aircraft had been issued. It was as if everyone had said, "It's about time!" Gone were hassles with newly arrived operations officers about the "right way." Down went the mishap rate. Almost everyone pronounced NATOPS "good," aside from some diehards who continued to grumble about lost opportunities for initiative.

NATOPS continued to develop. In December 1963, an F9F-8T NATOPS consolidating handbook information and flight and operating procedures was promulgated. There were more, many more, to follow. Frequent and regular NATOPS conferences under the auspices of the air type commanders helped to keep the manuals current and useful. One of the best summaries of NATOPS available was published in the August 1961 issue of *Approach:* "The new NATOPS program was developed by the users for the users. It will be modified as we go along by these same individuals. New tricks of the trade will be passed around quickly for expert evaluation and, if sound, for use by all hands. The end result will be increased operational readiness through increased safety brought about by improved pilot techniques."[14]

An interesting and important waypoint on the road to adoption of NATOPS was the cooperation among all the numerous naval aviation communities, between fleets, and with the Air Force. The Air Force had operated a standardization/evaluation ("Stan/Eval") program for many years, and the first Navy standardization evaluators actually took the Air Force course, learned the philosophy and methodology, and brought them back to the Navy, albeit somewhat modified.

In the beginning, each NATOPS manual was just one of a trilogy of books to be used by naval aviators. These were the *Flight Manual,* which had been around for a long time, covering the mechanics of the airplane—the "systems" in today's vernacular; the applicable NWP, which covered tactics; and NATOPS, covering techniques. Other manuals and technical orders were kept in the maintenance spaces, and pilots seeking answers to special problems often referred to them. Today, the three main manuals have all grown and have been combined into one.

Along with NATOPS came the aforementioned standardization instructors and evaluators, who covered everything from normal flight to emergency procedures, systems knowledge, and more. NATOPS was implemented quickly overall but built up gradually by aircraft type and it was incorporated in every Navy and Marine squadron and wing, afloat and ashore. Later, the system was expanded to LSOs, aircraft carriers, and other aviation ships, and a NATOPS *General Flight and Operating Instructions Manual* was issued. NATOPS is used for teaching in ground school and as a guide for both standard and emergency procedures in simulators, trainers, and in the air.[15] It's also the common denominator for readiness across fleets, type commanders, ships, and stations.

Today it would be hard to conceive of naval aviation without RAGs and NATOPS, but in the beginning it was hard to conceive of naval aviation standardized to such an extent without losing the spirit of innovation, a spirit that persists until this day. Nor could it have been foreseen that, due in large measure to effective RAG and NATOPS program, the all-Navy mishap rate would improve from 1,106 major accidents, 524 aircraft, and 387 people killed in FY 1958, the year before RAGs were begun and NATOPS was adopted, to only eleven major mishaps in 2009. It happened, and largely because of far-seeing souls who believed that dedicated training and standardization just might help. At the same time, it's hard to see any decrease in either individual or squadron initiative.

Very often, when old-timers are told that today's accident rate is only about one accident every hundred thousand hours, they are at first incredulous. Then came the questions of how and why. The answers might be better leadership, better selection, better personnel management, improved integration of aviation medicine, better aircraft and systems, better maintenance and supply, angled decks and mirrors, the replacement training concept, or NATOPS. The answer is not singular. These all helped, but central among the reasons are most certainly the establishment of RAGs[16] and the effective use of NATOPS.

10

The Doc

Aerospace Medicine—Flight Surgeons and More

A doctor who flies best understands the pilot.
Jeffrey R. Davis et al., eds., Fundamentals of Aerospace Medicine

The contributions to aviation safety by aerospace medicine are legion but, sadly, seldom highlighted.[1] Despite lack of fanfare, flight surgeons and other medical professionals—such as aerospace experimental psychologists, aerospace physiologists, aerospace optometrists, physiologists, and others—have been making flight safer and increasing readiness since the beginnings of naval aviation. While those contributions don't stand out in history as much as the development of jet aircraft or angled decks or the establishment of RAGs or NATOPS, aerospace medicine has in fact played a continuous and extremely important role. Aerospace-medical professionals have labored under the "radar horizon," but like the dripping of water on a rock over time, their cumulative efforts have added up to priceless contributions to increased operational readiness, mission accomplishment, and reduced mishap rates. They represent an extremely important chapter in the history of naval aviation safety.

The naval aeromedical profession has much in common with the community it serves, a group of self-assured, type-A personalities. In that community are not only aircrew but also maintainers, suppliers, Navy civilians, and families. Beyond medical qualifications, all members of the aeromedical profession have a deep interest in, if not love of, flying. All have received a basic orientation in flying: some no more than a few flights in the backseat of a primary trainer; others have gone through the full undergraduate flight training syllabus and received pilot or naval flight officer wings. Once designated as flight surgeons or as practitioners of allied specialties, most would just as soon stay in naval aviation the rest of their careers. This desire sometimes generates problems, however. Just like the naval aviators they support, flight surgeons have officially established career patterns. Periodically, they are called upon to rotate to nonaviation duty stations, like hospitals, naval base dispensaries, or Military Treatment Facilities (MTFs). Like naval aviators rotating to desk jobs ashore, their tendency is to go reluctantly and not to understand that the assignment is good for both the long-term professional development of the individual and the profession as a whole. In the case of flight surgeons the "white-shoe boys," the doctors who seem to spend their entire careers inside naval hospitals and are seen to dominate the Medical Corps, are the villains. Yet, arguably, without at least the grumbling support of those "white shoes," there might never have been such a thing as a School of Aviation Medicine or a residency in aerospace medicine in Pensacola, Florida.

That's where novice naval aeromedical personnel learn that the responsibility for meeting the medical, physiological, and psychological challenges facing naval aviators begins with them. Their principal mission and vocation is to keep naval aviation healthy and aviators fit to fly. They have been doing just that and making contributions to improving Navy-Marine aviation safety since the 1920s, when they first earned their flight-surgeon wings, with help from the Army.[2]

From 1926 to 1934, the Navy trained its own flight surgeons at the Naval Medical School in Washington, D.C. Between 1933 and 1938, the Army again assumed responsibility for Navy training. Finally, in 1939, training was put under the auspices of the Medical Department at NAS Pensacola. In 1946, the U.S. Navy School of Aviation Medicine was established; its name was changed to U.S. Naval Aerospace Medical Institute (NAMI) in 1965.

While early efforts concentrated on ensuring that only the most physically fit were inducted into naval flight training, from the beginning flight surgeons assisted in mishap investigation as well. Early on, the physical phenomena brought on by high-altitude flight, the effects of the forces of gravity, the science of night vision, the development of survival equipment, and the general physical conditioning of flight crews became parts of their portfolio. Their efforts, both individually and collectively, have led to safer and better procedures and much else besides. In particular, they have led the way to better training and equipment; to systems more capable and easier to use and maintain; and, most important, the development and application of the art and science of mishap prevention.

Naval aviators have a dichotomous relationship with their flight surgeons. On the one hand, the aviator knows deep down that the flight surgeon has his or her interest at heart, but on the other hand, the pilot or NFO assumes that any hint of physical or mental ailment, even a slight cold, just might give the flight surgeon cause for grounding him or her. Naval aviators can seldom tolerate that. So they hide such conditions from the flight surgeon, at least until something like a painful ear block from a descent with a head full of phlegm prompts one to cry out to the "Doc." That ambivalence about flight surgeons goes as far back as initial selection for flight training, when it seems to the prospective aviator that the flight surgeon is doing all he can to weed the candidate out. Even though proven apocryphal, the idea that "Doc's" aim is to weed out is a cardinal precept among prospective and newly designated aviators. All sorts of stories circulate as to how to circumvent

FLIGHT PHYSICAL EXAM. Foundation, *Naval Aviation Museum Foundation Quarterly*, with permission

any problems that might show up, whether during that first physical examination or in subsequent annual checkups. Thus, the flight crew's relationship with the flight surgeon starts out ambiguous and often continues that way for years. In fact, Dr. Isaac H. Jones, one of the Army's first aviation examiners, wrote in 1917, "It may take 100 years to convince pilots that keeping them physically fit to continue flying was the main purpose of flight surgeons, because pilots feel that doctors are determined not to let them fly if doctors can find a way to prevent them."[3]

Spotty relationships notwithstanding, the fleet flight surgeon's motto is, "Keep 'em flying, safely." Flight surgeons are continuously weighing risk and benefit. They understand the relationship between the aviators they support and themselves, and they strive to keep aircrews mentally and physically fit in order to keep flying. They continually ask themselves, "Am I comfortable allowing this aviator to step into a multimillion-dollar machine paid for by the taxpayers, a machine that will carry other aircrew, passengers, live ordnance—and maybe fly over civilian population centers?" They reason, "The Navy/Marine Corps have invested thousands of hours and millions of dollars training these aviators, and my job is to keep them flying if at all possible, and remove them only if they have the potential to pose a risk to themselves or others."[4]

That purpose is well-stated on the Naval Aerospace Medicine Institute website:

> The naval flight surgeon practices preventive medicine first and foremost. He or she is the natural interface between the practice of medicine, the science of safety, and the profession of aviation.

Through successful aviation medicine programs the flight surgeon promotes aviation safety, decreasing the potential for aircraft accidents. This is accomplished by a dedicated search for those problems—physical, mental, environmental, and man-made, which compromise safety in the air and in the workplace. To accomplish the job, the naval flight surgeon makes regular visits to squadron spaces, constantly assessing squadron esprit, safety consciousness, and the mental health of the aircrew and critical support personnel. Additionally, the flight surgeon flies with the squadron as aircrew to observe in-flight stressors and crew coordination. The process of promoting safety begins with the uncompromising selection of quality personnel. It extends through their training and into the fleet workplace, including the ground support personnel who ready the planes for flight. The training of a naval flight surgeon, therefore, includes subjects ranging from the physiology of flight to industrial medicine, environmental hazards and the investigation of aircraft accidents. The responsibilities of a naval flight surgeon in fast-moving, highly sophisticated operational forces are broad and ever-changing. The naval flight surgeon recognizes that safety hazards do not come to the clinic for identification but must be sought out. Thus, the establishment of good rapport with operational personnel is essential to safe completion of the operational mission.[5]

That purpose is well and good, but that rapport has first to survive the candidate aviator's initial meeting with a flight surgeon, a meeting fraught with concern on the part of the candidate. The concern is warranted. Flight-candidate selection was one of the very earliest and most important tasks of the flight surgeon, and it continues so today. From the beginning, it was universally agreed that good physical and psychological makeup were prerequisites to subsequent acceptable performance by an aviator, though some of the early requirements might give the modern-day person a chuckle. For example, in 1917 certain British physicians concluded that the best indicator of flying ability was the ability to ride a horse.[6] Yet most of the other early requirements made sense and persist to this day: tests of eyesight, coordination, equilibrium, and ability to withstand stress among them. In more recent years, other tests have been incorporated in the initial flight physical, the result being that once inducted, few aviation candidates ever drop out of training for physical or psychological reasons. That doesn't mean to say that some won't develop such problems later, but those will be found out and treated, with the principal aim of getting the aviator flying again.

Early in aviation, it was recognized that in addition to physical qualification there was an aptitude dimension to the problem of initial selection. Until 1940, there wasn't a good way to measure such aptitude, but in that year the then-recently inaugurated School of Aviation Medicine in Pensacola started what was known as the "Pensacola Study of Naval Aviators," later better known as the "Thousand Aviator Study," under the auspices of Dr. Ashton Graybiel. Subjects were administered a wide variety of tests thought to be promising predictors of success in the flight syllabus. In the end, two tests, the Flight Aptitude Rating (FAR) and the Aviation Qualification Test (AQT) were adopted. Some modifications to those two tests have been made over the years, but the FAR and AQT remain the best predictors of success in flight training.[7]

Because of rigorous and proven screening and testing it undergoes, the naval-aviator population seldom faces anything more than transient illnesses. From time to time a rare psychological problem, such as fear of night flying, might arise, and there have been isolated instances of alcohol affecting judgment, but such incidents have not had a significant effect on the mishap rate. In other words, inadequate or improper selection, testing, and screening have not been among the causes of high mishap rates, nor has there been room for improvement in selection, screening, or testing that would be reflected in a decrease in rates—all such success accruing to the credit of aerospace medicine professionals.

Beyond initial examinations and testing, it was recognized early in the history of manned flight that environmental and physical challenges to aircrews were quite different from those of earthbound activities. Dealing with them involved the medical, and later the full aeromedical, profession. It wasn't long before that involvement became one of the most important endeavors toward the preservation of life and equipment and the improvement of the efficiency of the human operators, the pilots. Thus, there was established continuing physiological training and development of personal equipment designed to minimize environmental effects.

A principal concern of aviators and physicians alike has from the beginning been the effects of operating in an alien environment and subjecting oneself to physical phenomena not usual on the Earth's surface. To conduct the training necessary for survival in that environment, an array of special devices and installations has been developed and is run by aviation medical personnel. All such training has its roots in some past difficulty—perhaps a mishap, perhaps a near miss—and each element was established to minimize chances of a similar event happening again, or if it did happen, provide a means to recover. Over the years the number of lives saved, mishaps avoided or mitigated, and needless outlays precluded through such training have been considerable, accounting for part of the steep downslope in mishap rates in earlier years.

One of the first of those phenomena to be addressed was lack of oxygen at altitude. As early as the twentieth century, Paul Bert learned that by sucking on

> Dr. Ashton Graybiel was, before undertaking his groundbreaking work in naval aviation medicine at Pensacola, first and foremost an eminent cardiologist. At Harvard University in the late 1930s he developed methods for measuring cardiovascular performance and coauthored with Dr. Paul Dudley White a text, *Electrocardiography in Practice,* that served as a standard from the 1940s to the 1960s.
>
> During World War II he studied the effects of fatigue and cardiovascular fitness on the performance of Navy and Marine pilots and initiated the groundbreaking "Thousand Aviator Study," which continues to this day. From 1945 to 1970 he served as the director of the Naval Aerospace Medical Institute (NAMI), and then, until 1980, he headed the Biological Sciences Department at the Naval Aerospace Medical Research Laboratory (NAMRL). During the latter period he performed experiments on how acceleration affects the organs of the inner ear, the circulatory system, and muscle control.
>
> Largely because of his work at NAMI and NAMRL he is considered by many to be the "godfather" of modern naval aviation medicine.

ASHTON GRAYBIEL
Foundation, *Naval Aviation Museum Foundation Quarterly*, with permission

oxygen he could overcome the effects of hypoxia; he thus became known as the "father of altitude physiology." Some years later, in 1918, a low-pressure chamber was built at the Air Service Medical Research Laboratory at Mineola, New York, to investigate and train for high-altitude flight. Building on that work, from World War II until recently the effects of lack of oxygen were demonstrated to flight candidates and aircrew in a low-pressure chamber.[8]

Other phenomena affecting the human body were also addressed early on, and each of the personal protection systems in use today can be traced to some past mishap or near-mishap experience. One example is escape. Bailout training was practiced well before World War II but became obsolescent when the first jets came along. It was medical personnel working with engineers that enabled the first American ejection from a jet, in 1946. Since then, aerospace medical personnel have continued to work hand in glove with engineers developing successive models of ejection systems, so that now it's inconceivable that a high-performance tactical jet aircraft would be built without a zero-zero ejection seat (that is, one in which an aviator could survive ejection at zero altitude, zero speed—stopped on the ground). Along with the seat have come trainers that instill in aircrews the confidence that should the unexpected happen they can live to tell their stories and fly another day. That's only the start, however. Today there is training for physical conditioning, water survival, night vision, effects of acceleration

EJECTION-SEAT TRAINER. Foundation, *Naval Aviation Museum Foundation Quarterly*, with permission

(G forces), and spatial disorientation, as well as the aforementioned effects of insufficient oxygen and ejection, bail-out, and parachuting.

That physiological training for naval aviators and aircrew begins in flight school and continues throughout one's career. It encompasses a wide range of subjects, all important to the individual, safety of flight, or both. The training may be under the direct supervision of an aeromedical safety officer (AMSO), an aviation physiologist who has been through the Aviation Safety Officer course, or even a flight surgeon, but together they determine what the training is to be and the frequency of any refresher courses or exercises.

Another area of flight surgeon effort also has its roots in past difficulty: personal equipment. Starting with the development of seat belts and the provision of oxygen supply and head protection, flight surgeons have been continually involved and concerned with personal protection. Today, there is a wide array of such equipment in use in naval aviation, ranging from the now rather basic fire-retardant flight suit to ever-improving head protection (helmets), oxygen systems, anti-G suits, escape systems, special equipment for operations in cold weather, flotation gear, and survival kits. Almost all appeared genesis because a flight surgeon saw a problem that had to be solved or else, with the aerospace medicine laboratory network backing him up, took the many personal-equipment improvisations rising from the fleet and engineered them into workable solutions to given problems. Thus, first lap belts and then shoulder harnesses were developed. Oxygen masks replaced sucking on tubes running from oxygen bottles. Hardhats replaced cloth helmets. The list of improvements prompted by need and then shepherded to operational and safe effectiveness by the aeromedical community is extensive. A particularly notable event was the design of the first equipment to mitigate the effects of acceleration, the G-suit, during World War II.

Flight-deck and line personnel also benefited. It's enlightening to see a film of World War II carrier operations with crewmen darting about in dungaree trousers, short-sleeve shirts or sleeves rolled up, and with cloth helmets or none at all, most without hearing protection. Compare it with a film made today: sleeves buttoned down, flotation jackets, cranial helmets with the best ear protection available. Flight surgeons and other aerospace medical personnel have worked diligently and continually to improve all of these systems, for flying and ground or deck personnel alike.

In the end, however, like so much of what the aeromedical community has done and continues to do, improvements have incremental effects on mishap rates; they don't cause sudden shifts. Such items and more are essential to the long-term well-being of aircrew (and ground crews), enhance operational effectiveness, and offer protection in the hostile environment above the solid ground or the flight deck, but don't necessarily enhance the published safety record. Nevertheless all are important, and any story of the history of naval aviation safety would be incomplete without mentioning them. Everything listed above, and others, is in a state of constant improvement, improvements most often stemming from experience in mishap or near misses. Without aeromedical involvement, whether by a squadron flight surgeon or a laboratory, or something in between, or all the above, many of the well-known improvements might never have been made, and the mishap rate would have been reflective of that.

At the unit level, the flight surgeon not only observes and makes recommendations for equipment improvements but observes and monitors the physical well-being of aircrew and their support personnel. Maintaining good health and personal physical fitness has long been recognized as essential to being a competent naval aviator, and achieving and maintaining that fitness is widely understood to be the responsibility of the individual. Yet, along with the unit commander, the flight surgeon is in arguably the best position to advise as to the adequacy of the individuals' programs, and from the earliest days flight surgeons have taken seriously this responsibility. They recognize full well that "an aviator, like the aircraft he flies, requires preventive maintenance. . . . [H]e must be physically fit to meet the combination of skilled perceptual-motor performance requirements, an alien environment, unusual stresses and little tolerance for error."[9] Efforts in this area, though quite important, have been subtle and largely taken for granted. The number of lives so saved or mishaps so prevented is difficult to calculate; suffice it to say that involvement of leadership, the individual, and the flight surgeon in promoting health maintenance has helped force the mishap rate ever downward over the years.

Unfortunately, even with perfect selection criteria, comprehensive physiological training, healthy minds and bodies, and the best of personal equipment, accidents still happen, and they must be investigated. Mishap investigation, as noted, was one of the very first employments of the flight surgeon beyond initial physical screening. It was soon recognized that no investigation could be called complete without the assistance of a medical person, ideally a medical person experienced in aviation matters, a flight surgeon, or in some instances another aeromedical professional. From those early investigations, there stemmed not only a medical citation as to the cause of death or injury but also, very often, recommendations to prevent that cause in the future; think seat belts, crash helmets, a reliable supply of oxygen, anti-G suits, and even cockpit layout. Thus, that there was a Medical Safety Division in the very first Naval Aviation Safety Activity is no coincidence.

While any mishap investigation strives to pinpoint all the causal factors in order to facilitate the learning of lessons, it's often difficult for nonmedical team members to identify faults or errors in the human/machine interface. The easy way out used to be to call it "pilot error," a flight-crew mistake, and move on. Fortunately, even from the very early years the flight surgeon on the mishap investigation team frequently insisted on going beyond that and looking into *why* the pilot had made the error. Even in so-called material failures, some sort of human error was often one of the causal factors. Perhaps some aspect of training was missing or inadequate and had increased the risk of human error. Perhaps someone had misused something, or had not maintained or serviced it, or had designed it improperly, or had reworked it below standards. Feedback from such discoveries served to facilitate training and provide input to scientists and engineers in the development and manufacture of new aircraft and modifications to existing aircraft.

These findings by aeromedical professionals became known as "causal related human error" and became part and parcel of aircraft mishap investigations. Not that the flight surgeon didn't make contributions elsewhere—he absolutely did—but in this particular area his work proved to be of most significance. Even so, beyond accident investigations, in laboratories and in field medical facilities flight surgeons and their colleagues sought answers to problems, ideally before they *became* problems. An early indication of such aeromedical contributions is a 1955 *Naval Aviation News* report of collaboration between the Aeronautical Medical Laboratory in Philadelphia and the Bureau of Aeronautics on the "art of instrumentation" and on attention paid to the pilot's information requirements in the development of new instruments.[10] Such efforts, as well as advocacy by flight surgeons and other aerospace medical professionals for identifying mishap causal factors beyond "pilot error" led directly to the concept of "human factors." That combination, coupled with spin-offs from aerospace research, produced what today has become a principal front in the reduction of numbers of mishaps. As such, it has become a subject of ever-increasing importance in naval aviation readiness and safety.

It all began in the earliest days of aviation, when delineation of procedures and tailoring of equipment was haphazard and the perceived need for them low. But even then, early human-factors acolytes, usually aeromedical personnel, urged standardized procedures and proper location and shaping of cockpit instruments, levers, and handles. They also came up with a number of innovations designed to reduce confusion and stress in the cockpit. Yet between 1955 and 1964, 72 percent of all naval mishaps continued to include a human-error causal factor. This underscored a real need to design and implement a system that could define issues and provide correctives in the area of human involvement so that appropriate training and equipment modifications could follow. Fortuitously, increasing postwar collaboration between the Aeronautical Medical Laboratory and BuAer led to growing focus on the subject of personnel error, soon to be called "human factor error."

As it turned out, the timing of the effort meshed nicely with earlier work of aeromedical personnel and with efforts of the Air Board,[11] Safety Center–sponsored symposia, and other colloquia. One of the most important payoffs from that collaboration was development of a general human-error framework. Existing accident databases were restructured and new investigative methods designed. As a direct result, the part played by human error in mishaps soon began to come into focus. In November 1963, the importance of human factors was stressed by Rear Adm. Edward C. Outlaw, then commander of the Naval Aviation Safety Center, at an International Air Safety Seminar in Athens, Greece.[12] Then, in August 1969, in a talk before the Aerospace and Undersea Medicine Program at MIT, Capt. Frank H. Austin, MC, USN,[13] made the following observations.

- "There is need for a valid easily obtainable monitoring index for determining the physiological and psychological condition of aviators *before* the commencement of a flight."

- "Since human factors persist in causing over 55 percent of all naval aircraft accidents our job in naval aviation is to continue attacking these factors with all the resources available to us."

He then described the Navy's Human Error Research and Analysis Program (HERAP).[14] HERAP took inputs from all sources but especially from aeromedical personnel throughout the fleet and the laboratories. The HERAP data was then analyzed and promulgated to end users—fleet operators, maintainers, logisticians,

> Capt. Frank Austin was one of the few doctors who qualified not only as a flight surgeon but also as a naval aviator. In addition, he was the first flight surgeon to graduate from the Test Pilot School at Patuxent River, Maryland.
>
> Between 1959 and 1963 he served as both flight surgeon and instructor pilot with Air Group 4 and VF-174 at NAS Cecil Field. While attached to VF-174 he also served short periods of temporary duty attached to NASA in connection with recovery of Project Mercury missions. From 1963 to 1965 he served as senior medical officer in USS *Enterprise* (CVAN 65).
>
>
>
> CAPT. FRANK AUSTIN
> Foundation, *Naval Aviation Museum Foundation Quarterly, with permission*
>
> In 1968 he became Head, Aeromedical Branch, Naval Safety Center, in Norfolk. There he was a key player in the development of a system for classifying human-factor elements in aircraft mishaps. In particular, he must be given great credit for introducing the Navy and Marines, and eventually the Air Force and the FAA, to the importance of human factors.
>
> Tours as force medical officer on the staff of Commander, Naval Air Forces, Atlantic Fleet and as director of aerospace medicine in the Bureau of Naval Medicine followed in short order.
>
> He retired from the Navy in October 1978 but continued as a forceful and talented aerospace medical professional in both NASA and the FAA.

depots, and manufacturers. That data in turn, even if sketchy, was used to modify and improve flight operations, maintenance, the supply chain, the various manuals, and even design and manufacturing. The percentage of cases in which human errors contributed to mishaps soon began to fall. Thus, the developing discipline of human factors began to be seen as important and increasingly to be looked to for answers as to how the mishap rate might be reduced even further. To facilitate those answers, a number of aerospace medicine people, researchers, and scientists collaborated to construct a system for investigating human error that would produce even more detailed and actionable data than did HERAP. It was and is called the "Swiss-Cheese Model of Human Accident Causation," published by James T. Reason[15] in 1990 and amplified by Scott Shappell, Douglas A. Wiegmann,[16] and others. (It is discussed more fully in chapter 11.)

Today, largely as the result of early efforts by aeromedical personnel, human factors is discussed in every preflight brief throughout naval aviation. Moreover, the overall effort is a major component of the Naval Aviation Safety Program in all its facets, including aviation maintenance and design safety, as discussed in chapters 12 and 13. The human-factors framework is now used within not only the Navy and Marine Corps but also in other military, commercial, and general aviation sectors as a way to examine systematically underlying human causal factors and improve aviation accident investigations.

In addition to all the above, aerospace medicine goes far beyond its work in squadrons, air wings, ships, and staffs. One example is the long-running Repatriated Prisoner-of-War (RPOW) study, carried out by the Naval Operational Medical Institute in Pensacola and patterned somewhat on the Thousand Aviator Study. Capt. Robert E. Mitchell, MC, USN, who had worked on the Thousand Aviator effort, was the principal organizer of the RPOW study, using some of the same tests used in the earlier effort, augmented with tests developed later. Captain Mitchell also arranged for recruitment of a comparison group, people who had backgrounds in combat similar to the RPOWS but had not been taken prisoner. The study continues to this day; results thus far tend to show that selection and aeromedical training undergone by RPOWs help them tolerate and survive their long-term incarceration. In fact, it is reported that as the study population ages, more abnormalities are turning up among the comparison group than in the RPOWs, perhaps because of an immeasurable "survival of the fittest" factor.

In a broader sense, aeromedical science, research, and development have been critical to both the safety and the steadily increasing reliability and performance of people, airplanes, and systems. Much of that work is conducted at somewhat out-of-the-way laboratories and other research activities little noticed by the larger community. Nonetheless, not only the Navy and Marine Corps have benefited but so too have the other services, NASA, the NTSB, the FAA, and international bodies as well. The end result of all that effort has been lives and equipment saved and operational efficiencies, whether military or commercial, raised to ever-higher levels.

Besides all their other contributions, aeromedical personnel, when integrated with the larger naval aviation community, have often made unexpected contributions to nonmedical aspects of safety and readiness. Whereas those engrossed in routine, day-to-day activities sometimes miss opportunities for safety and efficiency standing in plain sight, the flight surgeon, with his outside perspective and his talents of observation honed by years of medical practice, can often see them. One example typifies, although there are many more. In the mid-1960s, a number of sailors working near the bow catapults of aircraft carriers were getting blown over the side by jet blast or prop wash or by just plain making a misstep. It was two flight surgeons on carriers, one in the Atlantic Fleet carrier and one in the Pacific, who, simultaneously, realized that injuries, if not lives, could be saved by erecting a simple net around the edge of the flight deck adjacent to the bridle arresters. The advent of nose-tow catapults did away with the need for bridle arresters and nets, but in its day the suggestion preserved lives even though the developers, and the number of sailors they saved, are unknown.

> Dr. Robert E. Mitchell was commissioned as a Navy ensign in 1944, then attended McGill University in Montreal, where he earned his degree as a doctor of medicine. After internship, residency training, and designation as a flight surgeon in 1955, he joined the research division of the School of Aviation Medicine in Pensacola for the first of three tours of duty there.
>
> During these tours he was heavily involved with Dr. Ashton Graybiel in the "Thousand Aviator Project," designed to track the careers and lives of a thousand naval aviators over an extended period to assess the impact of such a career in both personal and professional terms. Begun in 1940, the study continues to this day.
>
> From 1958 to 1960 he was the senior medical officer in the aircraft carrier *Shangri-la*, and from 1965 to 1966 he was the air wing flight surgeon for the 1st Marine Aircraft Wing, flying combat missions in Vietnam.
>
> Returning to Pensacola, he headed the Medical Sciences Department of the Naval Aviation Medical Research Laboratory from 1970 to 1975, after which he took command of the entire laboratory. In 1973 he was instrumental in the establishment of a program to assess the health of Navy and Marine prisoners repatriated after the Vietnam War and in 1976 established a parallel Comparison Group Study.
>
> In 1982 he was elected an honorary member of the Vietnamese Prisoner of War Association (NAM-POW); the organization installed a plaque in his honor in the National Museum of Naval Aviation in 1986. In 1989 he was elected an honorary member of the Pioneer and Early Naval Aviator's Association, the Golden Eagles.

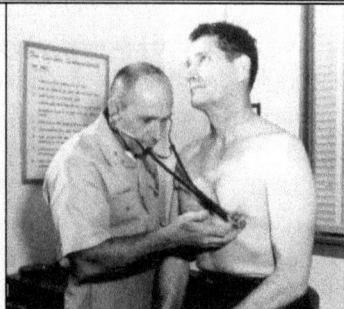

CAPTAIN MITCHELL AND JOE FOSS
Foundation, *Naval Aviation Museum Foundation Quarterly*, with permission

When it comes to contributions to safety, aeromedical personnel don't often get the recognition they should. For the most part they worked behind the scenes, at least until the Navy recognized the value of human factors, and that happened fairly recently. In what we've discussed one can see all sorts of contributions, but they were incremental in nature. In the personnel area, the establishment of physical and mental criteria for aircrew, a test to measure aptitude for flight, and emphasis on physical conditioning come to mind. In the area of flight equipment, safety harnesses, helmets, oxygen systems, G-suits, and more were developed and later perfected by aeromedical personnel. The naval aerospace medical community has made major contributions to naval aviation safety from almost the very beginning, but especially since the last half of the twentieth century.

Perhaps feeling ignored by the larger aviation safety community, or perhaps for other reasons, flight surgeons themselves have only infrequently advertised the good work they do. Unfortunately, what telling there is comes in the form of "preaching to the choir," in meetings and symposia of their colleagues, with few "operators" in attendance. For example, the Aerospace Medical Association holds annual scientific meetings and symposia and publishes a monthly journal. Unfortunately, few nonmedical people ever attend such meetings or read the journal, a cornucopia of information about the entire spectrum of aerospace medicine.

In summary, naval aerospace medicine is a long-standing and extremely important element of naval aviation safety. Because its specific contributions occur in small increments over long periods, they are often overlooked. Yet, without that long involvement and many contributions of naval aerospace medicine to safe performance, the dramatic progress made in saving lives and equipment and enhancing readiness would not have happened. Moreover, even as aircraft, their systems, and their sensors become more reliable and "user-friendly" as predictive maintenance[17] measures up to its potential, and as training for aircrew, maintainers, and the whole support network becomes more focused and appropriate to the task, it will likely be the human part of the naval aviation system in which the greatest progress will be made. When that happens, the now-underappreciated people of naval aerospace medicine will at last be fully recognized.

FLIGHT SURGEON WINGS. *NHHC*

11

Discovering Human Factors

Nothing could be fairer than to call it pilot error.
Anonymous

Man/machine interface has long been one of the most difficult and riskiest elements in aviation. The science of human factors deals with that interface. The concept is not new. It's just that until the late 1960s human factors in aviation, particularly naval aviation, were not categorized as such. Instead, mishap-cause factors involving people were listed as pilot error, maintenance error, or some other catchall term. The science of human factors as we know it today was just not that important. What was important was to get the machine off the ground, execute the mission, then get back to ship or station without breaking the aircraft or harming the crew. Now, because of lessons learned from analysis of human error, today's Navy and Marine pilots can marvel at their predecessors who had to learn by doing—that is, strap in, start up, and go. Even if benefiting from some preliminary orientation, such as a flight in a dual-piloted aircraft, they might still have to raise flaps and landing gear with a crank, operate the radio (if any) by use of a handheld microphone, and land with no shoulder harness, often prompting an unwanted launch of the pilot's face into an ill-positioned gunsight.

Things now are different—much different. The human-factor component is central to design, maintenance, mishap prevention, and, when and if they happen, mishap investigation. Often somewhat surprisingly to older naval aviators, human factors are an important subject covered in every preflight brief. Equally significant is that the subject is an important facet of any discussion of a change in procedures and that it is front and center in aircraft design, maintenance, and support. Such focus has played a significant role in achieving an ever-decreasing mishap rate and bodes to become even more important in the future.

In naval aviation before the 1960s, when a human made a mistake that led to a mishap or near mishap, the cause was usually listed as just that, some sort of error by a human: by the aircrew, a maintenance person, or a poorly operated or poorly designed system. The corrective action for such an error was either to ground or fire the humans involved or admonish and retrain them. Little or no attempt was made to share "lessons learned" with the fleet or industry, except for the odd event discussed by "Grampaw Pettibone" or published in A*pproach, Crossfeed,* or *Mech*,[1] or in individual experiences passed on at happy hours. Even the expression "human factors" was not much used among fleet operators.

The term was used elsewhere, however, especially in academia and laboratories, such as the Navy's Aeronautical Laboratory in Philadelphia; among engineers in BuAer; in the aerospace medical community; and among design engineers and leaders at the Naval Safety Center.[2] An especially significant watershed was, as we saw in the last chapter, Rear Admiral Outlaw's speech on human factors in Athens in November 1963. The sum total of these efforts by the growing community of those aware of the importance of human factors gradually began to pay off. Spreading awareness of the issue and feedback from mishaps and incidents facilitated by the Safety Center led to newer aircraft, designed not only to increase combat efficiency but to minimize human hurt and preserve equipment. Where possible, human-factors lessons learned became the bases for modifications to older aircraft as well.

Industry too recognized the importance of human factors. In fact, in many instances it led the Navy and the rest of the military. Yet no matter where first recognized, human factors required a new degree of specialization to be applied. From that requirement arose the discipline of "human engineering." In the early days of aviation, that effort took a decided backseat to aeronautics, structures, propulsion, electronics, and every other sector of the profession. Nevertheless, those few who worked as human engineers, often assisted or prompted by medical investigators, persisted and made progress. Unfortunately, in Navy and Marine squadrons that progress was often limited to little more than whatever local corrective action might be taken to address the specific cause of a mishap or an injury.

It wasn't that the topic was thought unimportant, however. From the earliest days of aviation, when the perceived need for careful delineating of procedures and tailoring of equipment was low, early human-factors specialists, usually aeromedical personnel (as we saw in the last chapter), urged standardization and proper location and shaping of cockpit instruments, levers, and handles. They also came up with numerous innovations designed to reduce confusion and stress in the cockpit. Progress was slow, however, and what was known about human factors tended to be ignored. Had it not been overlooked, it might have underscored the real need for a system that could define issues and provide correctives in the area of human involvement. There were other, more pressing matters at the time, however, such as training and standardization. (See chapter 9.) But when the Navy-Marine mishap rate fell so far that it became increasingly asymptotic, in the late 1950s and early 1960s, the opportunity to delve into human factors arose.

Even before that, during World War II, a group of psychologists and engineers had been assigned to assist in the configuration of aircraft instruments and controls. They easily found a great deal to do. Much of the early growth in what came to be called human factors derived from their work. Their goal was to design aircraft to match, as far as possible, human limitations; at first they concentrated on making displays, controls, and spaces fit human operators.[3] Because of the exigencies of the war their results were mixed, but their efforts and their science grew evermore important to both operational effectiveness and safety.

Their work was soon reflected in the design of several postwar aircraft, of which the Douglas AD Skyraider, while not the first aircraft built with consideration for human engineering, is a prime example. Designers of airplanes before the AD had considered things like the placement of instruments, controls, operating levers, and switches, but in the AD all that was pretty much put together. Numbers on instruments were sized for comfortable and instant reading. Landing gear, flap, and dive-brake controls were designed to look like the items they controlled, and those controls moved in the same directions as did, respectively, the gear, flaps, and dive brakes.[4] Such considerations were a giant step forward for not only efficiency but safety. That was only a beginning, however, as even after that there were shortfalls. Douglas, the company that had built the Skyraider, and the BuAer engineers who oversaw it managed to produce the A-4D Skyhawk with two look-alike T-handles for emergency use and place them in close proximity. One would disconnect the hydraulically actuated controls, allowing the pilot to revert to mechanically connected controls in the event of a hydraulic failure. The other would deploy an emergency generator. In an emergency situation, grabbing the wrong handle was eminently possible and could be disastrous. The Skyhawk was otherwise an outstanding attack aircraft, and such complications, whether in the Skyhawk or other aircraft, could be mitigated by training. But that was only the beginning and the lesser part of a bigger problem. Most design shortfalls could be fixed, given enough time and money; more difficult was convincing leadership that something other than grounding pilots for poor "headwork" might be needed to fix the problem.

Design problems aside, from the beginnings of aviation, because "pilot error" was the most common cause, accidents were often written off as the cost of doing business, an attitude that prevailed through much of the 1950s. (See chapter 2.) The fact is that human error had been implicated in well over half, some studies say over 70 percent, of all aircraft accidents, military and civilian. Yet few accident-reporting systems, the Navy's included, were designed around any particular framework for identifying human error in particular cases. Therefore, there was little data to use in human-error analysis, making it difficult to prove that there were any identifiable and specific problems to solve, let alone any attempt to solve them. Besides, in the 1950s such efforts as screening for commanding officers; providing more reliable aircraft, engines, and systems; transitioning to angled decks, steam catapults, and optical landing systems in carriers; and establishing the

NATOPS and RAG systems were in hand and could be more quickly implemented. The problems these concepts solved seemed to loom larger and be more solvable than all the facets and complications of what we know today as human factors.

Nevertheless, there increasingly developed between the Aeronautical Medical Laboratory and BuAer collaboration that led to growing focus on the subject of "personnel error" (later, human-factor error). Concurrently, civil aviation, supported by a wide range of psychologists and behavioral scientists, also began concentrating on the problem. As it turned out, as we saw in the last chapter, the timing was good.

Based on this top-level interest and the growing importance of the subject, the Naval Aviation Safety Center, as noted in chapter 10, established a Human Error Research and Analysis Program. HERAP took inputs from all sources but disproportionately from aeromedical personnel throughout the fleet and in the laboratories.[5] The HERAP data were analyzed in order to determine root causes, and the findings were promulgated to end users, fleet operators, maintainers and logisticians, and depots and manufacturers. That information in turn, though often sketchy, was used to modify and improve flight operations, maintenance, the supply chain, the various manuals, and even design and manufacturing. The percentage of human errors contributing to mishaps soon began to fall. Thus, the developing discipline of human factors began to be more and more looked to for answers as to how the mishap rate might be reduced even further.

While HERAP was first used under the aegis of the Naval Aviation Safety Center, it was not the only human-factors program.[6] In fact, in 1957, separate from naval aviation, a Human Factors Society was founded. That society was principally concerned with human information processing and control. Only later did the discipline grow to include physical performance.[7]

Meanwhile, an Englishman, Elwyn Edwards,[8] drew on the record of civilian accident investigations and developed a model of human factors in operations and design called the "Software, Hardware, Environment and Liveware" (human operators), or SHEL, model. With it mishaps could be better analyzed, and the 70 percent or so of causes once categorized simply as "human errors" could be parsed into workable subsegments and corresponding solutions or fixes sought. Existing accident databases were soon thereby restructured, and new investigative methods were designed.

Both HERAP and the SHEL model were increasingly useful in codifying human errors, and by the last decade of the twentieth century techniques had refined those errors into their constituent elements. More importantly, it was realized that a better way to analyze accidents than the concept of a "mishap chain" was to see the mishap as actually the result of a number of failures, both active and latent, occurring within complex operations. To visualize this process (as we saw in the last chapter), James T. Reason proposed the "Swiss-Cheese" model.[9] The

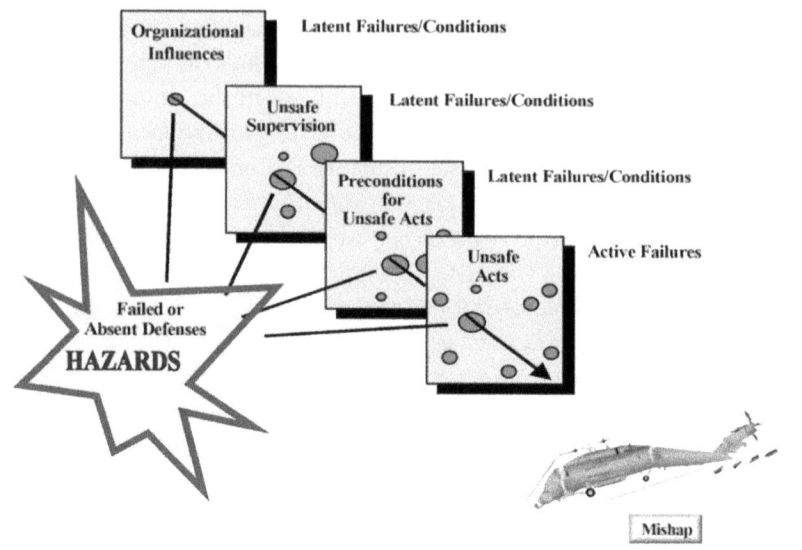

Figure 11-1 Swiss-Cheese Model
Naval Safety Center

metaphor was of several slices of Swiss cheese put together, each hole representing a failure of some sort. When several holes lined up, a situation existed wherein an accident might happen.

Later, Shappell and Wiegmann, whom we met in chapter 10, refined this classification into "Skill-Based," "Judgment," "Decision Making," and "Misperception" errors. Later, they adjusted their categorization of human factors analyses to include "Organizational Influences," "Unsafe Supervision," "Preconditions for Unsafe Acts," and "Unsafe Acts."[10] (See figure 11-1.) The taxonomy produced proved to be an excellent tool for analyzing the causes of a mishap, improving investigations by systematically examining the underlying human causal factors. Recognizing the utility of analysis based on such a model, the Department of Defense (DOD) developed and promulgated a standard code with supporting criteria. The DOD Human Factors Analysis and Classification System (HFACS)[11] defines, standardizes, and facilitates the use of "nanocodes," the HFACS subcategories of the four main tiers of failures and conditions:

- Acts
- Preconditions
- Supervision
- Organizational Influences

Mishap investigators could then review and populate these nanocodes with their findings. Using them as entry points, appropriate corrective actions could be devised and implemented.

It was immediately recognized that HFACS was applicable not only to flight safety but to naval aviation maintenance safety, aircraft systems safety, and design safety. Today, the use of HFACS has led to unprecedented improvement in aviation safety overall. In fact, it wasn't long after its promulgation of and acceptance by accident investigators and fleet users that looking at human-factors issues became an element of every Navy and Marine preflight brief, in hopes of identifying hazards before they were encountered and thus minimizing the potential for mishap. If even after all that preparation there should be a mishap, nanocodes are identified and assessed, and lessons learned are promulgated in a variety of media. In addition, squadrons and other aviation units have human factors councils, identifying human-factor problems. Then, importantly, in however they are identified, human-factor shortfalls have become an increasingly critical element in aircraft design. Indeed, HFACS is now applied far beyond naval, Air Force, and commercial aviation to a wide range of safety efforts, in other forms of transportation, manufacturing, medicine, and more.

The science of human factors has also enhanced an important relationship between the flight surgeon and the aircraft designer. In earlier times, when physicians tried to deal with engineers, they were very often turned away. Only grudgingly did designers accept from medical people help in solving problems in the human/machine interface. Yet, once they started working together, usually after the human-factors-based analysis of an accident, the mutual benefits exceeded all expectations. Tremendously improved man/machine interface and safer aircraft and procedures resulted. Thus, design, maintenance, operations, and medicine have combined to move the Navy-Marine mishap rate to unprecedentedly low levels.

Surprisingly at first glance, since the adoption of human-factor analysis as a principal element of safety promotion and aircraft-accident investigation the percentage of error attributed to humans has actually risen, from 72 percent in the late 1950s to 80–90 percent today. Human causation is now therefore the single greatest mishap hazard. This should not really be surprising, however; many of the other leading cause factors have either been eliminated or significantly reduced. On the other hand, using the principles of human-factors analysis, mishaps can now be assigned realistic and accurate causes, such as organizational influence or supervisory or preconditioned errors, all formerly grouped as "pilot error."

To guide operational units in the practice of HFACS, the Naval Safety Center has promulgated to all units a pocket-sized, flip-chart-format guide entitled *DOD Human Factors and Classification System (HFACS)*. The introduction to that guide reads in part:

Human error remains the leading cause of Navy and Marine mishaps. Mishaps are rarely attributed to a single cause but are often the end result of a series of errors, sometimes called the "Swiss Cheese Model." Root cause analysis can be performed in many different ways, but it always comes down to first asking why something occurred. Start with the problem, asking what prompted the problem to happen in the first place. Then keep taking it further and further until you can pinpoint specific processes, policies or procedures that didn't work. It all comes down to asking, "Why?" until you see a pattern in the problem.

This tool can help identify the starting point of the investigation.

In this same flip chart the benefits of HFACS are listed as follows:

- Structured Analysis of Human Error.
- Gets to the "Why" . . . not just the "What?"
- A new data driven approach.
- Can be used for more than operational purposes.

Today, awareness of the role of human factors and the implementation of routines to reduce errors arising from them, supplemented by mishap investigation in accordance with the Human Factors Analysis and Classification System model, have been major reasons for the reduction of the Navy/Marine mishap rate to the unprecedented lows now enjoyed. It would not be an understatement to declare that the recognition of the importance of human factors in aircrew, maintenance, systems, and design was one of the major achievements in naval aviation safety in the late twentieth century.

12

Maintenance and Supply

Don't worry, Chief. If you can show me how to start it, I can fly it.
Anonymous

For many years, what later came to be known as "maintenance error" was not often recognized as such. Very often, "pilot error" and other more obvious shortcomings were blamed as the cause of mishaps. It wasn't until the advent of more detailed and professional accident investigation, the recognition of the role of human factors, system safety, NATOPS and RAGs, and the joining of maintenance and supply in a common effort that circumstances beyond the pilot or other aircrew came to be more often assigned as reasons for a mishap. When that finally happened, the long tradition of designating any mishap as "pilot error" came to be suspect. There came the realization that, perhaps, maintenance, or supply, or even design, or some other condition beyond the ability of the pilot to control was at fault, at least partially so. The first newer suspect as a possible culprit beyond pilot error was maintenance.

While maintenance capability and philosophy had changed in many ways since the beginnings of naval aviation, by 1950 there were three levels of naval aviation maintenance: squadron, intermediate, and depot. At the squadron level, the commanding officer was (and is) responsible for aircraft maintenance—for ensuring that aircraft, engines, the various aircraft systems, and all their component parts are in suitable, reliable, and safe readiness to fly.[1] In a Navy or Marine squadron, the maintenance officer has most often been a line officer, a pilot (or in later years a naval flight officer) and of sufficient seniority to be a squadron department head. To his department were assigned the majority of the squadron's enlisted people, sailors or Marines, most of them graduates of an "A" school. Some of the more senior petty officers and sergeants were also graduates of a "B" school, a course specializing in certain more complicated equipment. Although the maintenance officer had a number of division officers assigned to his department, the key individual was the maintenance chief, a chief petty officer or senior sergeant (usually a master chief or master gunnery sergeant) with long experience in maintenance and leadership. In the 1950s, supporting the maintenance chief and his leading petty officers or noncommissioned officers was a library of technical publications issued by BuAer; however, most often the principal "technical pub" was either in the maintenance person's head or carried in the maintenance chief's wheelbook. (See chapter 2.)

For the more complicated maintenance issues, requiring specialized technical knowledge or more capable testing equipment, squadrons could turn to intermediate maintenance facilities: fleet aircraft support squadrons or their Marine equivalents, headquarters and maintenance squadrons, or, on board ship, the V-6 Division, a part of the Air Department. A downside of that arrangement was that both the FASRON and V-6 depended on the temporary assignment of specifically trained hands from the very squadrons being supported. This organization lacked a clear chain of accountability and was often the source of inefficiencies, misunderstandings, and disputes between squadrons and FASRONs or V-6 Divisions.[2]

Support beyond the capability of the FASRON came from a either a government-owned repair and overhaul facility staffed by government employees and a few specially trained sailors and Marines or a contractor aircraft-overhaul facility, either of which was likely to be far enough removed from the squadron to make misunderstandings not unusual. By and large, they did good work, but from the squadron's point of view, there was often insufficient quality inspection, and response times were almost always slower than was wanted.

Despite its growing shortcomings, however, the maintenance system worked well in its early years. Many repair parts were common among aircraft types and manufacturers. But when jets, radar, and more complicated electronics came along, the system faltered and sometimes contributed to mishaps.

In the 1950s, in supply, unlike maintenance, the principal responsibility lay outside the squadron. Each squadron was allowed some specified minimum number of spare parts, usually delivered as a "spares kit" and often limited to consumables. The squadron was supposed to requisition anything else from either the host naval or Marine Corps air station supply or the ship's supply department. Those commands' "allowance lists," the list of items they could stock, were drawn up and designated by a combined Bureau of Supplies and Accounts (BuSandA) and BuAer effort.[3] They consolidated lists of parts common to one or more aircraft and became known as AVCALs, Aviation Consolidated Allowance List, tailored to each ship or air station on the basis of the assigned aircraft and on either historical or projected usage or both.

Only items on the allowance lists could be kept on hand, and they could be issued only in accordance with certain regulations and using a signed, standardized form. Because they viewed the system as cumbersome, with complicated paperwork and anticipated delays, squadron maintenance chiefs often took matters into their own hands and built up by various means their own unauthorized little supply departments, most often in a cruise box or two, jealously guarded by that same chief and his crew. The seemingly cumbersomeness of the process also prompted cannibalization—robbing parts from other aircraft in a "down" status or from the remains of a mishap. That worked well for the most part, and many a skipper and maintenance officer put a blind eye to the telescope when it came to cruise-box supply, but again, that worked only so long as aircraft, engines, and systems were simple. Just as with maintenance, when jets and electronics and other sophisticated systems came along that system began to fail, and failed big-time. Not enough of those more sophisticated replacement components could be carried in a cruise box, and cannibalization became impractical.

There was another serious shortcoming to cruise-box supply. Parts obtained through "cumshaw"[4] or pirated out of aircraft designated to be struck were never accounted for in the supply system. Thus no usage was reported, so no replacement orders could be generated. To make matters worse, consumers often tried to bypass what they saw as an unresponsive procedure, one that served only to delay the flight schedule. Not only would this attitude in the long term jeopardize the readiness of the unit, but it tempted squadron COs, maintenance personnel, and pilots to launch an aircraft with a component performing either not up to par or not at all. How many 1950s mishaps were due to something like that is unknown,[5] but there are enough "sea stories" to confirm that it did happen, and often.

As if cumshaw maintenance and supply weren't fraught with enough problems in and of themselves, the advent of newer and more expensive aircraft along with their increased lists of parts (many of them unique to one aircraft type), special support equipment, and needs for extensively trained maintenance personnel caused a near crisis in naval-aviation readiness, let alone safety. Consider this quote from an article in *Naval Aviation News*: "Aircraft maintenance is now a complex billion-dollar-a-year business. Compared to the fighters of 1940, the fighters of today are five times as heavy, have six times as many inspection items, 10 times as many switches, 20 times as many valves, 60 times as many electron tubes,[6] require ten times as many items of support equipment, and cost about 89 times as much."[7]

Such aircraft could hardly be safely maintained out of wheelbooks or cruise boxes. It was recognized early on that even in material failures, evidence might show that someone had misused something, or had not maintained or serviced something, or had made or reworked something below standards. To address the growing problem, smart people dedicated to improving both safety and readiness came together and took steps to identify and overcome the many shortcomings in both maintenance and supply.

One of the earliest steps was the establishment of a Naval Air Technical Support Facility, under the auspices of BuAer, to set standards and control all aircraft drawings and technical manuals. Then in late 1954, under the aegis of the Inspections Requirements Branch at the Naval Air Test Center at Patuxent River, BuAer established standard check-sheet forms organized by systems. The following year, in one of the earliest attempts to collate fleetwide failure information, the Failure or Unsatisfactory Report (FUR) system was initiated. FURs, each in one of four categories, were submitted to the Aviation Supply Office (ASO), in Philadelphia, on IBM cards.[8] Then, in 1956, a group met in BuAer to develop an integrated Naval Aircraft Maintenance Program. Under the program squadron people would perform all direct maintenance required to keep their aircraft mission-ready, while ships and stations would provide the required facilities, installed equipment, parts, and other supporting services. Six levels of maintenance, A through F, were designated.

Noting that BuAer's efforts, while an excellent step forward, did little for the personnel and training aspects of the maintenance problem, the DCNO (Air), Vice Adm. Robert Pirie,[9] convened a group (the "Pirie Board") in 1957 to consider them. Unsurprisingly that board discovered many aviation-personnel shortcomings, including the fact that some three thousand maintenance officers were "missing," having "disappeared" into other assignments.

In 1962, even while BuAer and OPNAV were struggling to solve problems as they knew them, the Department of Defense established military specifications and standards and a "federal stock number system." This provided a common language across what had been a myriad of "stovepipes" and created a near revolution, a good one, in the stocking and ordering of spares. Meanwhile the Naval Air Technical Training Center (NATTC), under the aegis of Rear Adm. Fitzhugh Lee, developed the "Memphis Plan," a scheme to utilize better the graduates from NATTC. The Pirie Board not only immediately adopted and promulgated the Memphis Plan, underscoring the need to improve the utilization of personnel and training materials, but added several major changes, including standardization of aviation maintenance organizations. Also established were career programs to provide for increased specialization or subspecialization in maintenance for aviation-designated officer personnel and an aviation maintenance officer program. Capping these efforts, CNO in 1959 directed the disestablishment of the FASRONs and development of a comprehensive maintenance program.

Those who developed this new program had several things working for them. First, they had the results of the Pirie Board and Memphis Plan. Second, they had as possible models Air Force Manuals AF66-1 and AF67-1, which DOD had ordered the Navy to consider. (Although the Navy evaluators agreed that the manuals contained some good ideas, they rejected, in keeping with long-standing Navy practice, the concept of separate maintenance and operational chains of command.) Third, the Navy and Marine Corps had by now successfully implemented the RAG and NATOPS systems, which included training of maintainers.

Fourth and perhaps most important, the principal OPNAV action officers were Cdr. Leo Hamilton,[10] an aviation maintenance officer, and Cdr. Eugene Grinstead, a Supply Corps officer, both assigned to the DCNO (Air) staff. These two

Vice Adm. Eugene "Gene" A. Grinstead, SC, USN (Ret.), began his distinguished Navy career as a seaman apprentice in 1942, was a UDT (frogman) officer during World War II and then an iconic supply officer—retiring in 1984 as a vice admiral and director of the Defense Logistics Agency.

In every career position over forty-two years, he was recognized for revolutionary budget initiatives and logistics policy changes that resulted in dramatic improvement to fleet readiness at lower costs.

He was the father of the Aviation 3M program and the NISTARs program, which automated Navy distribution centers for the first time since World War II. His recommendation to use the working capital fund for procurement of aviation repairable components led to fully funded shipboard, air station, and wholesale repair-part inventories for the first time in naval history. This single achievement took aircraft readiness on board carriers from unsatisfactory levels to record highs that continue to this day.

VICE ADM. EUGENE GRINSTEAD
Defense Logistics Agency, with permission

In 1968 Captain Howard Goben, USN (Ret.), was the Navy's first designated Aeronautical Maintenance Duty Officer (AMDO) in the U.S. Navy.

He was designated as a naval aviator and commissioned ensign, USNR, in March 1944. He soon saw combat action in the Philippines and at Iwo Jima while flying the TBF Avenger torpedo bomber with Composite Squadron 77 on board USS *Rudyard Bay* (CVE 81).

After the war he had various duties in squadrons, staffs, and aircraft carriers, making numerous carrier deployments to the Pacific and Mediterranean. He was also a flight instructor, served ashore at FASRON 11, Atsugi, and Kangnong (Korea), and attended General Line School, the University of Mississippi, and the Navy Aviation Safety School, University of Southern California.

He headed the Aircraft Maintenance Technical Advisory Team, Naval Air Force Atlantic Fleet, NAS Norfolk, followed by assignment as Head, Fleet Aircraft Maintenance Division, Bureau of Naval Weapons, Washington, D.C, in 1963 and 1965. There his efforts were key to the development of what became the Naval Aircraft Maintenance and Material Program (NAMP), sometimes called the 3M Program. That was followed by duty as Head, Aircraft Maintenance and Material Division, Office of Deputy Chief Naval Operations (Air) from 1965 to 1971, where he continued to work the NAMP and 3M.

In 1971 and 1972 he was Head, Advanced Logistics Division, Naval Aviation Integrated Logistics Command at Patuxent River, followed by assignment as Head, Aviation Maintenance Division for Commander, Naval Air Force, U.S. Pacific Fleet.

His final assignment was as Officer-in-Charge, Commander Fleet Air Western Pacific Detachment, NAS Cubi Point, Philippines, 1973–75. He retired on 1 July 1975.

exceptional, experienced, and dedicated officers saw from the outset that the new concept had to improve the documentation of maintenance actions at all levels; provide for precise configuration and document control, to ensure that the right parts were correctly replaced; and focus on improved maintenance quality control. Hamilton, Grinstead, and Howard Goben, head of fleet maintenance in the Bureau of Naval Weapons (BuWeps), along with a lot of help from throughout the maintenance and supply establishments, were key to the development of what became the Naval Aircraft Maintenance and Material Management Program, the NAMP, sometimes called the 3M Program, made effective in 1959.[11]

In July 1959 the all-Navy/Marine mishap rate was 25.7 major accidents per hundred thousand flight hours, with 461 aircraft completely destroyed and 309 people killed.

NAMP was in itself basically a planned-maintenance and data-collection system, but from the very beginning it also:

- Established a standardized maintenance organization and system.
- Designated maintenance-activity work levels.
- Implemented calendar-driven inspections.
- Provided for "progressive aircraft rework" (PAR) instead of overhaul.
- Established a component-repair system, including ground handling equipment.

It also established a system of maintenance-data collection, accounting for man-hours, maintenance, and production. This data, in turn, improved quality control, local maintenance and material management, budget justification, and aircraft readiness and utilization:

- It markedly improved the availability of aircraft that were fully operational and certified *safe to fly*.
- It set up an organization that provided discipline, procedural rigor, and commonality of language and procedures for all maintenance actions, regardless of scope.
- It prescribed a common "maintenance action form" (MAF), which recorded:
  - The nature of a system or component failure, completion of a calendar inspection or special inspection completion, and other things.
  - The technical manuals, tools, maintenance skills, and parts required to correct the problem.
  - A method of recording information that maintenance control could use to order parts.

The recording of parts usage was an extremely important part of this process, in that, inter alia, it provided the substantiating documentation for future procurement. More important, and from a readiness and safety point of view, an unusually high demand for any one part or for a part not previously known to fail frequently flagged the need for special attention, investigation, and, perhaps, a redesign of the item itself. This in turn served to focus the attention of top management on special and emergency needs.

A critical and high-payoff aspect of the 3M Program was the establishment of a Supply Support Center (SSC) within the Supply Department of the carrier or the Aviation Supply Division of the supporting NAS or MCAS. The SSC provided a single point of contact from which squadron or Aircraft Intermediate Maintenance Department (AIMD—discussed below) personnel could order required parts. The priority established by maintenance control determined the required time frame for delivery of the item, usually less than one hour. Once sufficient usage data were collected, the system would generate a requirement for the item to be carried in the ship's or station's allowance. This, in turn, facilitated timely delivery and markedly reduced the unsafe tendency to "make do" with an inappropriate or unsafe part, the source of a number of earlier mishaps. The 3M Program became the common language, and its accompanying manual the bible, of maintenance and supply throughout the fleet.

That was not the end of the story, however. In 1965, after just two years of 3M, its six levels of maintenance were consolidated into three, providing clean and clear organizational responsibility with two principal pillars: a Planned Maintenance System and a Maintenance Data Collection System, together known as the Maintenance Management System. At the same time, an Aircraft Maintenance and Material Branch was established in OP-05.[12] Then, in May 1967, the old V-6 Divisions in aircraft carriers gave way to new Aircraft Intermediate Maintenance Departments, followed in short order, in 1968, by the inauguration of a new "restricted line" community, the Aircraft Maintenance Duty Officer (AMDO, designator 152X), whose members were the first fully defined and full-time naval-aircraft-maintenance specialists.

The advantages of the new 3M system soon accrued to all of naval aviation: carriers, helos, Marines, and land-based naval aviation alike. The Naval Air Training Command was especially enthusiastic about the new system; in 1970, Vice Adm. Bernard M. Strean, Chief of Naval Air Training, saw fit to publish an article in U.S. Naval Institute *Proceedings* praising the virtues of, and describing the outstanding results his command had achieved through, 3M.[13] In the article, he reported that largely because of 3M the Training Command had posted an all-time-low accident rate, had improved readiness by 15 percent, and had won the CNO Safety Award for two of the last three years. At the same time, prodigious amounts of money and man-hours were being saved. Similar reports were coming in from throughout naval aviation, despite the high operating tempo and influx of new and more complicated aircraft and systems. One example of that new complexity was the Versatile Avionics Systems Test (VAST), first installed on board ship in 1968, which was required to support such new aircraft as the RA-5C Vigilante reconnaissance platform.

> By December 1970 the all-Navy/Marine mishap rate had been reduced to 13.5 major accidents per hundred thousand flight hours, with 264 aircraft completely destroyed and 231 people killed—the rate of ten years prior had been cut almost in half.

Nevertheless, and despite sanguine reports, there were indeed disturbing trends in 1969, 1970, and 1971. Some of the new and more complicated aircraft and systems coming into the fleet had significant reliability problems, aircraft such as the E-2C, AV-8, P-3C, F-14, A-7E, and S-3A, for example, and new and more capable (and more complex) helicopters. Not insignificantly, operating dollars available were in a continual rate of decline. The problem was exacerbated by less-than-adequate intermediate test equipment, severe shortages of trained sailors, and spare-parts shortages, due to severe underfunding. One of the results was that in 1970, as just a one-year example, 16 percent of all Navy/Marine accidents were the result of maintenance error, errors that, according to the Naval Safety Center, fell into five well-defined categories.

- Nonstandard administrative procedures
- Lack of supervision
- Ineffective quality assurance
- Questionable training
- Less-than-optimum utilization of manpower, equipment, and facilities

This performance, coupled with lessons learned over the preceding nine years of operating in accordance with the first 3M manual, prompted a major revision. Professional and dedicated maintainers and supply professionals rose to the occasion. The result was a new Naval Aviation Maintenance and Material Program, promulgated on 1 January 1971.[14] The list of actions is lengthy but includes the following.

- Promulgation of a NAMP rewritten into four volumes[15]
- Standardization of:
    - Three levels of maintenance organization
    - Allowance lists
    - Inspections
    - Ground support equipment

- Handbooks
- Definition of aircraft custodians
- Forms and reports
* Revision of support documents
* Inclusion of maintenance line items in contracts
* Maintainability and reliability specifications
* Refinement of contractor support of new aircraft
* Innovations in provisioning

Closely coordinated with the promulgation of the new NAMP was the establishment of a Naval Air Integrated Logistics Support Center (NAILC), at Patuxent River. This was yet another step toward improved coordination between maintenance and supply, and more was to come. Also, by 1980, the information and data generated by the NAMP was fast overwhelming the computational, analytic, and storage capabilities of the day, and a new system had to be developed. The answer was the Naval Aviation Logistics Information System (NALCOMIS).

> By the end of calendar year 1980, the all-Navy/Marine mishap rate was
> 5.94 major accidents per hundred thousand flight hours,
> with 112 aircraft completely destroyed and ninety-one people killed—
> a rate less than half that of ten years prior and
> less than a fourth of what it had been twenty years prior.

In addition, the introduction of the F/A-18 Hornet in the early 1980s brought more reliable avionics systems, plus a new concept in maintenance support: contractor support in partnership with organic or government support. An avionics repair facility (ARF) was established at NAS Lemoore and NAS Cecil Field to bring factory technicians planeside with the local AIMD. This reduced repair turnaround time, thereby reducing aircraft downtime and increasing readiness. Most important, the prime contractor had access to and "visibility of" the failures and was in a position to create fixes.

Historically, initial outfittings of spare parts for given aircraft types were procured after the aircraft were produced and delivered. This and consistent underfunding of appropriated spare-part inventory accounts resulted in unacceptable shortages of spare parts when the aircraft were introduced to the fleet. These inventory shortages compounded the "normal" aircraft-introduction problems associated with maintenance and supply. To alleviate shortfalls in aviation "repairables" (that is, failed components that could be returned, refurbished, and reissued), in the early 1980s OPNAV created an innovative funding mechanism. The Navy Stock Fund (a revolving/working-capital fund) was approved to "buy in" repairable components in year one, to be "bought out" with appropriated funds in year three. The result was that aircraft spare-part requirements became fully funded, procured, and positioned on board ships and air stations to support the flight operational schedules when the aircraft were delivered. Stock funding also fully funded follow-on spare-part replenishment driven by unexpected usage/demand rates. In 1985, over $2.5 billion was invested in aircraft spares, resulting in dramatically improved aircraft readiness in the late 1980s and continuing to this day.

Shipboard readiness as measured by spare-part shortages preventing aircraft from being operationally ready dropped from triple digits to single digits in the 1990s.

In the 1990s, contractor logistics support was further refined through the introduction of "performance-based logistics" (PBL) support contracts at both the component level and the aircraft or engine level, at the ASO. The PBL contracts focused on performance and reliability, rewarding the contractor for improved reliability as well as improved performance. This effort has continued within the Navy, the other services, and the Defense Logistics Agency. Also in the 1990s, the Ships Parts Control Center (SPCC) was merged with the Aviation Supply Office to form the Naval Inventory Control Point (NICP). For twenty-five years, the supply, maintenance, and aviation engineering officers at the NICP have worked with the failure records in the maintenance data systems to reduce failure rates of parts. While failure data closely approximates the demand data for new parts, it is more descriptive of the circumstances of failure. In fact, the purpose has been to find parts or assemblies that fail often and fix the causes as a means of reducing cost.

Safety is the derivative benefactor of this effort, because the failure rate is reduced, and because the need to take the aircraft apart to fix failures is itself a source of new failures and new weaknesses. Readiness has improved, costs have reduced, but more important, the benefit for safety has been phenomenal.

This effort has involved reengineering of parts and assemblies, adaptation of test equipment to isolate failures better, correction of maintenance publications, retraining of maintenance personnel, and an assortment of other actions envisioned in a program called "Integrated Logistics Support." A change in the law that allowed supply officers to use the Navy Stock Fund to pay for these corrections has accelerated this effort. These techniques have now been incorporated into PBL, resulting in contracts that reward reductions in failure rates, lower costs, better readiness, and improved safety of flight.

> *In calendar year 2000 the all-Navy/Marine mishap rate was 1.99 major accidents per hundred thousand flight hours, with twenty-four aircraft completely destroyed and forty-six people killed. This was a rate two-thirds of what it had been ten years prior and a twenty-fourth of what it had been in 1950.*
> *In 2000 the Safety Center turned its principal focus to motorcycle accidents.*

By no means did the focus on aircraft mishaps lessen. Indeed, by 2000, the Aviation Directorate of the Safety Center featured Aviation Maintenance as a principal branch, along with Aeromedical, Airfield Operations, Investigations, Culture Workshops, and the School of Aviation Safety. Media and Statistics were independent directorates, although closely aligned with all aspects of aviation safety, of course.

As we have seen, even before 2000 there was increasing recognition of the role of human factors in mishap investigation. This recognition began to remedy the excessive ascription of mishaps to "pilot error," when in fact the pilot, or aircrew, had been "setup" to fail by some other type of error, including maintenance error. The advent of HERAP (see chapter 10) served to facilitate analysis so that subsequent corrective action could be carried out. HERAP was subsequently modified to become "Human Factors" and later into the "Maintenance Extension" of the HFACS program, or HFACS-ME.[16] The governing instruction series, OPNAV Instruction 3780.6 lays down that "HFACS-ME facilitates the recognition of absent or defective defenses at four levels, including unsafe: Management Conditions (Organizational & Supervisory), Maintainer Conditions, Working Conditions, and Maintainer Acts."[17] The instruction goes on to note that this framework can then be used to identify targets for intervention and corrective action.

That framework was indeed soon transformed into a database that classified maintenance errors as resulting from "Supervisory Conditions," "Maintainer Conditions," or "Working Conditions." Each of those was further subdivided as errors resulting from actions or nonactions within each of the conditions. As a result, after only a modicum of analysis, the reason for a maintenance mishap could be identified as one of several conditions, such as poor or nonexistent maintenance procedures, inadequate or poor supervision, miscommunication, nonuse of instruction, use of outdated instructions, or violations of policy, procedures, or checklists. Corrective action could be taken on that basis.

The most significant aspect of this framework and associated analysis is that no longer must there be a mishap or near mishap before corrective action can be taken. The opportunity was quickly translated into planning and briefing on hangar decks and shop floors, and maintenance error was thus dramatically reduced. Because of this, with HFACS-ME the days of just calling it "pilot error" or "maintenance error" became matters for the history books, and the mishap rate fell some more.

The contributions of maintenance and supply to the tremendous improvement in naval aviation safety between 1950 and 2000 cannot be overemphasized. Those contributions, especially those of dedicated and professional maintainers and suppliers, have been significant. Without that dedication and professionalism, from airmen and privates, from chiefs and sergeants, from officers of all ranks, and from Navy civilians, the record achieved over those fifty years could not have been recorded, and the aircraft and lives saved would have been lost.

Yet, maintenance and supply did not stop improving in 2000. In 2005, the eight Naval Fleet Readiness Centers were created, combining the three remaining aviation depots (North Island, Cherry Point, and Jacksonville) with eight Naval Air Station Aircraft Intermediate Maintenance Departments, further streamlining the three levels of maintenance into two, with sailors working side by side with civilian and contractor personnel. This was the most significant event in naval aviation maintenance history since the introduction of the NAMP in the 1960s. In 2012 the program's name changed again, to the Naval Supply Systems Command (NavSup) Weapons Systems Support (WSS), to focus even further on readiness performance vice parts availability.

While pilots and aircrew have been awarded medals and ribbons by the gross in the last fifty years, they won those accolades on the backs of a legion of dedicated and professional maintainers and suppliers. The critical roles played by successive generations of aviation maintainers and aviation supply officers have been recognized with suitable breast insignia: Naval Aviation Supply Wings were authorized in 1984, Professional Aviation Maintenance Officer Wings in 2009. Even so, these people can never be thanked or recognized enough.

13

The Underappreciated
Aircraft, Aircraft Systems, and Design Safety

Essential parts of the revolution in naval aviation safety have been, first, the remarkable growth of reliability of aircraft and engines, control systems, and hydraulics and, second, the almost meteoric rise in the importance of avionics. The sum total of these contributions is reflected in both operational capability and safety. An included and less obvious factor has been the pace of acquisition of new aircraft and the ability of manufacturers to incorporate lessons learned.

Between 1950 and 2000, fifty-one different aircraft models were introduced into naval aviation by way of first flights. Some models lasted only a short while, but others continued to operate in the force for many, many, years. Remarkably, twenty-eight of those fifty-one models were first flown between 1950 and 1959. It took the next forty years for the other twenty-three to make their first flights.[1]

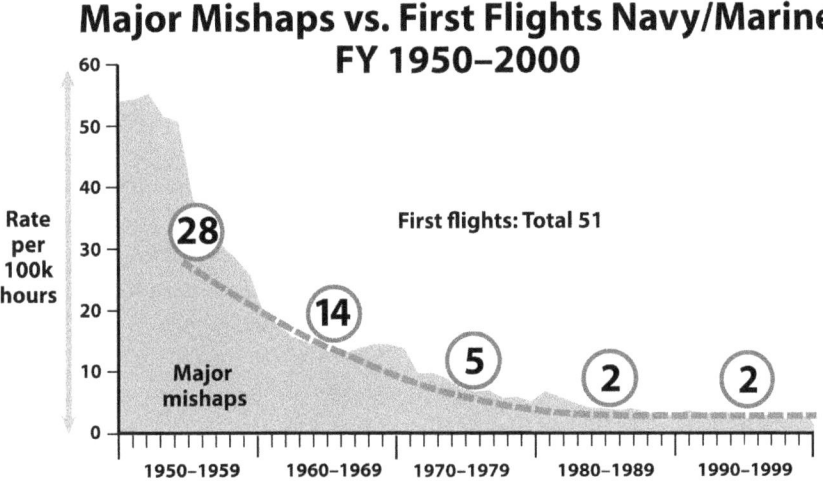

Figure 13-1 Graphic major mishaps vs. first flight
Data from Rausa's Pistons to Jets, created by Guy Arceneaux

The resulting profile is amazingly similar to the profile of figure 3-3 in chapter 3. This gives immediate rise to the question of whether the slowing pace of aircraft introductions was itself a major contributor to the gradual reduction in number of Navy/Marine mishaps between 1950 and 2000.

Early on, some of the newly introduced aircraft, especially the jets, were difficult to master. All the new aircraft, props, helos, and jets had technical problems. There was little maintenance knowledge about most of them, and only nascent supply support. The jets had special problems. With their straight wings, as they approached the sound barrier they encountered the problem of compressibility, poorly understood at the time. They had engines that were not always reliable and very often had inadequate response times. Electronics available were rudimentary by today's standards, largely the same as used at the end of World War II. These trends, coupled with widespread lack of standardization and flight discipline (see chapters 2 and 9), created an environment where the mishap rate was bound to soar, and it did.

As new aircraft entered, the inventory distractions abounded. Despite their historic performances in World War II, the dawn of the Cold War prompted serious questions about the roles of the Navy and Marines and particularly of naval aviation. (See chapter 2.) Could jets operate routinely off aircraft carriers? Could carriers survive in the atomic age? Were Navy/Marine aircraft capable of reaching potential enemy targets and surviving? To these challenges and others like them the leaders of naval aviation, officers who had fought World War II in the Pacific, engineers in the Bureau of Aeronautics, up-and-coming test pilots, and aircraft and engine manufacturers all responded with a resounding "Yes!" They then focused on making it happen.

Introducing so many new aircraft in such a short period of time was one of the major problems. Not sure which technologies would best meet future challenges and believing that time was of the essence,[2] the Navy attempted to reduce risk by letting multiple contracts to different aircraft companies in hopes that at least one of the designs would be viable. Additional risk was incurred by ordering series production of various models before flight testing was complete.[3] The upshot was that only a handful of the many models developed and tested had long tenures in the fleet; pilots seemed to be in an almost constant familiarization stage, never a particularly safe situation and undoubtedly a major contributor to the high accident rate of the 1950s.

The first jets flown by naval aviators, generally test pilots, were either experimental in nature or had been originally produced for the Air Force. One of the earliest was the Ryan Fireball, powered by a prop in the front and a jet in the back. The Chance Vought F7U-1 Cutlass was first flown in 1948 but soon proved to be a bit ahead of its time, although a later model was marginally successful.[4] More successful were the McDonnell FH-1 Phantom I and the North American FJ-1, the latter a carrier-capable aircraft that became the model for the highly successful Air Force F-86 Sabre. Soon the FH-1 was replaced by the much more capable F2H Banshee, and the FJ-1 was overtaken by the F9F-2 Panther.[5] Props still carried the load, however. F4U Corsairs and AD Skyraiders populated the carrier decks, with even a few TBMs used for antisubmarine patrol and utility.

The F3D Skyknight also appeared in both the Navy and Marine inventories in the late 1940s. This two-place twin-engine night fighter was deployed on board carriers in detachments of four aircraft but never made it as a full-fledged component of the carrier air group. (See chapter 5.) Instead, F3Ds were often shore based; nevertheless, they more than proved themselves during the Korean War, where they were flown by both Navy and Marine pilots from airfields in South Korea.[6]

In addition to all the other inadequacies, there were major problems operating jets from straight-deck aircraft carriers. Typical jet engine acceleration and thrust dictated that deck launches such as had been used by World War II fighters were out of the question. By today's standards, the thrust of the early jets was abysmally low. Even in 1951, the thrust of the single Pratt & Whitney J48 used in the F9F-2 Panther was only 6,250 pounds.[7] This meant that the hydraulically operated H-4 catapults then in use were only marginally capable of launching a fully fueled Panther, let alone one carrying any significant external load. Fuel was another problem. At first the carriers didn't carry what came to be known as "jet fuel," so aviation gasoline (AvGas) modified with a dollop of fuel oil to lower the temperature of ignition to a level more suitable to jet engines was used. To top it all off, jets were forced to use procedures for launch and recovery developed for the all-prop air groups of World War II.

Jets weren't the only innovation. While the very first helicopters had been flown during World War II, they had been used only for rescue. Marines, however, began early to develop the concept of "vertical assault" and during the Korean War showed dramatically the utility of the helicopter, which expanded to include medical evacuation, logistics, and more.[8] During that war, "some twenty-five thousand wounded were evacuated from combat areas by helicopter, and troops and supplies were moved in by the same method to places that would have been otherwise inaccessible."[9] Very soon, helicopters' capabilities multiplied until no air group, no ship, and no air station wanted to be without at least a detachment of them. Types of rotary-wing aircraft multiplied, and in 1951, Kaman Aircraft flew the first jet-powered helo.

Ashore, the P2V Neptune, designed before the war but resurrected in 1945, was the principal aircraft fulfilling the long-range patrol and ASW missions; it was also tested as a nuclear-weapons-delivery aircraft and was successfully launched, as a demonstration, from an aircraft carrier.[10] The Neptune could not be recovered aboard a ship, so a new aircraft capable of carrier operations and able to carry the huge nuclear device of the day was developed.[11] The North American AJ Savage fulfilled that mission until smaller nuclear weapons became available, at which time the F2H Banshee and the AD Skyraider took over the job. After losing the nuclear role to the smaller (and in the case of the Banshee, speedier) aircraft, the AJ continued deploying with carriers until the mid-1950s as a tanker.

By the start of the Korean War in June 1950, the Navy/Marine aircraft inventory had begun to sort itself out and stabilize. The larger carriers were outfitted with Panthers, Banshees, Skyraiders, and one or two helicopters. There were also detachments of Banshees specially equipped for photo reconnaissance and guided-missile control[12] and Skyraiders equipped for night attack and airborne early warning, respectively. Smaller carriers carried AF Guardians, radar-equipped TBMs, and helos. The patrol force was reasonably well stabilized with the Neptune and the sea-based Marlin. Marines counted jets, props, and helicopters in their inventory, with the latter continuing to increase in importance. For all types, succeeding generations rapidly followed, one after the other. Still, the big challenge was posed by jets, especially jets operating from aircraft carriers.

Beyond problems with straight decks and marginally capable catapults, the first generation[13] of carrier-capable jets arrived on the scene with traditional elevators instead of stabilators (in which the entire stabilizer, on either side of the rudder, is movable). Irreversible hydraulic flight controls with artificial feel were yet to come, as were redundant hydraulic systems and pitch-and-yaw-stability augmentation. Even ejection seats and air conditioning were still in rudimentary stages. Couple those lacks with the need for aircrew and maintenance personnel to learn a new aircraft for each deployment or more often, frequently with inadequate or nonexistent flight and maintenance manuals, and it's no surprise that the mishap rate seems to reflect so closely the rate of introduction of new aircraft.

Meanwhile, the aviation industry faced its own challenges. Conceiving, designing, and producing the aircraft and systems needed by the Navy and Air Force to meet the rising threats of the Cold War and by the civilian world to meet global transportation needs, taking advantage of the plethora of new technologies coming available, and converting or expanding manufacturing plants to accommodate the new systems—doing all this at the same time was a herculean task for the whole industry. Then, there was the growing understanding of high-speed aerodynamics, the availability of newer and more powerful power plants, and the opportunity to take advantage of rapidly developing computer power and avionics. In fact, the accommodation of electronic gear became a critical factor in designing new combat planes.[14] New management techniques enabled aviation, particularly the military aviation communities, to produce and to put into operation aircraft with ever-increasing performance.

Some of the similarities in mishap experiences of the several sectors of aviation depicted on the charts in chapter 3 reflect this. In the military services in particular the years immediately following World War II were tumultuous and heady, because of the need to meet new requirements, both operational and bureaucratic, and to comply with new ways of doing business. Driven by expensive electronics, complex designs, and exotic materials, let alone new requirements for unprecedented speed and maneuverability, costs went ever higher. In an attempt to keep budgets under control, something called "commonality" in design was implemented. Nevertheless, costs continued to grow, and another concept, "concurrency"—acquiring production tools and support equipment while the design was still on the drawing boards—came into vogue. These ideas, and others, were aimed at speeding up the acquisition process and reducing costs. Both goals often proved elusive, if not out of reach.[15]

All this notwithstanding, new engines and electronics systems were indeed developed, tested, and brought into the fleet in numbers seldom seen since. Propeller-plane production continued, but jets, then jets with swept wings, entered the fleet. Engines soon morphed from centrifugal flow to axial flow to high bypass, to gain higher operating pressure and better performance. New and more capable (and more difficult to maintain) electronic gear had to be accommodated. In the meantime, older designs continued in the fleet. The Lockheed P2V Neptune (see above) was a case in point. At the same time, helicopters came into their own, first with reciprocating engines but soon with gas turbines. Guided missiles arrived in the inventories both as weapons carried by airplanes and as stand-alone means of both offense and defense. Computers and electronics made their debuts in design, manufacture, navigation, control, and other realms. Between 1950 and 2000, there was literally a revolution in aircraft and in their systems, engines, and avionics. The effect of this revolution on aviation safety was tremendous.

The uncertainty about postwar roles and missions of the several services (see chapter 2) and lack of clarity about the future direction of commercial aviation led to uncertainty in the aviation industry itself. With the termination of wartime contracts, each firm had to decide whether to continue exclusively as an airframe or engine manufacturer or to seek diversification into nonaeronautical fields; whether to aim for military or commercial markets or both; what to do about new developments such as guided missiles, jet propulsion, vertical takeoff and landing, and high-altitude supersonic flight.[16] Expressing a typical dilemma, the Convair engineering department stated in April 1945, "Work has just started on possible airplanes for supersonic speeds. Practically no aerodynamic data are available in this speed range, and what there is isn't consistent."[17] In addition, once they did get to designing they found that the greater complexity of airplanes built for high-altitude, high-speed flight demanded attention to the minutest details and consequently unprecedented costs. It was an entirely new environment, one faced not only by the industry but by the services as well.

As a result, some aviation corporations consolidated, while others switched into other lines of business or closed all together. Most of those that stayed soon recognized the new imperatives and focused their research and development on improvements in operational performance, producibility (including automated production systems), use of new materials, and maintainability. The importance of electronics (and computers) grew, and as the industry took advantage of new concepts and new materials with each succeeding generation, aircraft became more capable and safer.

There were exceptions to this steady improvement in safety, to be sure. Over its lifetime the F-8 Crusader had more than its share of mishaps, and the RA-5C Vigilante wasn't far behind. But there weren't many such exceptions. Even with them in the mix, the naval aviation safety record continued to improve.

In addition to all the numerous systems improvements, industry also increasingly partnered with customers, the armed services, and commercial airlines in a practice that became known as "systems safety." In the late 1960s, industry and the services began to apply systems safety to design and production of new aircraft, later to operations at the squadron level.[18] The concept called for a risk-management strategy based on identification, analysis of hazards, and application of remedial controls using a systems-based approach. Its purpose was (and is) to ensure that safety is considered from the earliest stages of design through the procurement of a weapons system, in order to eliminate, or at least minimize, personnel hazards and material failures or malfunctions throughout the life cycle of the system or component. In a number of areas this approach merges with the science of human factors (see chapters 10 and 11), where its application to aircraft and aircraft-systems manufacture, aviation maintenance, and supply has proven to be a key ingredient in naval aviation safety improvement.

One of the most rewarding contributions of systems safety from an overall safety standpoint has been the accommodation of lessons learned all the way from the factory assembly line to the flight line to the cockpit. The "Anymouse" (see chapter 2) system, trouble reports, mishap reports from increasingly thorough aircraft accident investigations and their recommendations, and lessons learned all find their way into the systems-safety processes of producers, maintainers, and operators. It should be noted that systems safety is far different from traditional strategies of control, or attempt at control.[19] At the minimum, systems safety facilitates the incorporation of redundant or backup systems and of safety and warning devices and is an essential element in devising emergency procedures. It encompasses "design for safety," a concept and practice that embraces:

- The design of the vehicle, all components and systems.
- The development of the operating procedures provided to the human operator.
- The development of maintenance procedures for the vehicle, its components, and systems.

- The consideration of human factors, the bridging of knowledge about physiology and psychology to what has been learned about design and engineering.

A contractor who undertakes to design a new military aircraft bases that design on, inter alia, the customer's desires, military design specifications (MIL-SPECs), federal aviation regulations, and the contractor's knowledge and lessons learned in previous projects. Also included are the safety considerations of the design, whether it be for normal, abnormal, or emergency operations—that is, safe operation when single or multiple failures have occurred and there may be failures in both operating and maintenance procedures. Some of the concepts involved in this pursuit of safety are:

- Careful arrangement of components and systems to avoid catastrophic consequences of failures.
- Addition of caution and warning systems for the crew.
- Addition of systems, such as fire-detection and suppression systems, that can overcome potentially catastrophic failures.
- Redundancy, the provision of a backup in the event of failure of a primary component or system.
- "Similar redundancy," such as an additional hydraulic system.
- "Dissimilar redundancy," such as an air bottle for emergency deployment of landing gear.

To evaluate designs for safety, several analytical tools are used. Among them are:

- Qualitative Risk Assessment: a procedure that categorizes the severity of an event, from catastrophic to safe, on one scale, and the probability of occurrence, from frequent to extremely unlikely, on the other.
- Failure Modes and Effects Analysis (FMEA): a systematic procedure for projecting the effect of a failure of a component or system on the operation of the vehicle.
- Fault-Tree Analysis (FTA): a systematic procedure for projecting the failure of component or system on other components or systems in the vehicle.
- Software Independent Validation and Verification (IV&V): a systematic procedure for ensuring that software programs that generate commands for flight-control and flight-management systems work the way they're supposed to and that no combination of software-generated commands can lead to a catastrophic event.
- Probabilistic Risk Assessment (PRA): a systematic procedure combining FTA and FMEA to determine the probability of a catastrophic event for the entire vehicle.

These evaluations are used also in other safety design efforts, some mandated and some not, such as preliminary design reviews, critical design reviews, "graybeard" reviews, nonadvocate reviews, and by independent review teams. Along the way, of course, the various components and systems are tested.

While the efforts described above are well known and well accepted by both the industry and the military, the systems are not static. For example, there is continuing effort to utilize lessons learned early in the design process with the participation of suppliers at every stage. There is increasing emphasis on human factors in design, especially in the crew interface.

That is not to say that design errors never figure in the analysis of a mishap. The May 1972 edition of *Approach* tells of two T2B mishaps wherein, while the student pilots were blamed, the landing-taxi light switch on the left console was only two inches from, and of the same lift-lock construction as, the fuel-transfer switch. A pilot flying formation at night, especially a novice pilot, could very easily activate the wrong switch. The design was, indeed, corrected, but only after the fact, after two aircraft had been lost. At least the lessons learned from the incidents prompted changes, even if some nineteen months later. More attention paid to what we today call "human factors" might have precluded those mishaps.

Just as they have in accident investigation and maintenance, human factors have been increasingly important in design, especially since World War II and the advent of jets. In the earlier days, human-factors engineers, erstwhile "human engineers," were afterthoughts in the design process, if thought of at all. When BuAer began closer cooperation with flight surgeons; when the Naval Safety Center began providing hard data from the Human Error Research and Analysis Program (HERAP); and when, even more recently, the Navy-inspired Department of Defense Human Factors and Analysis Classification System (HFACS) came into being, human factors and human engineering were even more fully integrated into the design process. This process becomes iterative as feedback from the user becomes available. Whether that feedback is anonymous ("Anymouse") or comes from "unsatisfactory reports," reports of near misses, mishap investigations, or something else, more accurate data bases of component and system failure rates can be developed, and systems designers can take corrective action. Such corrective action range from workspace interface through display and instrument-panel and control design to overall configuration. The results of all the above, and more, are ever safer, more capable, and more maintainable aircraft and weapons systems, facts reflected in the declining mishap rate over the last fifty years, especially since the advent of HERAP and HFACS.

One of the more obvious and important outgrowths of increasing focus on human factors has been in the realm of cockpits and displays. A pilot of the 1950s transported into a cockpit of 2000 or 2015 might well feel lost. Gone are the "steam gauges"—dials, lights, and counters. Instead, there are multifunction electronic displays that can call up multiple pictures with the flick of a button on the control stick or side-stick controller. A heads-up display projected onto the windscreen can show targets, navigation routes, airspeed, landing approach information, fuel state, engine operating conditions, and more. None of this replaces a good scan of the cockpit displays, which comes only as a result of intensive training, but it facilitates safe flight in ways that are not yet fully understood.

One final factor in the slowing of the pace of introduction of new aircraft is the combined roles of the Congress and the Department of Defense. The unprecedented growth in requirements and oversight of the services and the conscientious design and production of military aircraft by manufacturers is, of course, all under the aegis of directives, often complicated directives, from DOD and of oversight, sometimes even interference, from Congress. To some extent, this oversight is historical, and, indeed, as far as Congress goes, it is rooted in the Constitution. Still, it can be, and often is, a process that delays acquisition, or even acquisition of the best. An example in the context of aircraft and systems procurement can be found in various laws and directives that began to descend upon the services and their suppliers in the late 1950s, as military procurement began to consume a larger and larger part of the nation's budget and several acquisition scandals were publicized.

At least partially as a result of this, Congress, but also the Office of the Secretary of Defense (OSD), began to direct that specific procedures be used in the development and acquisition of weapons systems, including aircraft. In fact, ostensibly to ensure careful analysis of the relationship between technical reality and procurement practices, there was developed a "weapon process" that called for four major phases of weapons-systems procurement: conceptual, definition, acquisition, and operational. OSD staff were evermore deeply involved in each phase. This was followed by establishment of OSD boards and issuance of instructions that called for even more new directives, standing boards, and meetings to review and offer guidance in preparation of requests for proposals, associated statements of work, and so forth, sometimes down to the smallest of details. Paperwork grew in inverse proportion to aircraft, engine, and systems production. Likewise, the people count rose, with more people supervising more people, while unit output went down and cost went up.

In many cases, these procedures were beneficial to the procurement system, but in others they merely served to delay an already-slowing process, often adding an unnecessary level of bureaucracy to an already overstacked overhead. All other effects aside, this slower process meant fewer first flights for Navy and Marine aircraft, thus contributing in an unexpected way to something desirable—more time for better learning and familiarization, thus safer operations overall. This is reflected in figure 13-1, above.

To say there has been a revolution in naval aviation since 1950 would be the grossest of understatements. In parallel with the rest of aviation, naval aviation has seen the advent of aircraft and propulsion systems with ever-increasing performance, reliability, and safety. Likewise, control systems, hydraulics, and avionics have made their own contributions. That naval aviation is by any measure safer than it has ever been is the result of all these developments and others. The contribution of each is reflected not only in operational capability but also in safety.

While the pace of acquisition of new aircraft may not appear at first to affect the safety of the force, the data suggest the opposite. When the frequency of delivery of new airplane types was high, so was the all-Navy mishap rate. As the frequency slowed in later years, the accident rate fell commensurately. Obviously this was not a purposeful mishap-prevention effort. Not all the political, bureaucratic, and technical challenges of bringing new aircraft into the fleet were laid on because of safety. Instead, it's an example of the phenomenon of unintended consequences. The sum total of those consequences led to a slower pace of introduction of new aircraft, which meant that aircrews, maintainers, and logisticians had more time to become expert in each, without having to learn several different models of aircraft in a very short time. In other words, they had time to climb the learning curve before beginning all over again. The unintended consequences of the imposition of new bureaucracy worked toward the overall good with regard to safety, even if less good with regard to acquisition expense, time to production, and matching the capabilities of the potential enemy.

This phenomenon of fewer new aircraft contributing to an improvement in the mishap rate did not rise to greater importance than the efforts of the safety center, the implementation of RAGs and NATOPS, angled decks, improved maintenance and logistics management, or the increasing professionalism and contributions of aerospace medicine. Nevertheless, system safety, "Design for Safety," and the many other efforts to improve have not been fully appreciated and are among the principal reasons the naval aviation safety record had improved so dramatically during the last fifty years of the twentieth century.

14

Making Believe
Simulators and Synthetic Trainers

An aircraft behaves as it does because it is obedient to the laws of aerodynamics. Difficulties arise in trying to duplicate this behavior in a ground-based assemblage of machinery and electronics which is not subject to the laws of aerodynamics. The perfect simulator would duplicate in every detail a particular aircraft's responses, handling characteristics, and sensations of flight. But, since nothing—including naval aviators—is perfect, most pilots continue to resent and revile these marvelous machines that take all of the danger, and most of the fun, out of flight training.

Lt. Cdr. C. A. Wheal, RN

In fact, some would say a good simulator check ride is like successful surgery on a dead body.

Anonymous

Aviation simulators today can replicate in great detail almost every phase of flight, from simple familiarization through sophisticated multiplane maneuvers to air combat, close air support, antisubmarine warfare, and more.[1] Their use is extensive, and intuitively, one would conclude they can and should make major contributions to flight safety. The trouble is that there are few studies and even less data to back up such conclusions. A search of the literature and an informal survey of pilots reveal that there is a general consensus that flight time and simulator time are somehow related to aircrew morale, readiness, and flight safety, but hard facts are few and far between. The need for such facts rises each time budget cuts are proposed and increased simulator time is recommended as a substitute for flight time, largely on the basis of presumed cost savings. There are other factors, however, factors such as the relationship of simulator time to unit readiness and aircrew morale and, of most importance, the relationship of simulator time to flight safety.

In the early twenty-first century one takes for granted simulators of all sorts: in movies and on television, in theme parks, museums, computer games, medical and dental training, driver education, and in industry, including the operation of complex machinery. One expects to see it in all phases of flight instruction, whether commercial or military aviation or space,[2] and in the operation of military ground vehicles, surface ships, submarines, and much, much more. Such was not the case in the mid-twentieth century. At that time, there were only a handful of aircraft simulator types. Subsequently, there has been an explosion of simulators for a plethora of services around the world in applications never imagined in midcentury. In the military services, the use of simulators for training has spread far beyond aviation, and concurrent with the spread of the internet, far-flung links have enabled simulation of naval battle-group and land force division-sized operations as well.[3] Yet, aviation training is where the use of simulators has found the most widespread application.

That may be because it was in aviation that the concept first took hold. For example, when Hap Arnold[4] began his flight training with the Wrights in 1911, "Instruction began on a crude sawhorse-mounted 'simulator' in which the student pilot learned how the controls moved."[5] Something like that was necessary because by today's standards, the Wright controls were incredibly complicated and difficult to manipulate.[6] Nevertheless, even with simpler controls many a flight student would, and still does, repair to his or her quarters to sit in a chair with a broomstick or small wheel and practice a maneuver learned that day or scheduled to be learned the next—a simulator in its most basic form.

As effective as such drills might be in undergraduate pilot training, something more was required for familiarization in the increasingly sophisticated aircraft of the 1930s. It was Edward A. Link, private pilot and son of an organ manufacturer, who designed the first mechanical flight simulator, known as the "Pilot Maker" in its day but later universally as the Link Trainer.[7] Begun as a basic "stick and rudder" trainer with no instruments, the early Link was at first relegated to amusement parks as a special sort of ride. Not until flying at night and in all weather became requirements, and not until turn-and-bank and airspeed indicators and a compass were added, did it become a premier vehicle for teaching and practicing instrument flight. Soon it spawned other special-use devices, but the basic trainer remained the Link, used by the thousands to train pilots in instrument flight in the United States, Britain, Germany, and Japan before, during, and after World War II. From it grew the sophisticated digital systems trainers used by all the air forces and airlines of the world today.[8]

The Link and other early synthetic trainers were based on the assumption that the most critical element of any trainer was movement—that is, that in order to fly safely one's senses had to be trained to know whether one was straight and level, climbing, diving, or rolling when unable to see outside. Thus, trainers were built to replicate the sensations of actual flight, with the ability to turn, climb, and dive. Edward Link achieved this "movement" by a complicated system of bellows much

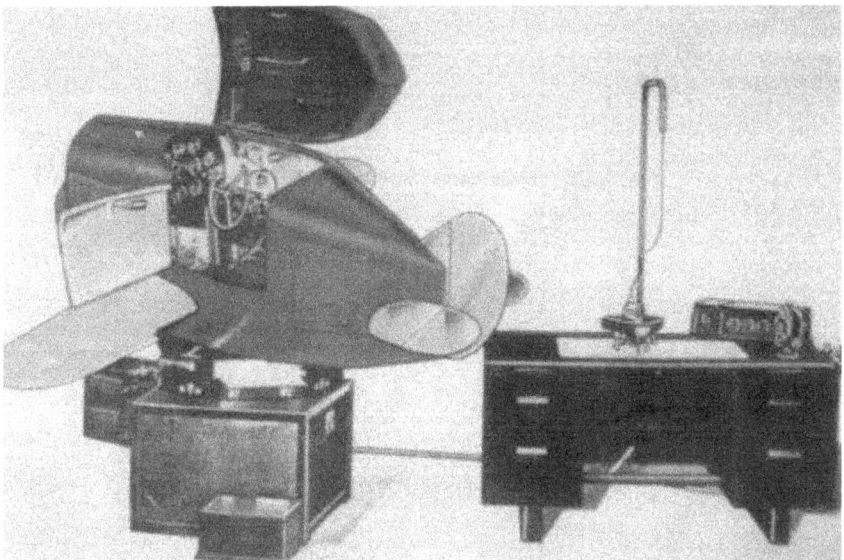

LINK TRAINER. *NHHC*

like those used in the manufacture of musical organs, the industry in which he got his start. Even when it was generally concluded that it was the not the human eye or muscles that controlled the sensations of flight but the sensory perceptions of the inner ear,[9] Link and his contemporaries continued to deliver simulators that would turn and bank, nose-over, nose-up, climb, and dive. The fact is, they did work, and they served the purposes of the day, even though there were a number of well-known shortfalls.

For example, according to Rolfe and Staples,[10] the first description of the trainer made no reference to instruments: "The device was primarily intended to demonstrate to students the effect of the controls on the attitude of the simulated 'aeroplane' and to train them in their coordinated operation. The simulated effects of the ailerons, elevators and rudder were independent. They did not represent the interactions present in the real aeroplane." Even when electricity replaced the bellows system, simulators continued to move. Motion in simulators is complicated and expensive, and thus some stationary "simulators" continued to be built, mostly as part-task trainers. Yet, that was the beginning of the discussion, "To move or not to move?" To this day, it has not been settled.[11] Thus, both systems will be found in the armed services, the airlines, and even in ab initio[12] training, although the latter tends toward the simpler and less-expensive stationary trainers, if such equipment is used at all.

Link Trainers played a key role in naval aviation training in the years before and during World War II, especially as the Navy faced requirements to train

Rear Adm. Luis de Florez poses while Wheeler Williams works on his bust in 1948. Today the bust is displayed in the de Florez Building at the Naval Air Warfare Center Training Systems Division in Orlando, Florida. *Naval Air Warfare Training Systems Division, Orlando*

rapidly growing numbers of new pilots. Nevertheless, the story of simulation in naval aviation would not be complete without the story of Rear Adm. Luis de Florez.

From April 1941, when then-Commander de Florez became head of the new Special Devices Desk in the Engineering Division of the Navy's Bureau of Aeronautics, he championed vigorously the use of "synthetic training devices" to increase readiness. Throughout World War II, his section developed numerous innovative training devices, including some that used motion pictures to train aircraft gunners, a device to train for precision bombing, and a kit with which to build model terrains to facilitate operational planning in the field. He even collaborated with Capt. P. V. H. Weems, a noted Navy navigation researcher, inventor, and instructor, to build a celestial-navigation device. One of his other major achievements was an operational flight trainer for the large and multicrewed (i.e., with a crew of several people) PBM-3 Mariner seaplane.[13] As his section grew in size and importance to the Navy, it became the Special Devices Division; in August 1946 the division was commissioned as the Special Devices Center at Port Washington, on Long Island, in New York. Today, that center has grown even more in scope and numbers of people and has moved to Orlando, Florida, where it is known as the Naval Air Warfare Training Systems Division of the Naval Air

Systems Command.[14] Unfortunately, de Florez did not leave behind many writings and has apparently no biographers; nevertheless, we know him by his work, by the high regard in which he was held by his seniors,[15] and by a speech that sums up his vision.[16] His real legacy was in training systems, not only flight trainers but gunnery trainers, radar trainers for night fighters, trainers to introduce aviators to automatic pilots, and others.

Luis de Florez left active duty right after the war, but those who went through naval aviation flight training in the 1950s and later benefited significantly from the work done by him and by the center he established on Long Island. Simulations of many sorts were integrated into the flight-training syllabus. Flight students practiced bailing out into a net from a stationary SNJ (the primary trainer used in the Naval Air Training Command in the 1950s) with engine turning at high power; experienced in the Dilbert Dunker what it was like to ditch an aircraft; learned how to see better at night in the night-vision trainer; and were exposed to the symptoms of hypoxia in a low-pressure chamber. Meanwhile, the aforementioned Link Trainer remained ubiquitous, for instrument training. For many years, naval aviators had received a modicum of instrument training, but real expertise was gained only by a relatively few night-fighter, attack, and transport pilots. It was not until the early 1950s that everyone was expected to be proficient in instrument flying. (See chapter 4.) All pilots then had to be acquainted with "blind flying" and airways navigation, which meant, of course, that newly designated naval aviators had to be trained to so qualify. Thus, the Link Trainer became even more important than it had once been.

The Link instrument-panel and radio controls used by pilot trainees mimicked faithfully the instruments and controls of the SNJ. Control manipulation produced motion; closing the Link's hood gave good practice for flying the patterns that were required in the actual airplane and for navigating low-frequency radio ranges. It was, in fact, a simple form of analog computer, empirically based. It was adequate for its day but hardly a simulator in today's sense.

As aircraft grew in performance and became equipped with evermore sophisticated technologies, a simple analog-based "blue box" (as Links were known, being painted blue) trainer would hardly do.[17] Therefore, in parallel with growth in aircraft technology and performance, training moved to electronic and digital computers; simulators grew more and more capable and sophisticated. Many had hydraulic actuators. Very soon, fault-insertion capabilities were incorporated,[18] fidelity improved, and computer-generated cathode-ray-tube images were installed. As a result of all these improvements, we now have part-task trainers, fixed-base trainers, motion-based trainers, computer-based trainers, procedural trainers, operational flight trainers (OFTs), weapon-systems trainers (WSTs), six-degree-of-motion trainers, night-carrier-landing trainers (NCLTs), LSO trainers, and other specialized and mission-rehearsal trainers, many capable of

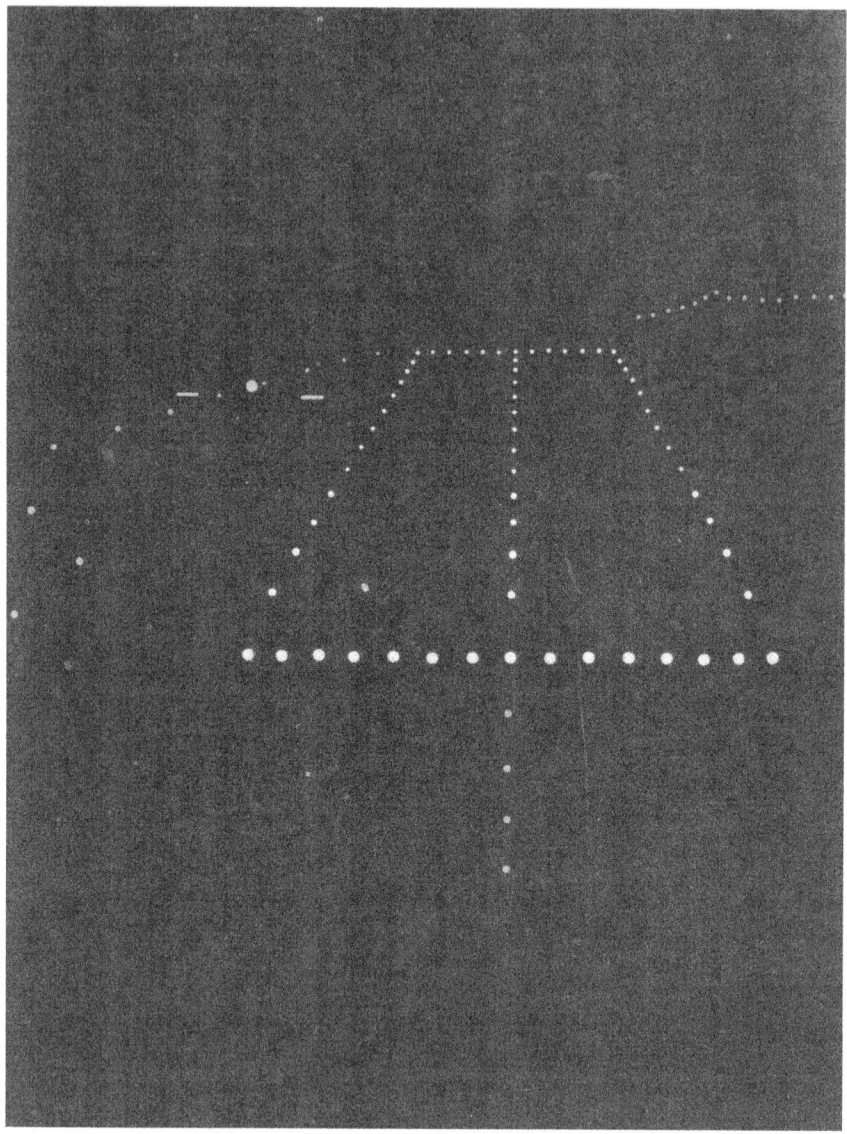

NCLT PILOT VIEW. *NHHC*

being networked over high speed links. This list, while seemingly extensive, does not, it should be noted, address trainers used in maintenance training, support-personnel training, engineering design and testing, or psychological and medical research.

In any case, the flight simulator had arrived at its modern form by the end of the 1960s.[20] Improvements since then have largely been refinements to the basic principles established before that time, although fidelity and the number of applications do grow with each new generation of simulators. One question remains unanswered, however: What is the optimum balance of flight time and simulator time versus morale, readiness,[21] cost, and safety? How does one find that right balance?

Any discussion of the relative merits of simulator and live training seems to break down into the following arguments by the advocates. They say the use of simulators will:

- Enhance safety
- Lower training costs
- Trade off (reduce) required flight time
- Require fewer support aircraft
- Provide for more accurate professional grading.

Unfortunately, it's not quite as cut and dried as all that. While the list rings true on the surface, the first and most important problem with it is that time in the simulator does not count for promotion and pay purposes or as "flight time," a measure near and dear to aviators of all stripes. Second, there are not enough simulators in the inventory to cover all the requirements for readiness and safety. The constant need to apportion procurement dollars between aircraft and simulators is weighted heavily in favor of aircraft. Third, it has been shown repeatedly that while simulators are good for honing certain techniques, they fall far short in the area of realistic practice involving psychomotor skills. Finally, the need to support constantly changing aircraft configurations and missions means either an increase in cost or a decrease in individual simulator fidelity.

With regard to the latter, consider that beyond basic systems familiarization and performance characteristics, it has been shown that the effectiveness of simulator training is based not only on the simulator fidelity and configuration but on a number of other variables as well. While the transfer of skills to a student can be quite large at the beginning of training, it tends to diminish as time goes by, as readily depicted in the traditional learning curve. It is also affected by any number of factors, such as total flight experience, time in the type aircraft simulated, type of mission, etc. Though a formula for measuring training transfer has been developed, there remain the questions of the cost/benefit of simulator training versus the cost/benefit of similar training airborne and of safety.

After long observation, there is general consensus that instrument flight, NATOPS and instrument checks, or new equipment or procedures can be better learned and practiced in a simulator than in flight, particularly if an OFT is used. Also, when a student is first beginning to fly or a pilot is checking out in a new aircraft, especially the newer and higher-performance aircraft of the 1950s, the chances of mishap were much reduced by time in a simulator. In fact, although in a somewhat different environment, commercial air operators rely completely on simulators for initial indoctrination, refresher training, and periodic flight checks. In the armed services, simulators lend themselves quite well to combat-mission rehearsal, especially with regard to unit and multiunit training. Networked weapons-systems trainers are especially effective for multicrewed aircraft and formations of single-pilot aircraft.[22] In that regard, research shows that simulations are used for, and payoff most frequently for, events that involve analysis of input data, such as occurs in ASW training. They are used least often for, and have least payoff for, events that require attempts to replicate situational or environmental conditions, such as in strike warfare training.

In any case, the consensus begins to come apart when using simulator time in lieu of flight hours is proposed. In addition, the limited availability and the difficulty of keeping simulators in step with operational developments and requirements lead to major and deleterious effects on their utility. Because of that limited availability and differences with modernizing aircraft and changing tactics, simulators are more apt to be found in training and replacement squadrons, where priority is given to students as opposed to fleet aircrew. In fact, the majority of simulator use outside the Naval Air Training Command is in the fleet replacement squadrons; fleet squadrons use simulators only about one hour per crew per month. At the same time, a significant amount of simulator time goes unused, and there are noticeable differences in use among the tactical air communities and helicopter and patrol squadrons. Much of this difference can be attributed to differences in missions and between small crews, sometimes a single pilot, and larger crews that need extensive training for mission coordination. In addition, once beyond a certain minimum flight time in any given period, the value of simulator training rapidly diminishes. Some scholars sum it up this way:

- Simulation is effective in such areas as introduction, practice, "switchology," procedures, NATOPS, and rehearsal.
- Live training may be needed for learning perceptual-motor skills.
- Simulators are not substitutes for flight time. They provide complementary and supplementary training to reduce deficiencies brought by increased complexity and task load.
- Pilot experience is a factor in simulator value. A synergy exists between simulator and flight hours for young pilots, by which rehearsal in a simulator should precede actual flying. Experienced pilots can show currency in various areas using a simulator without having to fly them.
- The kind of platform is also a factor in simulator value. The tasks required of certain aircraft—such as fighter, rotary-wing, and tilt-wing—place a premium on sensory inputs and situational awareness and thus

require more flying time. Other aircraft have more tasks that can be done in simulators.
- Tactics are a factor in simulator value. Weapons delivery can be learned and evaluated in simulators. Crew coordination works well in the simulator, but force-on-force simulations currently leave something to be desired.
- The learning of complicated or difficult procedures is facilitated through the use of appropriate simulators. For example, an evaluation in 1969 and 1970 of a sample of fleet carrier pilots in one of the first NCLTs found a measurable improvement in the performance of simulator-trained pilots over that of non-simulator-trained pilots, in terms of fewer technique wave-offs and a higher rate of successful carrier landings.[23]
- Negative training—learning bad habits—needs to be avoided. Simulators can become predictable and teach inappropriate responses. Simulators may also give a false sense of accomplishment.
- Funding is insufficient for procurement and for keeping simulators up with fleet aircraft. This creates a situation where simulators are often out of date and thus far less useful for learning and practice beyond the basics.

There is inevitably another "long pole in the tent," however, and it's a very long one: time in the air goes into the logbook, and simulator time does not. As we've noted, flying hours in the logbook are gold in the bank for the naval aviator. Absent any other context, the more hours one has logged, the more regard in which he or she is held. The conventional wisdom is the more flight hours logged, the better the chances for screening for more prestigious assignments and promotion. Only the number of carrier-arrested landings, or perhaps combat missions, can trump flight hours for a carrier pilot. Thus, as valuable and as money-saving as simulator time might be, it is seldom seen by either the participants or their seniors as being as important as time in the air. While almost everyone recognizes that a little simulator time reduces the amount of actual flight time required to qualify a new pilot or on a new piece of equipment, any fleet pilot would be most reluctant to substitute simulator time for actual flying. To enforce such a practice beyond certain limits would adversely affect both morale and retention.

Bottom line: simulators are not a be-all-and-end-all but, if properly employed, can enhance both readiness and safety. While most of the evidence for the above may be more anecdotal than scientific, there has been at least one book-length report on the subject, a study commissioned by the Navy and conducted by RAND, as well as several studies conducted by the Center for Naval Analyses (CNA) at the direction of the staff of the CNO, and at least one paper written as a thesis at the

Naval Postgraduate School;[24] since none of them were ever acted upon, however, their results must be cataloged as inconclusive.

Another study, *The Use of Flight Simulators in Measuring and Improving Training Effectiveness*,[25] addresses only reserve patrol plane crews. It found that such part-time aviators have very little skill loss over time and perform as well as their full-time counterparts, as measured by substantial increases in evaluation scores as simulator time is accumulated. This could well be because, except for pilots, the duties of a patrol-plane crew are not especially dependent on motor skills. In any case, another more recent study expanded the universe of effort to include regular crews in tactical air and helicopter communities, where motor skills most certainly are important. Unlike the reserve-patrol-plane study, *The Contribution of Aircraft Simulators to the Training and Readiness of Operational Navy Aircraft Squadrons*,[26] addresses the utilization of simulators by a sampling of East- and West-Coast fighter and helicopter pilots and crews. The conclusions are interesting, even if only inferentially addressed to safety. Among them are the following.

- Even as presently configured, simulators hold a great deal of untapped potential. They could make major contributions in procedural and decisional skills, but as presently configured and utilized they do not.
- The potential to train perceptual motor skills effectively in current simulators is limited.

In the first conclusion, the phrase "as presently configured" most certainly reflects the lack of updates that might keep simulators faithful to the aircraft they are designed to simulate. Further, the study found that, consistent with the latter conclusion, most simulator training falls into the procedural skill category, with very little decisional-skill training available. This is most likely because few simulators are well suited for the maintenance of perceptual motor skills. Additionally, experienced aviators are attuned to subtle nuances of actual flight that simulators do not replicate. All of this results in simulators being used relatively little to train operational squadrons. In fact, the data presented by the study showed that only one hour is spent in a simulator for every twenty or thirty hours of flight training, and most of that is for NATOPS and instrument checks.

Yet another study, *Flying Hours, Simulators and Safety: A Look at Flight Safety Trends*,[27] concentrated on Navy and Marine fighter and attack flying. A most comprehensive CNA effort, it points out that the value of simulators is recognized in training and readiness manuals and confirms that simulators are used by fleet squadrons for NATOPS checks and emergency procedure training, apparently to good effect. In particular, the study notes, the simulator offers the ability to generate hazardous flight scenarios in a safe ground environment. The study also observes that the NCLT is an obvious contributor to safety, but it does not report any data to prove it. Nor are there any data on the effect of simulator hours on mishap rates. Unfortunately, since neither the Safety Center nor any other Navy/Marine agency collects simulator use data, it's difficult to know how mishap rates might vary with simulator experience.

Lack of data notwithstanding, it is widely agreed that the use of simulators in aviation began with the notion that, at least up to a point, pilot time in a simulator would indeed enhance safety, since the risk of loss of life, limb, or aircraft in a simulator is zero, even while practicing what could otherwise be hazardous maneuvers. In fact, there is no question among pilots that quality time in a simulator practicing procedures, especially emergency procedures, enhances safety. Ask any naval aviator whether or not simulator time makes him or her a safer pilot, and the predictable answer is, "Yes, but . . ."—the "but" meaning, "It could never take the place of actual flying." That attitude is beginning to change, however.

Over the past twenty years, simulator fidelity, including concurrency with the parent aircraft, and capability to simulate multiaircraft tactics have grown almost exponentially. Thus, the use of simulators has gone beyond procedural task training to more complex skill training, such as air-to-air combat, cockpit resource management, mission rehearsal, formation flying, and more. Add the capability to network simulators, and team training in simulators becomes possible. For example, by way of "distributed mission training," a number of aircraft simulators can be networked, assisting markedly in developing team-member interaction skills. With such simulators in use, aviators' confidence in simulators has also grown. Unfortunately, like so much else with simulators (with the exception of the airlines),[28] there is little money to purchase adequate numbers of simulators or to measure their effectiveness.

As for mishap prevention, simulators have undoubtedly played a role, but the few studies that have been conducted have revealed nothing especially conclusive related to safety.[29] The one exception is that it has been shown that in multicrewed aircraft, simulator time is beneficial to readiness, which, of course, includes safety. There is also expert opinion derived from long experience that time in simulators that replicate especially hazardous flight experiences, such as NCLTs, enhances safety. Since night carrier landings represent one of the highest potentials for mishap, those opinions merit considerable weight. Thus, it might be concluded that appropriately configured simulators, used appropriately, can indeed enhance safety.

Based on the foregoing discussion, several conclusions can be derived with regard to the use of simulators.

- Simulators are well suited for initial familiarization with aircraft and weapons systems, instrument flight training, and periodic checks of qualifications in any given system.
- Whether or not simulator time can substitute for flight time in operational fleet squadrons might be determined with a comprehensive study,

but morale and retention and the likelihood of changing the culture that counts flight time as all-important will have to be addressed.
- Flight safety is clearly enhanced when a comprehensive simulator training program is in place and in effect throughout a unit, but the degree of enhancement is generally unknown.
- Lack of fidelity is a major problem, one that is forcing crews to discern between positive and negative training in simulators.[30]

Despite the absence of extensive hard evidence, it's quite reasonable to assume that the use of simulators of all types has in fact made significant contributions to naval aviation safety over the past fifty years. This was particularly so between 1950 and 1960, when jets came into the inventory in large numbers,[31] aircraft systems became more capable and more sophisticated, and the capability to fly all missions at night and in all weather from both ship and shore became a universal requirement. It was also during those same ten years that simulator technology matured and their use spread throughout naval aviation. Meanwhile, the Navy/Marine mishap rate nearly halved.

Clearly, the use of simulators of all kinds by novices and veterans alike in preparing for the entire range of flight, from initial familiarization to complex battle problems, has contributed markedly, even though in ways not entirely quantifiable, to both the readiness and safety of naval aviation.

15

On to the Twenty-First Century
ORM, CRM, and Culture Workshops

In the late twentieth century, as the major mishap rate moved toward zero and traditional cause factors diminished in number, there was opportunity to concentrate on accident-prevention efforts theretofore neglected. The growing awareness of the importance of human factors was taking greater hold, but such new concepts as Crew Resource Management (CRM) and Operational Risk Management (ORM) were not even considered, let alone well known, in naval aviation until the late 1980s, and their implementation was not widespread until the 1990s. Today, in addition to human factors, CRM and ORM are critical considerations from design, manufacture, support, maintenance training, flight operations, mishap investigation, and more. As more advances are made in naval aviation mishap prevention, they will undoubtedly come in CRM and ORM areas.

From the earliest days of naval aviation—indeed, from the earliest days of the Navy, Marine Corps, and Coast Guard—the mission commander has played a critical role in the execution of any tasking. In fact by regulation, he or she is ultimately in charge, responsible, and accountable. At the same time, he or she is supported by a crew, or at least one wingman, all of whom are duty bound to voice concerns when an operation is conducted without due regard to risk management or in an unsafe manner. This is a central precept of ORM and CRM.[1] For those who espouse "participatory leadership," leadership that creates a climate in which anyone can speak up and contribute when and if necessary, both CRM and ORM merely codify what has been their experience. Unfortunately, until the recognition of the importance of human factors, followed by the adoption of ORM and CRM as central to the successful accomplishment of any mission, participatory management was too often not practiced, and the concepts now known as CRM and ORM were too often not realized, arbitrarily ignored, or overlooked.

When CRM and ORM were introduced, for those whose experience in naval aviation was limited to the 1950s, 1960s, 1970s, or before, the terms "risk management" and "crew resource management" might well have come from some little-known psychology textbook or from Mars. The better squadrons and the better flight crews put into practice those disciplines even before they had names; no one called such practices that, nor were they as formalized as they later came to be. At the extreme, risk management might have been summed up in such slogans as "Don't flat-hat" and "Don't forget to switch fuel tanks." Crew resource management was often reduced to "Just sit there, don't talk, and read me the checklist when I call for it" or "Stay on my wing and keep quiet—when I want something from you I'll ask for it." The numbers of mishaps and near mishaps that resulted from such attitudes are incalculable; records weren't kept, although digging into mishap report narratives does give a flavor. Nevertheless, in the closing years of the twentieth century, as the Navy/Marine major-mishap rate moved ever closer to zero, commanders and analysts began looking at ways in which the rate might be lowered even more. The first attempt was termed Aircrew Coordination Training (ACT), but that soon morphed into CRM, with ORM following.

The Navy and Marine Corps adopted CRM after seeing the American commercial airlines succeed with it in the early 1990s. Its goal was to improve safety by improving coordination, communications, and awareness. In October 1996, the Air Board approved implementation of ORM throughout naval aviation followed in April 1997, with OPNAV and Marine Corps ORM instructions.

With top leadership on board, ORM was quickly incorporated into the curriculum at the Naval Aviation Safety School, adopted by management at the Safety Center, and implemented in ready rooms, maintenance spaces, and ultimately the rest of the fleet. Indeed, while CRM came to naval aviation via the airlines, ORM came from within the Navy and has now long since spread far beyond naval aviation, to the Air Force, and American commercial aviation, and is likely in the future farther afield. Improvements weren't immediate or dramatic, but an unexpected reward was that everyone, from lowest ranks to flag officers, soon realized they were part of the act. As appreciation grew of what ORM and CRM could do, readiness and morale improved apace. These were concepts to which many reacted with "Why haven't we done this before?" Of course, in those units where there had been good leadership, ORM and CRM weren't really anything new, but now they were codified, and the systems and procedures that came along with them cleaned up some loose ends and made even that leadership a bit better—and led to improved safety everywhere.

Tales of insufficient or inappropriate crew coordination are rife throughout naval aviation, indeed throughout aviation. In 1999 Wiegmann and Shappell (see chapter 11) had reported that "between 1986 and 1990, the most common of all aircrew causal factors was the lack of aircrew coordination or effective crew resource management."[2] Of some interest is that this same report observes that most tactical-air CRM mishaps involved CRM failures during nonroutine or in-extremis situations, while most of rotary-wing CRM mishaps involved failures during routine flight operations. Differences in aviation communities notwithstanding, these observations only scratch the surface of why there are shortfalls in crew resource management in the first place. Experts in the field write that the answer undoubtedly lies in the way pilots are trained.[3]

As Americans, we tend to focus on the individual as opposed to the group. Who won the spelling bee? Not, which was the best class of third graders in the school? Who won the Rhodes Scholarship? Not, which school was ranked at the top? In flight training, that individualistic orientation is reinforced. From the start the goal is to solo, not to work with another crew member. Later on, even in multicrewed aircraft, flight checks tend to be oriented to the individual rather than the crew. Individual competence is the sine qua non of flying.[4] Such attitudes are unlikely to change much in the near term, but in somewhat belated recognition of the importance of CRM, recent training has indeed begun to focus on improving trainees' behaviors and teamwork skills. Suffler, Salas, and Xavier list the CRM skills to be trained to in table 15-1.[5]

Building on early work by aeromedical personnel and academics and on the airlines' experience, the Navy and Marine Corps are today fully immersed in CRM, and sure enough, there is an OPNAV instruction that applies.[6] The stated purpose of the program according to that instruction is "to integrate specifically defined behavioral skills throughout Navy and Marine Corps aviation training, and to integrate the effective application of these behavioral skills into operational aviation procedures wherever appropriate. CRM training will increase mission effectiveness, minimize crew preventable error, maximize aircrew coordination, optimize risk management, improve recognition and recovery from errors, and serve to reduce mishaps that result from poor CRM."

Another way to understand CRM is to look at it as "human-systems integration" aimed at reducing crew-coordination failures, whether human to human or human to machine. While the architecture of naval aviation's CRM program is laid down by the instruction and is centrally controlled by Commander, Naval Air Forces (CNAF), with advice from the Naval Safety Center, each aviation unit is given latitude to tailor its own CRM program (administered by a trained CRM curriculum model manager) for its particular aircraft and mission. This is

Table 15-1 CRM Skills

COMMUNICATION	BRIEFING	BACKUP BEHAVIOR
Monitor mutual performance	Team leadership	Decision making
Task-related assertiveness	Team adaptability	Shared situational awareness

consistent with the fact that naval aviation, just like the broader Navy and Marine Corps, is divided into many separate subcultures. Adapting CRM to these separate subcultures, let alone to separate mission requirements, makes eminent sense.

The earliest application of CRM was in mishap investigation. However, it soon became very apparent that CRM would offer huge payoffs if applied before there *was* a mishap—thus the practice of briefing potential CRM issues before and after every flight. Not long after that practice was initiated, CRM was applied to maintenance, flight-deck operations, and other flight-support efforts as well. Today, CRM is an integral part of every maintenance procedure and preflight checklist, right along with mission, rendezvous, and recovery. Now defined as, "Supporting Mission Accomplishment through Enhanced Performance," CRM consists of seven skills, listed and discussed in the governing instructions. All are trained to in regular CRM sessions, and records of participation are maintained in individual NATOPS jackets. The skills are:

- Mission analysis
- Assertiveness
- Decision making
- Communications
- Leadership
- Adaptability/flexibility
- Situational awareness

Continuous training in and application of CRM has made naval aviation markedly safer. CRM works even better when paralleled with Operational Risk Management.

ORM[7] is the process of dealing with risk, including hazard assessment, risk decision making, and implementation of effective risk controls. ORM is based on the concepts that all hands are responsible for using ORM and that risk is inherent in all operations but can be controlled. Some would say life itself is a risk, but in the pursuit of mission, naval aviation may have to face more of it than most others. That should not include *unnecessary* risk, however. ORM is how safety, operations, and mission accomplishment are brought together to be managed as one, in order to avoid unnecessary risk while still accomplishing the mission, or, when avoidance is unattainable, to keep risk at an acceptable level.

It might be said that such a philosophy is common sense, but unfortunately, common sense did not always prevail. Recall the horrendous mishap rates of the 1950s and the unjustified risks taken that led to a majority of those mishaps. Most naval aviation leaders knew that unnecessary risks were being taken too often and responded by setting proper examples or coming down hard with discipline. But there was no standard methodology for identifying risk, except in the grossest of terms, or for minimizing the consequences in the event that risk taking, warranted or not, ended badly. For some time, references to "warranted risk" have existed in odd corners of policy and tactics, techniques and procedures, and folklore with regard to specific capabilities, but until the advent of ORM there was no overarching effort to be aware of risk and reduce it across the board. Today, it's recognized that through ORM risk can indeed be avoided or, where operationally necessary, be mitigated and made manageable, but ORM requires involvement by the whole crew, whom it holds duty bound to voice any concerns when an operation is contemplated.

These are particularly hard concepts for those who grew up in an environment where the one in charge was always right, but the Navy, Marine, and Coast Guard aviation communities have adopted ORM with gusto, and the ever-declining mishap rate reflects that. Intrinsic in that effort is the follow-on Navy-wide effort to:

- Accept risks only when benefits outweigh costs.
- Accept no unnecessary risk.
- Anticipate and manage risk by planning.
- Make risk decisions at the right level.

Recognizing and managing risk is what ORM is all about, writes Vice Adm. John P. Currier, U.S. Coast Guard, in *Proceedings*:[8] "The ability to recognize and mitigate risk is a critical component of mission success—and the sign of a true professional." If Vice Admiral Currier and others are to be believed, and most experts in the subject do agree, to recognize risk one must know the causes. The causes may be many, but those who have studied the phenomena generally list the following ten:

- *Change.* Sometimes referred to as the "mother of risk," because so much might flow from change—for example, last-minute changes of destination or target, generally under time constraints for planning.
- *Resource constraints.* "No spares available, but I won't need that instrument because it's VFR."
- *New technology.* "We don't have the manual yet, but I can work it out."
- *Complexity.* "Post-maintenance check flight, followed by a low-level navigation flight to night FCLP [field carrier landing practice]—no sweat."
- *Stress.* "Darn. I only got four hours' sleep. The wife wants me to pick up the kids at two, and I need this hop to practice for my NATOPS exam tomorrow."
- *Human nature.* "Who's he to tell me what to do and how to do it?"
- *High energy levels.* "Two day hops and a night low-level? Piece of cake."
- *Societal constraints.* "I've got an ear block, but I can't refuse to fly tonight, because I'll be called a wimp."

- *Environmental influences.* "I don't need an instrument clearance. If it's socked in when I get back, I'll use a standard 'self-penetration.'"
- *Tempo of operations.* "Two hops a day for two weeks? Let's go for it!"

ORM is designed to mitigate, if not eliminate, these root causes of risk. In a lecture room, the comparison of ORM to the traditional approach would look something like table 15-2.

Based on the above, a very useable recipe for implementation of ORM in the fleet has been developed and trained to. Its concept and definition, terms, and principles are the framework by which ORM has been and continues to be implemented throughout Navy, Marine, and Coast Guard aviation. Once installed, understood, and accepted, ORM becomes almost second nature, a process that has added significantly to mishap avoidance throughout naval aviation. "Process" is the operative word, in that that's what ORM is all about. It cannot be stressed too strongly: ORM is a systematic decision-making process, not a program. The process operates on three levels, embodying four principles, and can be implemented in five iterative steps, all as depicted below in figure 15-1, a slide from the Naval Safety Center.

The key to this entire process comprises the five steps depicted in the closed loop in figure 15-1. In practice today, every brief, whether for flight, major maintenance, or even a major flight-deck evolution, includes a section on ORM, including the five steps. When done right—and the more a unit practices the better it gets—it was forecast, ORM would achieve the following:

- An increase in the probability of completing a successful mission
- Expanded operational effectiveness
- Enhanced overall decision making
- Provide an aid to decision making
- Significant reduction in loss

All of these forecasts have come true. Naval aviation has never been as successful, more operationally effective, or had a better mishap record. Much of the more

Table 15-2 New and Old Ways Comparison

ORM	TRADITIONAL
Systematic	Random—individual dependent
Proactive	Reactive
Integrates all types of risk	Safety as afterthought
Common process/terms	Nonstandard
Decision risk vs. benefit	"Can do"

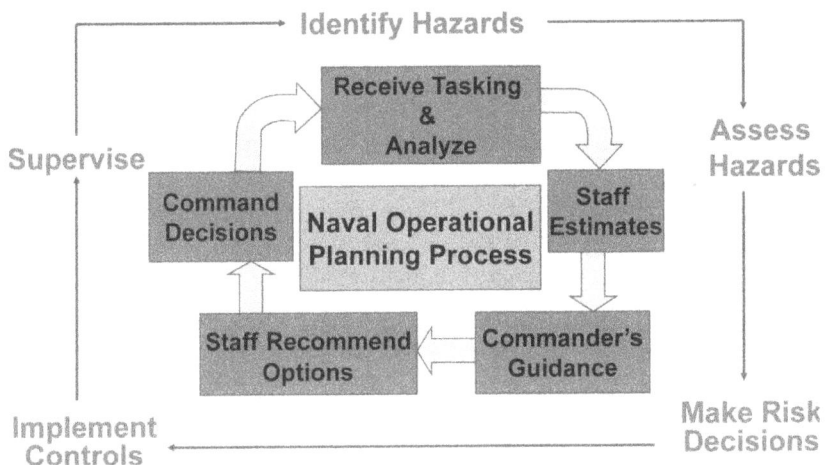

Figure 15-1 ORM Process Model
Naval Safety Center

recent improvement has come because of the implementation of CRM and ORM force-wide, but there is one more thing: culture.

Many naval aviators had an idea—this was long the topic of discussion at happy hours and in ready rooms—that the very culture of naval aviation was somehow at the root of the inability to eliminate mishaps. The "ace of the base," and "wannabe Mavericks" (like Tom Cruise in the movie *Top Gun*) exercised undue influence, especially on the younger aircrews—thus a growing readiness to begin an examination of culture. Conscientious commanding offices, assisted by human-factors acolytes, were the first to begin such examinations. Then, on 29 January 1996, an F-14 Tomcat crashed into a residential neighborhood on departure from Nashville International Airport. Both crewmen and three people on the ground were killed, and three homes were engulfed in flames. Directly relevant was that this was the fourth major mishap for that squadron in a year. This mishap was so egregious and attracted so much publicity that Adm. Frank B. Kelso, the CNO, personally ordered the Assistant Chief of Naval Operations (Air Warfare) to take action. In response, that leader turned to, among other avenues, the Naval Aviation Human Factors Quality Management Board (HF QMB).

That board, chartered to "reduce the human error flight mishap rate by 50 percent by fiscal year 2000," looked in turn to the Air National Guard (ANG), which had attributed its recent 50 percent decrease in Class A mishaps to the "Culture Workshop," a tool whereby the culture inside an organization can be quickly assessed. Based upon the ANG experience, the HF QMB recommended, and the

Air Board adopted, culture workshops (CWs) as a tool to help prevent mishaps. Commander, Naval Air Forces[9] issued CNAF Instruction 5420.2, which stated, "Experience has shown that degenerative organizational cultures often foster the development of unhealthy practices, or habits, which ultimately can contribute to or result in a mishap. The failure to correct underlying deficiencies often is an error of omission, vice commission, based on an inability to see the problem. The CW premise is that—safety exists on a foundation of trust, integrity, and leadership: created and sustained by effective communication."

At first culture workshops were voluntary. Soon they were required, but they are eagerly sought out throughout the force, which recognizes their value. The actual workshop process involves a trained facilitator from offsite, a local naval aviator, and a chief petty officer. They engage in individual discussions with squadron personnel, conduct three squadron-wide seminars, then debrief the commanding officer. In that frank and strictly confidential meeting, relative strengths or weaknesses are presented. Although it may seem a rather simple process, it has paid off in unexpected ways.

CRM, ORM, and culture workshops are relative latecomers in the history of naval aviation safety. Some of the principles they embody may have been implicitly followed in the past, but generally sporadically and only at the discretion of the commanding officer. If we could go back and reconstruct mishaps from years past, we would undoubtedly uncover numerous cases of poor crew-resource or operational-risk management and would most certainly identify cultural issues. Most probably, such mishaps were at the time attributed to "pilot error" or some equally facile cause. But now that naval aviation has adopted CRM, ORM, and culture as important concepts, all with the full backing of leadership at the highest levels, we can reasonably expect even further reductions in the all-Navy mishap rate in the years to come.[10]

16

Success

Summary and Conclusions

That American naval aviation reduced major mishaps from 1,488 in 1950 to only twenty-nine in 2000 and continued with an average of less than twenty per year for the next fifteen years is an amazing achievement. Even more significant, deaths due to naval-aviation mishaps decreased from 227 in 1950 and 536 in 1954 to 46 in 2000 and twenty in 2014. Over the same period the capability of the force improved dramatically, and naval aviation and its people covered themselves with distinction while bringing the fight to the enemy in five hot wars,[1] as well as maintaining readiness to fight day and night and in bad weather throughout the long Cold War, several less-intense conflicts,[2] and numerous contingency and humanitarian operations, near and far.[3] Of almost as much significance is that the all-Navy mishap rate fell to that of the U.S. Air Force and approached that of American commercial aviation, a most remarkable feat. That performance has continued; indeed, it has improved, despite continued fast-paced operations throughout a troubled world.

The underlying reasons for this feat have been described in preceding chapters. Based on those reasons, the following are the more obvious factors that led to that remarkable achievement. Other large and complex organizations might well benefit from the lessons learned by naval aviation during this long journey to success.

First on the list are the benefits accruing from the establishment of the Safety Center—in effect, a safety "center of excellence"—and its ensuing programs of investigations, analysis, reporting, education, and publicity.

The center itself was not enough, however. It took a perceptive and motivated person, Capt. James H. Flatley, to lay the basis for the innumerable improvements that ensued. Naval aviation derived incalculable benefit from his efforts. What he achieved shows that any organization with knowledgeable, dedicated, and effective leadership can and most likely will achieve success.

Sometimes overshadowed by Flatley's achievements was a revolution in personnel management, a three-pronged effort: selecting only the best performers for command, emphasizing safety education, and improving the training and status of safety officers. The result was bringing the best available leaders—the best-performing, best-trained, and best educated—to top leadership billets in operating squadrons and wings.

Resulting directly from that improved leadership and safety consciousness were the establishment of RAGs and NATOPS, a Naval Aviation Maintenance Program, and the streamlining of naval aviation supply.

Another asset that has been as important to safety consciousness as improved leadership has been the legions of people who make up the naval aeromedical enterprise and, increasingly, their allies, the human-factor analysts.

The transition to jets and the slowing rate of new aircraft introduction to the fleet had a marginal effect on the mishap rate, and it's hard to conclude that implementation of angled decks and other aircraft-carrier improvements had even that much effect, let alone more. They both most certainly contributed to improved operational effectiveness, but when it comes to mishap rates it must be remembered that a large percentage of naval aviation was non-jet and that not all Navy/Marine aircraft flew from aircraft carriers.

Likewise, the hours that Navy and Marine pilots spend in simulators add up to only a fraction of their flight hours, although simulators have proven most useful in certain phases of aviation training. Therefore, the effect of simulator time on the mishap rate must be considered minimal.

Other factors, such as system safety and improvements in aircraft design and equipment systems, improvements learned from progress in the larger world of aviation, were indeed important, but in general their effect was gradual and subtle, not the kind of thing that produces a dramatic sea change. Nevertheless, it's obvious that close monitoring of progress in safety in other enterprises must continue, if not accelerate.

More recently, CRM, ORM, and Culture Workshops are proving to be extremely beneficial to naval aviation safety and readiness. They are valuable tools in the leadership kit of today's commanding officers and safety officers. Because they are relatively new programs, they have not been significant in the successes achieved by the earlier programs, but they bode well for the future.

Regardless of which of all these events and changes may have had the most impact, their sum total has been impressive improvement in readiness and lives and aircraft saved. No longer do admirals lament, "Crashes will always be with us." No longer is the "Navy Hymn," played at funerals and memorial services, known better to aviators than any other song. No longer do accidents litter the ocean and the landscape.

Such signal achievements have been wrought by a stream of dedicated individuals motivated by a variety of purposes. Only a few of those people are remembered today for what they achieved. Some of their names are found in the foregoing text, some that should be there are not, but many contributed. Because of their collective efforts, naval aviation today is the safest it has ever been, with no diminution in either capability or readiness.

More importantly, today's Naval Aviation leadership, despite sustained high tempo operations worldwide, are proving quite capable of continuing to improve in both readiness and safety. Naval Aviation is in good hands.

Sky anchors aweigh!

Afterword

The research for this book was done in connection with fulfillment of obligations as the Ramsey Fellow at the Smithsonian Air & Space Museum, 2009–10. It has since been modified from a somewhat academic report to a narrative.

The original intent was to analyze the all-Navy (Navy and Marine Corps) major-accident rate from 1950 to 2000, with the aim of discovering the exact actions that led to the continuous improvements shown in tabulations of mishap statistics and thus providing a more precise history, as well as insight as to what future efforts might have the highest payoff. The method was to have been regression analysis, using mishap data as the dependent variables and specific changes in operating policies or material improvements as the independent variables.

To determine as precisely as possible the elements of the dependent variables, finite historical mishap data were required. Unfortunately, it turned out that, with some exceptions, the accident data that was sought does not apparently exist. Bits and pieces were located, however, and they have been used wherever possible. For example, for several years in the 1950s the staff of the Deputy Chief of Naval Operations (Air Warfare) compiled and semiannually distributed accident data. Also, the staff librarian at the Smithsonian Air & Space Museum retrieved from the FAA Library a sheaf of Naval Safety Center *Weekly Summaries* that were about to be discarded because of the disestablishment of that library. Additional, if sporadic, mishap data have also been extracted from back issues of *Naval Aviation News*. In addition, the occasional aircraft-mishap-board investigation has been made available and used to the extent possible under the law. Even so, neither the sum total of these nor any individual ones provides much more than unconnected data points. If the initial goal of this effort is to be fulfilled, the missing data are sorely needed.

In order to verify facts and opinions and to ensure clarity of my own observations, I engaged at least one expert in each field covered to review chapters as they were produced. Some of the individuals who helped are named in footnotes; others are listed below. My heartfelt thanks to them all.

Finally, special thanks are extended to my Ramsey Fellowship adviser and historian at the Smithsonian Air & Space Museum, Mr. Dominick Pisano; the Smithsonian Air & Space Museum librarian, Mr. Phillip Edwards; former Ramsey Fellow, mentor, and friend Vice Adm. Gerald Miller, USN (Ret.), deceased; Dr. Thomas C. Hone, historian and author; and Mr. Fred Rainbow of the U.S. Naval Institute.

Especially helpful were the friends and advisers, each of them subject-matter experts, who provided assistance on specific chapters, as follows:

- Chapter 10: Cdr. Walter Dalitsch, MC, USN
- Chapter 12: Vice Adm. Edward Straw, SC, USN (Ret.), and Capt. Larry Lavely, SC, USN (Ret.), deceased
- Chapter 13: Mr. Roger Schaufele, deceased, retired Vice President, Engineering, Douglas Aircraft Company
- Chapter 14: Mr. Henry Okraski, retired Senior Executive Service, formerly of the Naval Air Systems Command Training Systems Division, Orlando, Florida
- Chapter 15: Capt. James "Skip" Lind, USN (Ret.)

Also most helpful was the work done by Mr. Guy Arceneaux to provide the charts in chapters 3 and 13 and appendix 6, and by Ms. Carol Ann Dunn in arranging the bibliography and glossary.

Finally, this book would never have come to fruition without the encouragement and support of the Naval Historical Foundation, in particular its chairman, Adm. Bruce Demars, USN (Ret.); board members Rear Adm. William J. Holland, USN (Ret.), and Rear Adm. Richard C. Gentz, USN (Ret.); and the executive director, Capt. Charles T. Creekman, USN (Ret.). My most grateful thanks to them all, and to the entire Board of Directors of the Foundation for their support.

Appendix 1
Marine Aviation

Marines too routinely deploy on board ship, flying the same aircraft types and facing the same problems as their Navy brethren. In fact, squadrons are generally interchangeable, although naval aviators are oriented toward war at sea and projection of power from the sea while Marines are focused more on supporting Marines ashore, but both services are trained for both missions.

Marines tended to drift away from carriers and to bases ashore as Vietnam heated up, but a few squadrons still went afloat. VMF-212 flew F-8 Crusaders from *Oriskany* early in the war, VMFA-333 flew F-4 Phantoms from *America,* and VMA-224 flew A-6 Intruders from *Coral Sea.* Mostly they flew from shore bases in Vietnam, however. There were also two Mediterranean deployments of Marine A-4s while the Vietnam War was ongoing.

After the Vietnam War the Marines opted not to acquire the A-7 Corsair II and went for the Harrier. The Marines never adopted the H-60 either, and the Navy has yet to go for the V-22 Osprey. Still, Marines and Navy, and Coast Guard too, are the products of the same flight training, follow similar safety programs and maintenance philosophies, and participate in the NATOPS and RAG systems as well.

Marines continue to go to sea with the Navy, and Navy squadrons occasionally deploy ashore with Marines. Marine strike-fighter squadrons maintain their carrier qualifications and regularly deploy on board aircraft carriers. Marine AV-8 Harrier, V-22 Osprey, and Marine helos regularly go to sea, normally on board amphibious ships.

Appendix 2
Naval Safety Center Yearly Major Mishap Statistics

	Hours	Major Accidents		Destroyed Aircraft		Fatal Accidents		Fatalities		Cost
		No.	Rate*	No.	Rate*	No.	Rate*	No.	Rate*	
July 1–June 30										
1950	2,770,408	1,488	53.71	481	17.36	137	4.95	227	8.19	
1951	3,172,111	1,714	54.03	675	21.28	185	5.83	391	12.33	
1952	3,767,765	2,066	54.83	708	18.79	224	5.95	399	10.59	
1953	4,351,768	2,229	51.22	714	16.41	238	5.47	402	9.24	
1954	4,378,468	2,213	50.54	776	17.72	263	6.01	536	12.24	215,941,667
1955	4,352,496	1,662	38.18	611	14.04	225	5.17	366	8.41	224,009,174
1956	4,348,865	1,456	33.48	574	13.20	242	5.56	406	9.34	226,654,473
1957	4,251,109	1,298	30.53	613	14.42	243	5.72	358	8.42	292,429,185
1958	3,901,150	1,106	28.35	524	13.43	195	5.00	387	9.92	327,855,150
1959	3,491,481	896	25.66	461	13.20	176	5.04	309	8.85	310,511,478
1960	3,387,560	655	19.34	360	10.63	155	4.58	268	7.91	266,441,050
1961	3,512,603	603	17.17	336	9.57	146	4.16	279	7.94	287,767,506
1962	3,710,782	576	15.52	329	8.87	132	3.56	264	7.11	282,929,550
1963	3,528,760	513	14.54	277	7.85	109	3.09	216	6.12	280,688,030
1964	3,702,920	506	13.66	290	7.83	118	3.19	197	5.32	321,268,590
1965	3,653,734	457	12.51	287	7.85	105	2.87	226	6.19	350,962,720

(continued)

Appendix 2: Naval Safety Center Yearly Major Mishap Statistics *(continued)*

	Hours	Major Accidents		Destroyed Aircraft		Fatal Accidents		Fatalities		Cost
		No.	Rate*	No.	Rate*	No.	Rate*	No.	Rate*	
July 1–June 30 *(continued)*										
1966	3,739,856	476	12.73	296	7.91	105	2.81	232	6.20	384,267,230
1967	3,723,203	508	13.64	313	8.41	133	3.57	357	9.59	398,934,000
1968	3,626,458	513	14.15	335	9.24	130	3.58	427	11.77	470,413,000
1969	3,756,984	530	14.11	356	9.48	136	3.62	290	7.72	509,597,190
July-Dec										
1969	1,636,526	216	13.20	158	9.65	64	3.91	160	9.78	216,022,000
Jan 1-Dec 31										
1970	2,978,433	402	13.50	264	8.86	105	3.53	231	7.76	446,608,000
1971	2,790,773	258	9.24	180	6.45	64	2.29	117	4.19	335,424,000
1972	2,662,829	252	9.46	170	6.38	67	2.52	129	4.84	355,884,000
1973	2,371,502	206	8.69	144	6.07	50	2.11	122	5.14	328,430,000
1974	2,151,535	147	6.83	106	4.93	43	2.00	81	3.76	220,450,000
1975	2,141,506	137	6.40	94	4.39	34	1.59	67	3.13	264,571,000
1976	1,974,772	128	6.48	88	4.46	36	1.82	73	3.70	263,675,000
1977	1,981,328	107	5.40	104	5.25	41	2.07	119	6.01	321,952,270
1978	1,948,671	109	5.59	102	5.23	51	2.62	129	6.62	418,461,293

Year									
1979	1,911,859	103	5.39	95	4.97	41	2.14	79	4.13	311,350,936
1980	1,936,360	115	5.94	112	5.78	43	2.22	91	4.70	392,868,569
1981	1,966,464	95	4.83	87	4.42	40	2.03	83	4.22	394,687,158
1982	2,018,752	90	4.46	83	4.11	40	1.98	74	3.67	339,014,989
1983	2,004,069	87	4.34	88	4.39	39	1.95	100	4.99	521,954,461
1984	2,092,525	69	3.30	70	3.35	32	1.53	79	3.78	330,787,600
1985	2,136,109	73	3.42	69	3.23	28	1.31	82	3.84	363,283,189
1986	2,145,698	75	3.50	74	3.45	29	1.35	73	3.40	517,919,169
1987	2,236,533	69	3.09	68	3.04	25	1.12	65	2.91	673,475,807
1988	2,218,055	51	2.30	49	2.21	24	1.08	51	2.30	521,041,248
1989	2,270,479	51	2.25	51	2.25	25	1.10	93	4.10	558,392,168
1990	2,119,915	66	3.11	64	3.02	20	0.94	39	1.84	714,126,220
1991	2,145,049	60	2.80	63	2.94	24	1.12	77	3.59	787,472,099
1992	1,853,721	55	2.97	52	2.81	32	1.73	70	3.78	851,360,478
1993	1,745,376	53	3.04	53	3.04	23	1.32	54	3.09	871,552,883
1994	1,572,441	28	1.78	28	1.78	9	0.57	13	0.83	508,085,106
1995	1,569,329	34	2.17	30	1.91	13	0.83	17	1.08	663,357,025
1996	1,650,026	36	2.18	39	2.36	16	0.97	46	2.79	
1997	1,523,507	27	1.77	25	1.64	13	0.85	30	1.97	
1998	1,518,109	36	2.37	34	2.24	16	1.05	48	3.16	
1999	1,514,603	22	1.45	23	1.52	5	0.33	9	0.59	
2000	1,460,082	29	1.99	24	1.64	11	0.75	46	3.15	

*Per 100,000 flight hours.

Appendix 3
Navy and Marine Accident Reporting Classifications

"Navy Aircraft Accident, Incident, and Forced Landing Reporting Procedure," OPNAV Instruction 3750.6B of 20 May 1956, defines damage and injury classifications as follows:
    A — Strike damage (or lost)
    B — Substantial damage necessitating major overhaul of the aircraft
    C — Substantial damage, major overhaul not required
    D — Minor damage

Injury Classifications are:
    Class A — Fatal injury
    Class B — Critical injury
    Class C — Serious injury
    Class D — Minor injury
    Class E — No injury
    Class L — Unknown injury, lost and presumed drowned
    Class M — Unknown injury missing

At some point, possibly in 1980, 3750.6 was changed to incorporate the cost of damage and combine the damage and injury classifications. One of these revisions was summarized for flight mishaps as follows:

> **CLASS A SEVERITY:** Total cost of damage is $1,000,000 or more and/or involves destroyed aircraft and/or fatal injury and/or permanent total disability.
> **CLASS B SEVERITY:** Total cost of damage is $200,000 but less than $1,000,000 and/or involves permanent partial disability and/or hospitalization of five or more personnel.
> **CLASS C SEVERITY:** Total cost of damage is $10,000 but less than $200,000 and/or involves an injury of five lost workdays.

At some point, OPNAV Instruction 3750.6 became less tolerant of injuries in Classes B and C. The current OPNAV Instruction 3750.6R was updated for inflation on 1 October 2009:

> **CLASS A SEVERITY.** A Class A mishap is one in which the total cost of damage to DOD or non-DOD property, aircraft, or UAVs exceeds $2,000,000, or a naval aircraft is destroyed or missing, or any fatality or permanent total disability of DOD personnel results from the direct involvement of naval aircraft or UAV. Loss of a UAV is not a Class A unless the cost is $2,000,000 or greater.

Class B Severity. A Class B mishap is one in which the total cost of damage to DOD or non-DOD property, aircraft, or UAVs is more than $500,000 but less than $2,000,000 or a permanent partial disability or the hospitalization of three or more DOD personnel results.

Class C Severity. A Class C mishap is one in which the total cost of damage to DOD or non-DOD property, aircraft, or UAVs is $50,000 or more but less than $500,000 or an injury to DOD personnel results requiring one or more lost workdays.

OPNAV Instruction 5102.1D and Marine Corps Order P5102.1B for the *Navy and Marine Corps Mishap and Safety Investigation Reporting and Record Keeping Manual* contains the same or very similar definitions.

Appendix 4
Aviation-Oriented Safety Center Publications

CURRENT (AS OF AUGUST 2013)

- *Approach.* The Naval Aviation Safety Review; monthly (from 1955)
- *Weekly Summary* of major aircraft accidents. Printed and mailed until sometime in the 1990s, specific date unknown. Now promulgated on the Safety Center website.
- *Crossfeed.* Published monthly in two parts:
  - *Cockpit Crossfeed* is primarily for commanding officers and aircrew.
  - *General Crossfeed* is primarily for maintenance managers and maintenance personnel.
- *Mech.* A quarterly publication primarily for enlisted maintenance personnel and their supervisors (from 1961).
- *U.S. Navy/Marine Corps Aircraft Accident Statistical Summary.* To commanding officers and seniors twice a year.
- *Emergency Airborne Escape Summary.* Annual.
- *Flight Deck Awareness.* Carrier and amphibious versions.
- Occasional special issues on subjects such as Operational Risk Management and OPNAV Instruction 3750.

PREVIOUSLY DISTRIBUTED BUT NOW DISCONTINUED

- *Anymouse.* A periodic summary of "Anymouse" reports received.
- Flight Surgeon's Newsletter.

Appendix 5
Principal Carrier Alterations

SCB-27C

- C-11-1 steam catapults; 45,000 lbs. at 132 knots
- Mark 7 Mod 1 arresting gear; 45,000 lbs. at 140 knots
- Hull blistered five feet at each side; new beam 103 feet
- Escalator from hangar deck to flight deck
- Four ready rooms moved to second deck
- Deck-edge no. 3 aircraft elevator moved to starboard; 57,000 pound capacity
- Boat and aircraft crane forward of the no. 3 aircraft elevator
- Jet-blast deflectors at both catapults
- Nuclear weapons facilities
- Two hangar-bay division ballistic fire doors
- Jet fuel–tank storage and pumping
- Two starboard sponsons fitted for four five-inch guns.

SCB-125

- Angled flight deck
- Hurricane bow
- Primary flight control moved up and aft
- Barricade stanchions and engines
- Mirror landing system

SCB-110

- Similar to SCG-125 except as applied to *Midway* and *Franklin D. Roosevelt*

SCB-110A

- Similar to SCG-125 except as applied to *Coral Sea*

Appendix 6
Typical Straight-Deck Carrier Landing Pattern

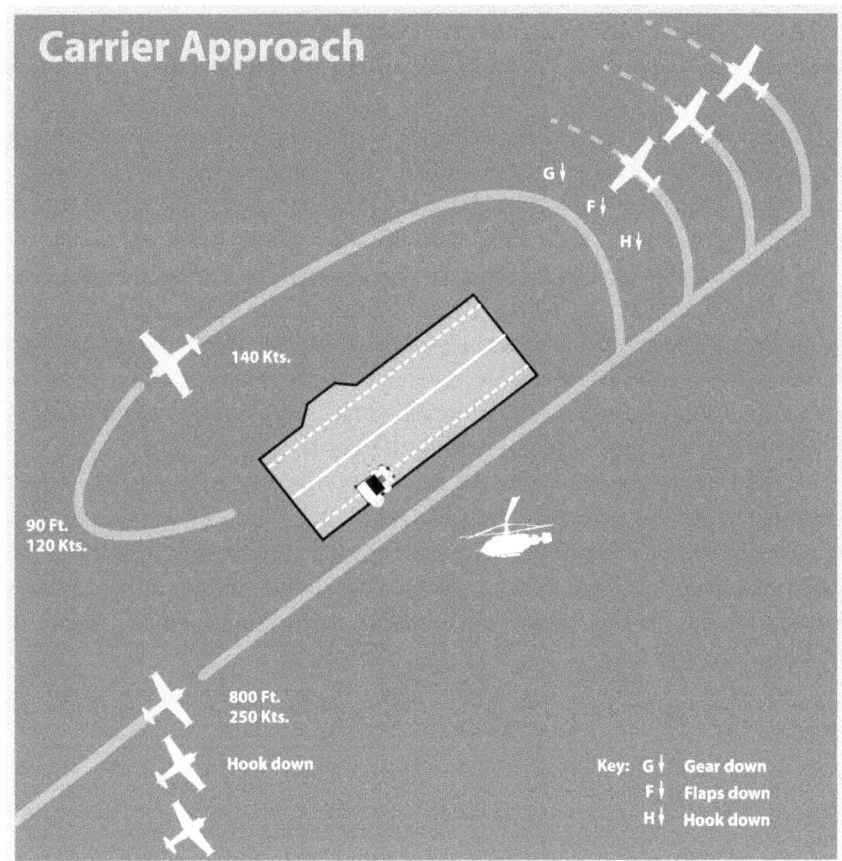

Figure A6-1 Straight-deck landing pattern
Created by Guy Arceneaux

The flat pattern was a procedure that took great skill, especially for a wingman to transition from having his eyes glued partly on his leader's wingtip light, partly on flying his own machine, partially on instruments, and partially on the carrier. It was only with the advent of the angled deck, the optical landing system, and radar control that a higher pattern with a more straight-in descending approach became more practical; it was much safer.

To prepare to enter the landing pattern, aircraft form into a right echelon, tailhooks down, descend to three hundred feet above the water paralleling the ship's course, and adjust speed to three hundred knots (180 for props). Once ahead of the ship (or when able to take interval on any preceding aircraft) the leader breaks off—that is, he makes a sharp, slightly descending left turn. The other aircraft continue on the ship's course, breaking individually at forty-second intervals.

As each aircraft breaks left it descends gradually to 125 feet, lowering landing gear and flaps, and slows to 125 knots, taking up a heading reciprocal to the ship's course.

When abeam the carrier's island the pilot commences a slowly descending left turn to the ship's course—the "Fox corpen," in the lingo of the day—meanwhile slowing to whatever his optimum airspeed is. He aims to be at the ninety-degree position (halfway through the turn) at an altitude of ninety feet over the water.

Continuing the turn and a slight descent, he endeavors to catch sight of the LSO with about forty-five degrees left in the turn to the ship's course. Once he sights the LSO he must heed his signals but must also be careful to continue to fly the aircraft precisely. When close to the end of the flight deck, if all is well in the eyes of the LSO, there will be a "Cut" signal. At that point the pilot sharply reduces the throttle to idle, lowers the nose a bit, and then flares to land.

If the tailhook catches a wire, all is well and the pilot is signaled by a deck crewman to taxi out of the arresting gear. If for some reason a wire is not caught, the aircraft will be stopped by a barricade erected athwartships forward of the arresting cables. A barricade engagement almost always inflicts some damage on the aircraft, but the pilot is most often unhurt, as are any aircraft or flight-deck personnel nearby.

Chronology

Events listed in this Chronology have been placed in accordance with data reported in various source materials and, wherever possible, cross-checked with Evans and Grossnick, Volume I.

1943 —	1 Jan	First emergency use of ground-controlled approach equipment; PBY Catalinas at NAS Quonset Point.
	18 Aug	Deputy Chief of Naval Operations, Air (DCNO (Air)) established by the Secretary of the Navy, with the responsibility for all aviation personnel and their training.
	4 Aug	Chief of Naval Air Intermediate Training directs that Aviation Safety Boards be established at each training center under his command.
	8 Nov	CNO extends aviation-safety-board directive to all primary and operational commands.
1944 —	3 Feb	Flight Safety Bulletin Number One issued jointly by DCNO (Air) and Chief, Bureau of Aeronautics (BuAer) announcing jointly their intention to issue consecutively numbered bulletins concerning the safe operation of naval aircraft. This will turn out be a forerunner of *Approach, the Navy and Marine Corps Aviation Safety Magazine*.
	5 June	DCNO (Air) directs the establishment of Aviation Safety Boards in all commands and the appointment of a flight safety officer in each squadron.
	14 July	A Flight Safety Council established by the joint action DCNO (Air) and the Chief of the Bureau of Aeronautics to plan, coordinate, and execute flight safety programs.
	6 Sep	Flight Safety Section established in the Office of the DCNO (Air) and assigned the direction and supervision of the aviation safety program.
	1 Dec	Naval Aircraft Factory Philadelphia began development of the slotted-cylinder catapult. This will later be married to the British development of the steam catapult and subsequently be adopted by the USN.
1945 —	Summer	"Anymouse" conceived by Lt. Cdr. Trgve A. Holl, VR-31 safety officer.
	5 Dec	Five TBM Avengers and one PBM with a total of twenty-seven men are lost on overwater navigation flight from Fort Lauderdale.

1946 — 7 Mar		CNO directs that GCA be adopted as the standard blind-landing system for the Navy.
	15 Aug	Instrument Flight Standardization Board established under the control of the CNO to determine means by which the instrument flight proficiency of pilots can be improved.
	1 Oct	Naval School of Aviation Medicine established at NAS Pensacola.
1947 — 4 June		CNO approves Ships Characteristic Board Change 27A designed to meet requirements for operating jets.
1948 — 4 June		First Air Board organized for the purpose of maintaining close relationships between the operating forces and planning agencies. Principal members to be DCNO (Air), Chief of BuAer, ComNavAirLant, and ComNavAirPac.
	29 June	Development of TACAN initiated.
1949 — April		Probe and drogue air refueling demonstrated by Flight Refueling Ltd.
	23 Apr	Construction of USS *United States* stopped.
1950 — 25 June		North Korean forces move into South Korea.
	3 July	USS *Valley Forge* and HMS *Triumph* launch first strikes in support of UN forces. First Navy kills as Panthers down two YAK-9s.
	July	First sea trials with steam catapult in HMS *Perseus*.
	28 Oct	CNO directs establishment of a permanent Instrument Flight Board at each station, air group and squadron. All Group I naval aviators to maintain a valid instrument rating as of eighteen months from that date.
1951 — 9 Aug		Angled deck first proposed at the Royal Aircraft Establishment in Bedford, England. After tests on board HMS *Triumph* similar tests held on board USS *Midway*. Both tests retain original arresting wires but use painted-on angled deck.
	October	Angled-deck project proposed by Lewis Boddington, U.K.
	November	U.K. Royal Aircraft Establishment proposed experiments for visual landing aids (mirror).
	2 Nov	Capt. J. R. Poppin, USN, director of the Aviation Medical Acceleration Laboratory (AMAL) at Johnsville, becomes the first person to ride the newly built human centrifuge.

	1 Dec	Naval Aviation Safety Activity established. Cdr. M. A. Peters assigned as first CO.
1952 —	February	First angled deck painted on HMS *Triumph*; touch-and-go trials.
	February	HMS *Perseus* steam catapult demonstrated to USN.
	1 Feb	CNO approves mod of Project 27A that includes more powerful arresting gear, higher-performance catapults, and replacement of no. 3 centerline elevator with a deck-edge elevator.
	March	Experimental mirror landing site erected at Farnborough.
	April	Testing of probe and drogue air refueling using the AJ-1 as a tanker and Panthers and Banshees as receivers.
	28 Apr	Navy announces that British-developed steam catapults will be adopted for use in the USN.
	8 May	Fleet Air Gunnery Unit (FAGU) established by ComNavAirPac.
	26–29 May	Feasibility of angled deck demonstrated on board USS *Midway*.
	17 June	Aviation Medical Acceleration Lab dedicated at the Naval Air Development Center.
	19 Nov	OPNAV Instruction 3750.6, "Naval Aviation Safety Program," issued.
	Sep–Dec	USS *Antietam* installs angled deck.
1953 —		Development of nylon safety barriers at Farnborough.
	12 Jan	First landings on board USS *Antietam* with angled deck.
	12 Jan	"Anymouse" implemented.
	March	First group of Air Force pilots enroll in USC safety course.
	4 May	CNO directs entire *Forrestal* class of carriers to be built with angled deck.
	17 July	R4Q crashes departing Whiting Field. Despite the death of forty-four, the investigation reports a cause of "Undetermined."
	2 Sep	Project 110, a conversion plan for *Midway* class promulgated. (Same as 27C except for C-11 catapult on the angled deck.)

	3 Sep	O-in-C Naval Aviation Safety Activity letter report to the CNO, the "Flatley Report," issued.
	1 Oct	USS *Hornet* completes angled-deck conversion. Last of nine *Essex*-class converted IAW Project 27A.
	October	First group of naval aviators enrolled in USC Aviation Safety Course.
	19 Nov	FAGU opened to both Pacific and Atlantic Fleet squadrons, "as a step towards increased emphasis and standardization."
	December	At the Naval Air Materiel Center in Philadelphia a Type C, Mark XI steam catapult, based on British design but at higher pressure, launches a 23,670-pound dead load to a velocity of 156 miles per hour. (This paves the way to *Hancock*'s receiving the first shipboard Type C, Mark XI, catapults in May 1954.)
1954 —	27 May	CNO approves Project 125, which in general provides for installing angled decks, enclosing bows and other changes in carriers that had earlier completed Project 27A modernization.
	1 June	First steam-catapult launch from USS *Hancock*. Cdr. Henry J. Jackson, in an S2F-1, is catapulted from *Hancock* in the initial operational test of the C-11 steam catapult. As tests continue throughout the month, a total of 254 launchings are made with the S2F, AD-5, F2H-3, F2H-4, FJ-2, F7U-3, and F3D-2.
1955 —	22 Mar	Navy R6D of VR-3 crashes and explodes on Pali Kea Peak, fifteen miles northwest of Honolulu, Hawaii, killing all on board. The loss of fifty-seven passengers and nine crew members makes it the worst-ever heavier-than-air crash in naval aviation.
	April	Naval Aviation Safety Activity redesignated as Naval Aviation Safety Center.
	4 Apr	Jet Transition Training Unit (JTTU) established at NAS Olathe, Kansas.
	July	First edition of *Approach,* replacing the U.S. Naval Aviation Safety Bulletin.
	22 Aug	First U.S. aircraft-carrier mirror landing. VX-3 begins operational evaluation of the mirror landing system installed

on *Bennington*. Cdr, Robert G. Dose, flying an FJ-3 Fury, makes the first landing with the device. Two days later Lt. Cdr. Harding C. MacKnight made the first night mirror landing in an F9F-8 Cougar. The squadron's favorable report will form the basis for a decision to procure the mirror landing system for installation on aircraft carriers and at certain shore stations.

12 Sep — All fighters in production ordered to be equipped for aerial refueling.

1 Oct — *Forrestal* commissioned.

9 Nov — The Chief of Naval Operations advises the Chief of the Bureau of Ships that each angled-deck carrier would be equipped with mirror landing systems and requests that equipment for twelve installations be procured during FYs 1956 and 1957.

1956 — 1 Mar — *Essex* completes angled-deck conversion, making her the eighth conversion since *Antietam*.

6 Apr — *Franklin D. Roosevelt* completes SCB 110, which includes angled deck.

25 Apr — CNO announces that mirror landing systems would be installed at all principal naval air stations to improve air traffic control and reduce landing accidents.

27–28 June — First annual Fleet Air Gunnery Meet at NAAS El Centro.

15 Aug — *Hornet* completes angled-deck conversion.

11 Oct — An R6D-1 of VR-6 on a scheduled Military Air Transport Service flight from Lakenheath, England, to Lajes, Azores, disappears over the Atlantic with nine crew members and fifty passengers on board.

1957 — 1 Feb — Lt. Cdr. Frank Austin, MC, USN, becomes the first Navy doctor to complete Test Pilot School.

13 Apr — Aviation officer distribution shifted from DCNO (Air) to CNP.

30 Apr — Naval Aviation Medical Center commissioned at Pensacola, combining the Naval School of Aviation Medicine and the Pensacola Naval Hospital.

	12 Aug	F3D Skyknight lands on board *Antietam* in first shipboard test of ACLS; more than fifty landings will be made between 12 and 20 August.
	28 Aug	Ground-level ejection seat demonstrated at NAS Patuxent River when Lt. Sydney Hughes of the British Royal Air Force successfully ejects from an F9F-8T while flying just above the ground at 120 mph.
1958	10 Mar	The Chief of Naval Operations approves a reorganization of carrier aviation that provides, inter alia, for a permanent replacement air group to be established on each coast and made responsible for "the indoctrination of key maintenance personnel, the tactical training of aviators, and conducting special programs required for the introduction of new models of combat aircraft." This reorganization was first directed in the fall of 1957, thus some apparent discrepancy in dates. Cagle describes it as a "squadron training system . . . modernized and streamlined by the establishment of the replacement squadron and air group concept." It's known today as the "RAG Concept."
	1 July	First joint CAA/Navy Radar Air Traffic Control Center (RATTC) commences operations at NAS Miramar.
	23 Aug	FAA established.
1959	5 Feb	In accordance with the Defense Reorganization Act of 1958, the position of Assistant Secretary of the Navy for Air is abolished.
	26 May	A concept of aircraft maintenance that provides for the assignment of responsibility directly to the unit having custody of the aircraft and for a gradual elimination of FASRONs is approved for implementation.
	15 July	Aviation Safety Division of OP-05 changed to staff position as OP-05F to act as principal adviser to DCNO (Air) in all matters of air safety and to coordinate the planning and implementation of aviation safety programs throughout the Navy.
	1 Dec	BuAer merged with BuOrd to become Bureau of Naval Weapons.

1960 —	25 Feb	An R6D Liftmaster carrying seven crew members, nineteen members of the Navy Band, and a team of twelve antisubmarine warfare specialists collides with a Brazilian DC-3 over Sugarloaf Mountain, Rio de Janeiro. The accident claims the lives of all but three on the Liftmaster and all twenty-six people—four crew members and twenty-two passengers—on board the airliner.
	March	CNO letter issued to major commands and operating forces relative to utilization of aviation safety officers.
	May	*Coral Sea* completes SCB 110, which includes angled deck.
	9 Aug	Letter from Commander Naval Aviation Safety Center to CNO, "Naval Aviation Criteria," sets the stage for NATOPS.
1961 —	June	Naval Training Device Center publishes *Improvement of Flight Handbooks*.
	10 July	First NATOPS manual promulgated: HSS-1.
	14 Dec	Completion of the installation of the Pilot Landing Aid Television (PLAT) system on *Coral Sea* (CVA 43), the first carrier to have the system. By early 1963, all attack carriers will have received PLAT, and planning will have begun for its installation in antisubmarine carriers and at shore stations as well.
1962 —	19 Dec	First shipboard test of nose-gear catapult, E-2 Hawkeye followed by an A-6 Intruder, on board USS *Enterprise*.
1963 —	18 Aug	Six A-4 Skyhawks lost while operating in the eastern Atlantic and Mediterranean. Three crash ashore when they are unable to find French divert field in the fog. One flies into a mountain, another hits the ramp on landing, and a third disappears on a routine flight.
	13 June	First fully automatic carrier landings completed with both flight controls and throttles operated automatically by signals from the ship. The event highlights almost ten years of research and development and follows by about six years the first such carrier landing made with test equipment.
1966 —	1 May	Naval Material Command established, with the Naval Air Systems Command as one of six systems commands.

1967 —		First *Medical Officer Newsletter* published, includes articles on hypoxia and dangers of SCUBA within a certain number of hours of flying.
	15 May	CNO directs establishment of Aircraft Intermediate Maintenance Departments in all aircraft carriers.
	15 Aug	The Aircraft Carrier Safety Review Panel holds its first meeting. Headed by Adm. James S. Russell, USN (Ret.), the panel is appointed to examine actual and potential sources of fire and explosions in aircraft carriers, with the object of minimizing their frequency and damage, and to propose further improvement in the equipment and techniques used to fight fires and control damage by explosion.
1968 —	28 Mar	Aircraft Maintenance Duty Officer (AMDO/152x) community established.
	3 May	Naval Safety Center with revised mission formed by combining the Naval Aviation Safety and the Submarine Safety Center, formerly at Groton. At the same time the Office of the Assistant CNO (Safety) is established.
1969 —	24 June	First operational hands-off carrier arrested landing using the AN/SPN-42 ACLS.
	1 Sep	Naval Aviation Logistics Support Center established at Patuxent River.
1970 —	21 July	OPNAV Instruction 4790.2, "Naval Aviation Maintenance Program," issued.
1971 —	8 Dec	CincPacFlt orders video coverage of the entire launch and recovery sequence of carrier operations.
	March	CNO establishes OP-02 and OP-03 in addition to OP-05. "The DCNO for Air inherited all the offices in the old OP-03 (DCNO for Fleet Operations and Readiness) that programmed aviation activities."
1972 —	4 May	Navy's first Night Carrier Landing Trainer (NCLT) established for the A-7 at NAS Lemoore.
1975 —	5 May	First Aviation Medical Officer class commences at Pensacola.

	19–20 Jun	Joint Aviation Safety Conference on Out-of-Control/Stall/Departure.
	13–15 Apr	Carrier Landing Performance conference.
	21 Oct	OPNAV Instruction 5102.1, "Safety Investigation," issued.
1977 —	1 Oct	Naval Aviation Logistics Center becomes operational at NAS Patuxent River.
1984 —	8 May	First Aviation Supply Wings awarded to Vice Adm. Eugene A. Grinstead Jr., Rear Adm. Andrew A. Giordano, and Commo. John H. Ruehlin.
1987 —	21 Dec	Changes to the Office of Chief of Naval Operations, required by the Goldwater-Nichols Department of Defense Reorganization Act of 1986, result in redesignation of the Deputy Chief of Naval Operations (Air Warfare) as Assistant Chief of Naval Operations (Air Warfare).
	31 Dec	For the first time in its history, the Naval Air Reserve Force, consisting of fifty-two operational squadrons and over four hundred aircraft, completes a full calendar year without a major aircraft mishap.
1991 —	27 Sep	In a televised address, President George H. W. Bush announces that the United States will unilaterally reduce nuclear arms, including the withdrawal of all tactical nuclear weapons from Navy ships. The order directs the withdrawal of Navy air-deliverable nuclear weapons from aircraft carriers and land-based naval aircraft, such as patrol planes, and the storage or destruction of these weapons.
	12 Nov	First Naval Air Training Maintenance Support Activity established at NAS Corpus Christi.
1992 —	22 July	Acting Secretary of the Navy Sean O'Keefe and the CNO, Adm. Frank B. Kelso II, announce a sweeping reorganization of OPNAV staff aligning the OPNAV staff with the Joint Staff. The scheme includes the merger of the Assistant Chiefs of Naval Operations for Submarine Warfare (OP-02), Surface Warfare (OP-03), Air Warfare (OP-05), and Naval Warfare (OP-07) into one staff under DCNO for Resources,

	Warfare Requirements and Assessment (N8). Director, Air Warfare (N88), becomes the new designation assigned to Air Warfare (OP-05).
30 Sep	AirLant's four functional wings—Helicopter Wings, Atlantic; Patrol Wings, Atlantic; Strike-Fighter Wings, Atlantic; and Tactical Wings, Atlantic—are disestablished in a sweeping change that eliminates an entire echelon of command in the administrative structure of naval aviation on the East Coast.
1993 — 1 Jan	After almost 50 years, OP-05 dies. In a reorganization of the OPNAV staff, the position of ACNO (Air Warfare/OP-05), becomes Director, Air Warfare (N88) and reports to DCNO (Resources, Warfare Requirements and Assessment)/(N8). The N88 billet is dropped from a three-star flag officer to a two-star.
1 Oct	The Naval Training Systems Center, Orlando, Florida, is redesignated Naval Air Warfare Center, Training Systems Division, although without a change of mission.
1994 — 20 Dec	Robert C. Osborn dies at the age of ninety at his home in Salisbury, Connecticut. For more than fifty-one years he had drawn the cartoon "Grampaw Pettibone" in *Naval Aviation News*. During World War II Osborn created the "Dilbert the Pilot" and "Spoiler the Mechanic" posters and the "Sense" pamphlets, which were disseminated throughout the fleet.
1995 — 1 Oct	The Naval Aviation Supply Office is disestablished at Philadelphia. The Naval Inventory Control Point, Philadelphia/Mechanicsburg, Pennsylvania, is established in its place. The new command takes over both the functions of the Supply Office and the Ships Parts Control Center at Mechanicsburg, which was also disestablished.
1997 — November	The Improved Fresnel Lens Optical Landing System completes shore-based technical evaluation at NAS Patuxent River, Maryland. The system is then installed on board *George Washington* (CVN 73).

Notes

Preface

1. The term "naval aviation" includes the aviation elements of the Navy, Marine Corps, and Coast Guard. It includes fixed-wing, prop, jet, tilt-wing, and rotary-wing aircraft, whether they fly from ships, land, or sea. The term includes officers and enlisted personnel and supporting government civilians. All uniformed personnel attend flight, maintenance, and safety schools under the aegis of the Naval Air Training Command; the Marines and Navy, for the most part, fly the same aircraft and deploy on board ships and ashore.

Chapter 1. Black as Midnight

1. Two steady, small, red lights atop the ship's mainmast.
2. See appendix 6 for a cartoon of the "flat" carrier landing pattern used in the 1950s and prior.
3. Vice Adm. J. J. Ballentine personal letter to Rear Adm. Rico Botta, Naval Air Material Center, 21 March 1952, box 13, J. J. Ballentine papers, Library of Congress Manuscript Division.

Chapter 2. Difficult Days

1. Personal email exchange with the author, March 2012.
2. Dave Bradford, comp., "Mad about Safety: 70 Years of Grampaw Pettibone," *Naval Aviation News* (Winter 2013): 10–15.
3. "'Anymouse's' Anniversary," *Approach* (November–December 2005): 4–5.
4. Jeffrey G. Barlow, *Revolt of the Admirals: The Fight for Naval Aviation, 1945–1950* (Washington, D.C.: Naval Historical Center, 1994).
5. *Valley Forge, Philippine Sea, Boxer,* and *Leyte.*
6. Mark L. Evans and Roy A. Grossnick, *United States Naval Aviation,* Vol. 1, *1910–2010* (Washington, D.C.: Naval History and Heritage Command, 2015), 593.
7. Capt. James H. Flatley, Commander Naval Aviation Safety Activity, letter to ComNavAirLant, 17 August 1953, Naval History and Heritage Command, Aviation Archives.
8. Vice Adm. John Jennings Ballentine, personal letter to Rear Adm. E. A. Cruise, 11 March 1954, box 13, J. J. Ballentine papers, Library of Congress Manuscript Division. One TBM landed on the parking ramp at Cartagena instead of the runway; another TBM, carrying passengers and mail, spun on

an approach to Naples Capodichino; a third nosed-up by taxiing too close behind a large multiengine transport; and a fourth went into instrument flight conditions while carrying passengers on a VFR flight plan.

9. John T. Hayward and C. W. Borklund, *Bluejacket Admiral: The Navy Career of Chick Hayward* (Annapolis, Md.: Naval Institute Press, 2000); Jerry Miller, *Nuclear Weapons and Aircraft Carriers: How the Bomb Saved Naval Aviation* (Washington, D.C.: Smithsonian Institution, 2001). These two books authored by distinguished naval professionals who were present at the time cover well the effort of the Navy in gaining a role in event of nuclear war.
10. Rear Adm. L. A. Moebus to Vice Adm. J. J. Ballentine and others, 17 July 1952, box 13, J. J. Ballentine papers, Library of Congress Manuscript Division.
11. Vincent Davis, *The Admirals Lobby* (Chapel Hill: University of North Carolina Press, 1967), 40–41.
12. Anonymous Air Force exchange pilot, "An Air Force Pilot Talks about Navy Operations," *Approach* (April 1977): 1–7.
13. Thomas P. Hone, *Power and Change: The Administrative History of the Office of the Chief of Naval Operations, 1946–1986* (Washington, D.C.: Government Printing Office, 1989), 48.
14. *Approach* (April/May 1990) interview with Vice Adm. James B. Stockdale describing how then-Commander "Red Dog" Davis, when CO of a Crusader squadron, had a standing order that all new pilots would spend two full days with him reviewing handbooks and schematics before they could fly.
15. All data cited herein are for non-combat-related mishaps. Combat mishaps are scored elsewhere.
16. In 1968 the Naval Aviation Safety Center merged with the Naval Submarine Safety Center and became the Naval Safety Center. Shortly thereafter surface, and still later shore, safety directorates were established at the center, all modeled on the successful aviation-safety efforts, including safety officers for all ships and shore stations.

Chapter 3. The Competition

1. "Part 121" is a shorthand for Title 14 of the Code of Federal Regulations Part 121, which covers commercial air flight. The term "FAR Part 121" may also be heard but, while formerly accurate, is today a colloquialism.
2. Tom Morrison, *Quest for All-Weather Flight* (Ramsbury, U.K.: Crowood, 2003), is an outstanding history of these developments.
3. The NACA was established in 1915 largely through the urging of then-captain William Moffett, the longtime chief of the Navy Bureau of Aeronautics. NACA was absorbed into NASA in 1958.
4. The NTSB originated in the Air Commerce Act of 1926, in which Congress charged the U.S. Department of Commerce with investigating the causes of

aircraft accidents. In 1940 that responsibility was given to the Civil Aeronautics Board's Bureau of Aviation Safety, but since 1967 investigation has been the responsibility of the NTSB.
5. That the figure 3-3 annotations may be arbitrary is underscored by a similar chart prepared by a flight surgeon wherein it is claimed, albeit somewhat tongue in cheek, that all improvements in the mishap rate have been due to a series of medical innovations.
6. Pat Patrick and Gregory N. Seuss, *Flying Hours, Simulators and Safety: A Look at Flight Safety Trends,* Report CIM 68.10 (Arlington, Va.: Center for Naval Analyses, December 1999).

Chapter 4. Beginning to Get It Right

1. "... And Then There Were None ...," *Approach* (September 1955): 4–11, a true story of eight Naval Reserve Cougar pilots who set out on a cross-country flight and ran into weather. Three returned to base. One landed at an abandoned airstrip. Two landed on highways. One landed on top of a dam, and one died.
2. Charles Roemer, "The Flatley Report Which Saved Naval Aviation," *Foundation* (Spring 1985): 56–61.
3. VMR-153 Aircraft Accident Report 2-53, R4Q, 17 July 1953.
4. A descent through instrument flight conditions without clearance from a controlling authority.
5. VC-3, Moffett Field, California, for Pacific Fleet night fighters; VC-4, Atlantic City, New Jersey, for Atlantic Fleet night fighters; VC-11, at North Island, California, for Pacific Fleet airborne early warning; VC-12, at Quonset Point, Rhode Island, for Atlantic Fleet airborne early warning; VC-33, at Atlantic City, for Atlantic Fleet night attack; and VC-35, at North Island, for Atlantic Fleet night attack.
6. O'Rourke, G.G. with E.T. Woldridge, *Night Fighters Over Korea* (Annapolis: Naval Institute Press, 1998), 11.
7. ComNavAirLant training officer, memorandum, to Vice Adm. Ballentine [then ComNavAirLant], undated, box 13, J. J. Ballentine papers, Library of Congress Manuscript Division.
8. Capt. G. G. O'Rourke, with E. T. Woolridge, *Night Fighters over Korea* (Annapolis, Md.: Naval Institute Press, 1998), is an outstanding description of Korean War night fighting and attendant problems.
9. Cdr. Walter Dalitsch, MC, USN, "Blind Flying: What We Didn't Know Didn't Kill Us . . . Most of the Time," *Approach* (January–February 2011): 6–8, is an excellent review of the history of instrument flying.
10. Physically qualified naval aviators less than forty-two years old.

11. FAWTUPAC was at first at Naval Air Station (NAS) Barber's Point but then moved to NAS Miramar, with a detachment at NAS Moffett Field. The entire squadron transitioned to VF(AW)-3 in 1958.
12. FAWTULANT's predecessor was VCN-2, initially at NAS Oceana, Virginia, but soon moved to NAS Key West, Florida, maintaining an Oceana detachment. In 1958 the squadron and its detachment were merged with VF-21 and VA-44, respectively.
13. YE/YG was a ship-based orientation and homing device.
14. Capt. Brett Easler and Cdr. Bruce Herman, "On Glide Path, on Course," *Naval Aviation News* (Summer 2014): 16–19. Also, "History of GCA in the Navy," www.gca-atc.org/USN, last accessed 2 August 2015, sets out the history of air traffic control, including the beginnings of GCA and the development of the Air Controller rating.

CHAPTER 5. NAVAL AVIATION'S TRANSITION TO JETS

1. Robert C. Rubel, "The Navy's Transition to Jets," *Naval War College Review* (Spring 2010): 49–59; Donald Davenport Engen, *Wings and Warriors: My Life as a Naval Aviator* (Washington, D.C.: Smithsonian Institution, 1997).
2. Because of difficult carrier suitability the Skyknight was eventually used mostly ashore and mostly by the Marines.
3. In fact, the A-4, albeit known as the AF-1B, is flying today from the Brazilian aircraft carrier *Minas Gerais*.
4. See Robert F. Dunn, "In-Flight Refueling," *Hook* (Fall 2010): 31–34.
5. An external fuel tank equipped with an air-driven propeller in the nose that drives a hydraulic reel system enabling the streaming of a hose with a drogue on the end so another aircraft can plug in and take fuel.
6. Robert F. Dunn, "The Angle of Attack Indicator," *Approach* (January–February 2011): 9–10.
7. Tommy H. Thomasson, *U.S. Naval Superiority: Development of Shipborne Jet Fighters 1943–1962* (North Branch, Minn.: Specialty, 2007), 123.
8. For FY 1950 the all-Navy major mishap rate was over fifty-three accidents per hundred thousand flight hours. In 1959 the rate was just under twenty-six accidents per hundred thousand flight hours. See appendix 2 for annual rates for all years.

CHAPTER 6. AIRCRAFT CARRIERS

1. Norman Friedman and Arthur D. Baker III, *U.S. Aircraft Carriers: An Illustrated Design History* (Annapolis, Md.: Naval Institute Press, 1983).
2. Barlow, *Revolt of the Admirals*.

3. Cdr. Hal Buell, USN (Ret.), "The Angled Deck Concept, Savior of the Tailhook Navy," *Hook* (Fall 1987). This is one of the very best descriptions of the development of the angled deck available.
4. Thomas C. Hone, Norman Friedman, and Mark D. Mandeles, *Innovation in Carrier Aviation,* Newport Paper 37 (Newport, R.I.: Naval War College Press, 2011); Norman Polmar, *Aircraft Carriers: A History of Carrier Aviation and Its Influence on World Events,* vol. 2, *1946–2006* (Washington, D.C.: Potomac Books, 2008).
5. *Antietam's* conversion was limited to the deck only—no steam catapults and no mirror landing system. Aircraft recovering aboard *Antietam* used the traditional, flat "paddles pass" until her decommissioning in 1963.
6. The conversions of seven of these ships, in addition to *Antietam,* were limited to the angled deck only. They did not receive steam catapults, nor did they get improved arresting gear. Most finished their service lives as CVSs and as such did not normally operate jets. One active *Essex*-class carrier, *Lake Champlain,* never got either the angled deck or steam catapults.
7. See Appendix 5 for descriptions of SCB Alterations, dates, and ships affected.
8. "Cut" is a signal given by the LSO, at which time it is mandatory that the pilot reduce the throttle(s) to idle power and land the aircraft.
9. Capt. Jerry O'Rourke, "Night Hookers, Part III," *Hook* (Fall 1988): 53.
10. Mishap damage caused while taxiing or moving aircraft around the ship but not serious enough to require filing a mishap report. Repair can often be effected locally.
10a. From these data, then, it's rather obvious that there were other factors contributing to making Navy and Marine skies safer. In fact, while angled decks did indeed enhance safety on the margin, their adoption did more for operational effectiveness than it did for safety.
11. William F. Trimble, *Wings for the Navy: A History of the Naval Aircraft Factory, 1917–1956* (Annapolis, Md.: Naval Institute Press, 1990). See also the excellent digest of the history of the catapult in the U.S. Navy in the February 1954 issue of *Naval Aviation News.*
12. Interestingly, USS *Gerald Ford* (CVN 78) is being built with electromagnetic catapults.
13. An expression referring to an older type of attitude gyro, which would tumble during more extreme maneuvers. To restore it to normal operation the pilot would "cage" it—that is, lock it in place. Once the aircraft returned to straight and level flight, the gyro could be uncaged—thus the expression.
14. Vice Adm. J. J. Ballentine, personal letter to Rear Adm. Rico Botta, Naval Air Material Center, 30 June 1952, box 13, J. J. Ballentine papers, Library of Congress Manuscript Division.

15. Rear Adm. Richard T. Gaskill, "Plane in the Water!," *Foundation* (Fall 2009): 20–29.
16. Thomasson, *U.S. Naval Air Superiority*.
17. Cdr. Edwin F. Stobie, "All Weather Landing System," U.S. Naval Institute *Proceedings* (July 1965): 156–59, is a comprehensive description of the SPN-10 system and its operation.

Chapter 7. Beyond Jets and Aircraft Carriers

1. OP-05, memorandum 30-84, 12 March 1984, Naval History and Heritage Command, Washington, D.C. [hereafter NHHC] Archives.
2. This accident was reported on in the famous "Flatley Report," covered in more detail in chapter 8.
3. Evans and Grossnick, *United States Naval Aviation*, 1910-2010, Vol. II, 93. "Aircraft on Hand."
4. Ibid., vol. II.

Chapter 8. The Catalyst for Improvement

1. This chapter, slightly edited, was published in *Foundation*, the Naval Aviation Museum Foundation (NAMF) journal, on 11 April 2013 (pages 16–27) and is included herein with the permission of the NAMF. The title "Naval Safety Center" encompasses not only the current enterprise of that name but its predecessors the Naval Safety Activity and the Naval Aviation Safety Center.
2. *Naval Aviation News* is the longest running naval aviation publication and continues to this day. It contains a plethora of information on all subjects (and their history) relevant to naval aviation. Back issues can be accessed at http://www.history.navy.mil/research/histories/naval-aviation-history/naval-aviation-news/back-issues.html (last accessed 23 August 2015).
3. ComAirPac and ComAirLant were later designated as Commanders Naval Air Forces Pacific (ComNavAirPac) and Atlantic (ComNavAirLant), respectively. More recently, they have been consolidated as Commander Naval Air Forces, with ComNavAirPac and ComNavAirLant as reporting commands.
4. In Group III were designated naval aviators who were physically qualified to pilot aircraft and were over forty-two. Group II aviators were those temporarily physically disqualified. For Group I, see chapter 4, note 9.
5. *Naval Aviation News* is known colloquially and throughout the U.S. Naval Aviation community as *NavAirNews*. Back issues can be accessed at https://www.history.navy.mil/research/histories/naval-aviation-history/naval-aviation-news.html.
6. Until 1959 the mishap rate was calculated as major mishaps per ten thousand flight hours. As of 1960 the calculation was changed to reflect major mishaps

per hundred thousand flight hours. All data and charts in this book have been stated in accordance with the latter definition.
7. "Air Force Safety Center," *U.S. Air Force,* www.af.mil/AboutUs/FactSheets/Display/tabid/224/Article/104488/air-force-safety-center.aspx, last accessed 5 August 2015. On 31 December 1971, the Air Force Inspection and Safety Center was inaugurated at Norton. Reorganization of the Air Staff in 1992 created an Air Force Chief of Safety, reporting directly to the Air Force Chief of Staff.
8. Steve Ewing, *Reaper Leader: The Life of Jimmy Flatley* (Annapolis, Md.: Naval Institute Press, 2002), is a comprehensive biography of James H. Flatley.
9. VMR-153 Accident Report 2-53, Naval Aviation Safety Activity letter NASA/P22/JHF/vc, serial 010, 3 September 1953, "Naval Aviation Accident Prevention Program, Discussion Of." Section 23 of the report does indeed indicate "Undetermined," but paragraph 33 states, "The Board concludes that the primary cause of this accident is pilot error." These contradictory statements only add to the inadequacy of the report.
10. Ibid. VMR-153 Accident Report 2-53, Naval Aviation Safety Activity letter NASA/P22/JHF/vc, serial 010, 3 September 1953, "Naval Aviation Accident Prevention Program, Discussion Of."
11. Ibid.; Ewing, *Reaper Leader,* 299; Roemer, "Flatley Report," 56–61.
12. Derek Nelson and Dave Parsons, *Danger: Life and Death Stories from the U.S. Navy's* Approach *Magazine* (Osceola, Wis.: Motorbooks International, 1991), 1–21, quoted by permission.
13. *Naval Safety Center School of Aviation Safety,* http://www.public.navy.mil/navsafecen/Pages/aviation/SAS/index.aspx, last accessed 10 December 2015, summarizes the history of the School of Aviation Safety.
14. OPNAV Instruction 3750.14 of 22 May 1959 stipulated, "All ships and stations concerned with the operation of aircraft and all operational squadrons shall have at least one naval aviator assigned as Aviation Safety Officer. This officer should be the direct representative of the Commander and shall be a graduate of the Aviation Safety Officer's Course at the University of Southern California."
15. A listing of current Safety Center aviation-oriented publications is given in appendix 4.
16. "A One-Stop Safety Shop for Sailors and Marines," *Hook* (Winter 2008): 33–38, an excellent recap of the current, organization, functions, and products of the Aviation Directorate of the Naval Safety Center.
17. To the regret of many, the "Anymouse" program is now defunct, ostensibly replaced by such efforts as Crew Resource Management and Operational Risk Management, both described in chapter 15.
18. The contributions of aviation medicine to the naval aviation safety record are covered in chapter 10.

19. Rear Adm. William O. Burch and Capt. Gale E. Krouse, "Reporting Facts for the Naval Aviation Safety Program," *Judge Advocate Journal* (September 1959): 3. When the article was published Rear Admiral Burch was the Commander Naval Aviation Safety Center, and Captain Krouse was director of the Judge Advocate General's Investigations Division.
20. Federal Tort Claims Act, 28 U.S. Code, 1346(b), 1988, 2671–80, and predecessor legislation.
21. Long-standing unofficial Naval Safety Center motto.

Chapter 9. Six Amazing Years

1. This chapter was published in the *Naval War College Review* 64, no. 3 (Summer 2011): 98–110, used with permission.
2. After about six weeks out of home port on one cruise in the 1950s, an unfamiliar commander came into the ready room, looked around, then left. After the door closed the pilots all looked at one another and asked, "Who was that?" It turned out to have been the CAG!
3. Evans and Grossnick, *United States Naval Aviation*, Vol. I, 285.
4. "Supersonic Checkout," *Naval Aviation News* (April 1955): 1–5.
5. "Crusader College Carries On," *Naval Aviation News* (June 1958): 22–23.
6. Ibid.; Evans and Grossnick, *United States Naval Aviation*, Vol. I, 221.
7. The now almost forgotten practice of gathering for camaraderie and drinks after a week of flying, usually on a Friday or Saturday night.
8. "Crash Program," *Approach* (August 1959): 16–19.
9. Capt. R. G. Dose, USN, "The Replacement Air Group Concept," U.S. Naval Institute *Proceedings* (April 1960): 135–38.
10. Engen, *Wings and Warriors*, 236–37.
11. Col. William T. Hewes, USMC (Ret.), "The High Dive," *Foundation* (Spring 2010): 96.
12. Ibid.; Engen, *Wings and Warriors*, 245; James L. Holloway III, *Aircraft Carriers at War: A Personal Retrospective of Korea, Vietnam, and the Soviet Confrontation* (Annapolis, Md.: Naval Institute Press, 2007), 149–51. These sources have different accounts of how NATOPS began. Admiral Holloway was then executive assistant to Vice Admiral Pirie; Engen was an air-wing commander.
13. Capt. R. J. Selmer, USN, "A Stan Man Speaks," *Approach* (October 1962): 1–4. The article was originally a speech at a Third Quarter ComFairAlameda Safety Council.
14. "New Standards for Naval Air," *Approach* (August 1961): 6. See also, "The One Best Way—New Standards for Naval Air," *Naval Aviation News* (August 1961):6-7.
15. "The 'New Approach' Continues," *Approach* (September 1972): 8–10.

16. The RAG acronym was officially replaced by FRS (Flight Replacement Squadron) in December 1963, but both terms are still used interchangeably.

CHAPTER 10. THE DOC

1. Much of this chapter was published in *Foundation* (Fall 2014): 74–85. Used with permission.
2. Davis, Johnson, Stepanek and Fogerty, eds. *Fundamentals of Aerospace Medicine* (Philadelphia: Lippincott Williams & Wilkins, 2002)
3. Ibid.
4. Cdr. Walter Dalitsch, MC, USN, personal note to author.
5. "Flight Surgeon Requirements and Training," *Navy Medicine Operational Training Center,* http://www.med.navy.mil/sites/nmotc/nami/academics/Pages/FlightSurgeon.aspx, last accessed June 2013.
6. Perhaps the idea that a flight candidate should be able to ride a horse is not as silly as one might think. For years many Americans thought a prerequisite for flying an airplane was the ability to drive a car. Then we found that Chinese and Vietnamese who might not be able to drive did quite well in the air.
7. The FAR is graded from 1 to 9. Over the years many basic flight-training instructors have found that flight students with FARs below 3 could not succeed, no matter how hard they tried. Curiously, those who scored 9 were also apt to have difficulties. That particular phenomenon has never been satisfactorily explained.
8. Today the training more often is done with a Reduced Oxygen Breathing Device.
9. *U.S. Naval Flight Surgeon's Manual* (Washington, D.C.: Bureau of Naval Medicine, 1969), 641.
10. "Aero Medical Men Study Flight Equipment," *Naval Aviation News,* 31 April 1955, 30–31.
11. The Air Board is a panel of the most senior active naval aviators, usually DCNO (Air), DCS (Air) USMC, ComNavAirLant, ComNavAirPac, the Chief of Naval Reserve, and the Chief of Naval Air Training. The board usually meets semiannually and sets policy for naval aviation in accordance with guidance set forth by the CNO and the Commandant of the Marine Corps.
12. Rear Adm. Edward C. Outlaw, USN, "Design Safety and Material Reliability," remarks delivered before the International Air Safety Seminar in Athens, Greece, November 1963. Complete text in Naval Aviation Safety Center Chronology of Highlights, Calendar Year 1963, NHHC Archives.
13. Captain Austin was on duty as the Head, Life Sciences Department at the Naval Safety Center at the time. See sidebar for other highlights of his most distinguished career. While others had identified and dug into what came to

be called the "science of human factors" even before Frank Austin, to him must be given credit for introducing the Navy and Marines and eventually the Air Force and the FAA to the importance of human factors.
14. The Naval Aviation Safety Center had, in fact, established the Human Error Research and Analysis Program (HERAP) in the late 1950s, but it had not heretofore received much publicity.
15. James Reason, *Human Error* (Cambridge, U.K.: Cambridge University Press, 1990). Reason's work involved operators of a nuclear power plant, but his observations have been found to apply as well to aircrew, maintainers, supervisors, and others involved in aviation.
16. Both Shappell and Wiegmann are aerospace experimental psychologists. Lieutenant commanders in the Naval Reserve, they did much of the work cited herein while assigned to the Naval Safety Center.
17. A mathematical approach to forecasting maintenance problems based on statistics gathered from past experience.

Chapter 11. Discovering Human Factors

1. Naval Safety Center publications, and see chapter 8.
2. Naval Aviation Safety Center, *U.S. Navy Safety Program,* Report RA 1–58 (Norfolk, Va., 2 February 1958), VI-6, discusses the human element in aircraft accidents, labeling them "personnel factors," a precursor to the category "human factors."
3. David C. Edwards, "Psychology of Aircraft Controls," in *Pilot Mental and Physical Performance* (Ames: Iowa State University Press, 1990), 47–58.
4. Rosario Rausa, *Skyraider: The Douglas A-1 Flying Dump Truck* (Baltimore, Md.: Nautical and Aviation, 1982), 11.
5. Capt. Frank H. Austin, MC, USN, "Operational Aspects of Aviation Medicine" (paper presented at the MIT Aerospace and Undersea Medicine Program Summer Session, 1969).
6. The CAA/FAA and the NACA/NASA had earlier embarked on their own human-factors programs.
7. Earl L. Weiner and David C. Nagel, eds., *Human Factors in Aviation* (San Diego: Academic, 1988), 5.
8. Barbara G. Kanki, Robert L. Helmreich, and Jose Anca, eds., *Crew Resource Management* (San Diego: Academic, 2010). Chapter 1, by Helmreich and H. Clayton Foushee, cites Edwards, but further biographical information on him is lacking.
9. Reason, *Human Error,* 199–209.
10. Scott Shappell and Dennis Wiegmann, *The Human Factors Analysis and Classification System: HFACS,* Report DOT/FAA/AM-00/7 (Oklahoma City: FAA Civil Aeromedical Institute, February 2000).

11. *Naval Aviation HumanFactors Program,* www.public.navy.mil/navsaf cen/pages/aviation/aeromedical/human factorshfacs.aspx, last accessed 10 August 2015, describes the Defense Department HFACS guidance, developed in large measure by Shappell and Wiegmann, including nanocodes.

Chapter 12. Maintenance and Supply

1. This organization is markedly different from that of the U.S. Air Force, where maintenance is performed by personnel in an organization separate from the flying squadron's chain of command.
2. FASRONs were first established just after World War II. Prior to that some squadrons were supported by Carrier Aircraft Support Units (CASUs), but only later in the war when squadrons were large and moved frequently from ship to ship.
3. Since the end of World War II Navy bureaus have undergone various changes in name and some modification in function. Thus the former Bureau of Aeronautics is now the Naval Air Systems Command, and the former Bureau of Supplies and Accounts is now the Supply Systems Command.
4. A Cantonese word for gratuity—or in many contexts, by extension, bribe.
5. An accurate account of how many of those mishaps might have been attributed to maintenance error is almost impossible to parse out of the data, because mishap investigation in the 1950s was not as thorough as it later became.
6. It should be noted that this was before the widespread use of transistors and chips.
7. Maj. Richard A. Bauer, USMC, and Lt. Leo L. Hamilton, USN, "Naval Aircraft Maintenance Program," *Naval Aviation News* (February 1961): 27–29.
8. An eighty-column card on which data could be recorded and retrieved based on a system of punched holes—now almost obsolete.
9. See chapter 9 for short biography of Vice Admiral Pirie.
10. Leo Hamilton became in 1968 one of the first one hundred to be selected as Aviation Maintenance Duty Officers.
11. V. J. Lemmon and W. A. Schroeder, "The Right Thing for Naval Aviation," U.S. Naval Institute *Proceedings* (January 1973): 23–27.
12. This was largely due to the efforts of Capt. Howard Goben, who, supported by then Rear Adm. Jerry Miller, was instrumental in the establishment of the Aviation Maintenance and Management Office, OP-514, as part of the DCNO (Air) organization.
13. Vice Adm. Bernard M. Strean, "The Naval Aviation 3M Program: Success or Failure?," U.S. Naval Institute *Proceedings* (September 1970): 86–88.
14. OPNAV Instruction 4790.2 series, "Naval Aviation Maintenance Program."
15. "Maintenance Management," *Approach* (April 1971): 26–31.

16. Cdr. John Schmidt et al., *Assessing Naval Aviation Maintenance Safety: Error Reporting, Data Management and Trend Analysis* (MS thesis, Naval Postgraduate School, Monterey, Calif., 2001).
17. Human Factors–Maintenance Extension is based on the "Swiss-Cheese model" developed by James Reason and modified by S. A. Shappell and D. A. Wiegmann. See chapter 11.

Chapter 13. The Underappreciated

1. Rosario Rausa, ed., *Pistons to Jets* (Washington, D.C.: Government Printing Office, 1986). Volume 2 of this 75th Anniversary of Naval Aviation Commemorative Collection is an especially clear and comprehensive report on this period and the years that followed.
2. See chapter 2 on the imperatives for naval aviation to gain a nuclear-delivery capability and meet the rising challenges of the Soviet Union, quite aside from the perceived need to cope with the rising influence of the U.S. Air Force.
3. Rubel, "The Navy's Transition to Jets," 53.
4. John B. Rae, *Climb to Greatness: The American Aircraft Industry, 1920–1960* (Cambridge, Mass.: MIT Press, 1968), 189. The later F7U-3 incorporated in air groups in the mid-1950s was much more successful, albeit with a high mishap rate.
5. David Noland, "Panthers at Sea, "*Air & Space* (June/July 2013), is an excellent review of Panther operations.
6. Capt. Gerald G. O'Rourke, "Korean Knights," in *Into the Jet Age: Conflict and Change in Naval Aviation 1945–1975*, ed. E. T. Woolridge (Annapolis, Md.: Naval Institute Press, 1995), 183–207.
7. Rae, *Climb to Greatness*, 192.
8. Roger E. Bilstein, *The Enterprise of Flight: The American Aviation and Aerospace Industry* (Washington, D.C.: Smithsonian Institution Scholarly, 2001), 90–91.
9. Rae, *Climb to Greatness*, 205.
10. Ibid., 177: "The Navy had been interested in this design in 1941 and had to suspend during the war. Eventually, 900 of them were built in seven major versions."
11. The "Little Boy" nuclear device weighed ten thousand pounds.
12. The Regulus surface-to-surface missile, which needed airborne guidance, was deployed in the mid-1950s. Specialized Banshees provided that guidance.
13. The term "first generation" is somewhat ambiguous but includes the jet aircraft the Navy and Marines had with which to fight with when the Korean War began: F2H McDonnell Banshees, F9F Grumman Panthers, and Douglas F3D Skyknights.

14. Bilstein, *Enterprise of Flight*, 94.
15. Ibid., 76, 80, 94.
16. Ibid., 174.
17. Ibid., 175.
18. Lt. Cdr. R. A. Hess, "System Safety and the Decision Maker," *Approach* (June 1973): 10–15.
19. Vice Adm. M. F. Weisner, "A New Approach," *Approach* (December 1971): 1.

CHAPTER 14. MAKING BELIEVE

1. First epigraph is from Lt. Cdr. C. A. Wheal, RN, "Simulators in Flight Training: A Pilot's View," U.S. Naval Institute *Proceedings* (October 1976): 50–57.
2. See Alan B. Shepherd, with Alan Bartlett, *Training by Simulation* (Washington, D.C.: Smithsonian Institution, 1965), for an overview of astronaut simulator training.
3. The website *National Center for Simulation,* www.simulationinformation.com, is a comprehensive overview of modern applications of simulation, last accessed 21 August 2015.
4. Early Army Air Corps aviator who rose to the five-star level as the Commander, U.S. Army Air Forces in World War II.
5. Walter J. Boyne, *Beyond the Wild Blue* (New York: St. Martin's, 1997), 11.
6. Frederick J. Hoover, "The Wright Brothers Flight Control System," *Scientific American* (November 1978): 132–40.
7. Lloyd L. Kelly, as told to Robert B. Parke, *The Pilot Maker* (New York: Grosset & Dunlap, 1970), v.
8. J. M. Rolfe and K. J. Staples, eds., *Flight Simulation,* Cambridge Aerospace Series (New York: Cambridge University Press, 1986), chap. 2, is a succinct history of flight simulators.
9. Ibid., 17, describes the consensus of opinion that arose both in Europe and in the United States in the mid-1920s. It wasn't until the 1970s that a new consensus emerged, that orientation depends largely on vision.
10. Ibid., 19.
11. David J. Allerton, *Principles of Flight Simulation* (Hoboken, N.J.: John Wiley & Sons, 2009), is a most thorough discussion.
12. A commonly used term (Latin, "from the beginning") for students learning to fly in general aviation.
13. Rolfe and Staples, *Flight Simulation,* 29.
14. *Naval Air Warfare Center Training Systems Division,* www.navair.navy.mil/nawctsd/, last accessed 7 August 2015.
15. Luis de Florez is mentioned in glowing terms for his contributions in the oral histories of such World War II leaders as Arleigh Burke, Harry Donald Felt,

Lloyd Mustin, Noel Gayler, Henry Miller, Joy Bryce Hancock, and John J. Ballentine.
16. "Synthetic Aircraft," an address delivered by Luis de Florez at a 26 January 1949 luncheon session of the Institute of the Aeronautical Sciences, a forerunner of the American Institute of Aeronautics and Astronautics (AIAA), later published in *Aeronautical Engineering Review* (April 1949).
17. Allerton, *Principles of Flight Simulation*, 3.
18. The Link operators could cause instrument, radio, and navigation facility failures, but there was no way to insert engine, system or flight-control faults as with other simulators.
19. *Note deleted.*
20. Rolfe and Staples, *Flight Simulation*, 35.
21. In some flight environments one might substitute "Proficiency" for "Readiness," but in Navy and Marine combat squadrons "readiness" to perform satisfactorily all mission requirements is the sine qua non.
22. John F. Schank et al., *Finding the Right Balance: Simulator and Live Training for Navy Units* (Santa Monica, Calif.: RAND, 2002), 55, 67: "Our research shows that simulations are used most frequently for events that involve the analysis of input data, such as occurs in ASW training. They are used least often for events that attempt to replicate situational or environmental conditions, such as occurs in strike warfare training."
23. Lt. Cdr. J. R. McDaniel, "NCLT, a Complete Approach," *Approach* (February 1972): 16–22.
24. Robert S. Roof, *Naval Aviation's Use of Simulators in the Operational Training Environment: A Cost Analysis Perspective* (thesis, Naval Postgraduate School, Monterey, Calif., 1996), available at https://calhoun.nps.edu/10945/32118.
25. Alan J. Marcus and Cdr. Lawrence E. Curran, USN, *The Use of Flight Simulators in Measuring and Improving Training Effectiveness*, CRM 86-27 (Arlington, Va.: Center for Naval Analyses, February 1986).
26. O. Kirn Malmin and Lyle A. Reibling, *The Contribution of Aircraft Simulators to the Training and Readiness of Operational Navy Aircraft Squadrons*, CRM 95-143 (Arlington, Va.: Center for Naval Analyses, September 1995).
27. Patrick and Seuss, *Flying Hours, Simulators and Safety.*
28. The airlines have a great safety record, as attested in figure 3-2 of chapter 3, largely owing to the confidence pilots have in simulator fidelity and FAA standards for simulator certification.
29. Patrick and Seuss, *Flying Hours, Simulators and Safety.*
30. Ibid. See also FAA Standards for Simulator Certification.
31. Rubel, "The Navy's Transition to Jets," 51–59.

CHAPTER 15. ON TO THE TWENTY-FIRST CENTURY

1. Vice Adm. John P. Currier, U.S. Coast Guard, "Risk Management for the Proficient Operator," U.S. Naval Institute *Proceedings* (August 2013): 18–21. In earlier days the term CRM meant "Cockpit Resource Management." "Crew" is now universal.
2. Douglas Wiegmann and Scott A. Shappell, "Human Error and Crew Resource Management Failures in Naval Aviation Mishaps: A Review of U.S. Naval Safety Center Data, 1990–96," *Aviation, Space and Environmental Medicine* 70, no. 12 (December 1999): 1147–51.
3. Kanki, Helmreich, and Anca, *Crew Resource Management*, 5–6.
4. Robert C. Ginnett, "Crews as Groups," in ibid.
5. Marissa L. Suffler, Eduardo Salas, and Luiz F. Xavier, "Why Is Evaluation of CRM Training Necessary?," in Kanki, Helmreich, and Anca, *Crew Resource Management*, para. 7.2.
6. OPNAV Instruction 1542.7 series, "Crew Resource Management Program."
7. This section on ORM is based in large part on an ORM training curriculum prepared and used by Capt. James "Skip" Lind, USN (Ret.), in educating naval aviation aircrews on the principles and nuances of ORM under the sponsorship of Commander, Naval Air Forces.
8. Currier, "Risk Management for the Proficient Operator," 18.
9. CNAF replaced ACNO (Air Warfare) as the Navy's "head aviator" while the issue was working.
10. In June 1997, the CNO, Admiral Johnson, stated, "ORM applies across the entire spectrum of naval activities, from joint operations and fleet exercises to our daily routine. We must encourage top down interest in the ORM process, from the flag level all the way to the deckplates."

CHAPTER 16. SUCCESS

1. Counted are the Korean War, the Vietnam War, two Persian Gulf wars, and Iraq.
2. Grenada and Kosovo are examples.
3. Principal among these were the Cuban Missile Crisis, the Jordanian crisis of 1969, and the Yom Kippur War of 1973.

Glossary

3M: Shorthand for Naval Aircraft Maintenance and Material Program
Ab initio: From the Latin for "from the beginning"
ACLS: Automated Carrier Landing System
ADF: Automatic Direction Finder
AFB: Air Force Base
AIMD: Aircraft Intermediate Maintenance Department
AirLant: Commander, Naval Air Forces, Atlantic Fleet
Air group: an organization of squadrons of varying types of aircraft assigned to one station or carrier. Now an Air wing
AirPac: Commander, Naval Air Forces, Pacific Fleet
Air wing: an organization of squadrons of varying types of aircraft assigned to one station or carrier. Formerly air group
AMSO: Aeromedical Safety Officer
AQT: Aviation Qualification Test
ARF: Avionics Repair Facility
ASW: antisubmarine warfare
Banshee: popular name for the F2H fighter aircraft, built by McDonnell Aircraft.
BASH: bird and animal strike hazards
Bolter: an attempted carrier landing that fails to engage an arresting cable, at which time the pilot applies full power and takes off, or bolts, then reenters the landing pattern
BuAer: Bureau of Aeronautics (earlier termed BuAero)
BuSandA: Bureau of Supply and Accounts
CAA: Civil Aeronautics Authority. The predecessor agency to the FAA was disestablished on 1 November 1958
CCA: carrier-controlled approach
Chocks: wooden wedges applied to each tire of a parked aircraft to keep it from moving
CNA: Center for Naval Analyses
CNAF: Commander, Naval Air Forces
CNO: Chief of Naval Operations
CRM: Crew Resource Management
Cruise book: a book of memories and photographs that tells the story of a ship and its crew, usually over the period of one cruise or one deployment
Cumshaw: a term derived from the Chinese meaning, loosely, something for which one could trade another item of equal value or importance or for a vague promise that it would be "paid for" for later
CV: aircraft carrier

CVA: attack aircraft carrier

CVAN: attack aircraft carrier (nuclear)

CVB: heavy ("battle") aircraft carrier. Applied to *Midway* class; the term is no longer used

CVN: nuclear-powered aircraft carrier

CVS: antisubmarine aircraft carrier

DCNO: Deputy Chief of Naval Operations

DME: distance-measuring equipment

Downwind: a course reciprocal to the heading of the wind

Dustpan lights: low, shielded lights mounted on either side of the carrier flight-deck landing area providing a modicum of illumination. Called "dustpans" because the shields are similar to inverted dustpans

FAA: Federal Aviation Administration. First formed as the independent Federal Aviation Agency, but on 1 April 1967 it was redesignated as the Federal Aviation Administration and made a part of the Department of Transportation.

FAGU: Fleet Air Gunnery Unit

FAR: Flight Aptitude Rating. Sometimes used, inaccurately, to mean "Federal Air Regulations"

FASRON: Fleet Air Support Squadron

FCLP: field carrier landing practice

Flatley Report: a sixty-four-page letter to the CNO with nine separate conclusions and a recommendation that all aspects of the Naval Aviation Safety Program be reviewed by a board headed by a flag officer

Flat pattern: a carrier landing pattern in which the aircraft starts its approach abeam the ship at 150 feet then makes a descending 180 degree turn to the ship's heading to arrive at the "Cut" position thirty-five to forty feet above the flight deck, where the LSO takes control. This is as opposed to the higher pattern used in a mirror, or lens, approach.

Flight Safety Foundation: an international non-profit organization founded in 1947 to provide impartial, independent, expert safety guidance and resources for the aviation and aerospace industries

FLOLS: Fresnel Lens Optical Landing System

Fresnel lens: large-aperture, short-focal-length light used to indicate glide path for landing aircraft, especially on board aircraft carriers. Often called a "mirror," referring to earlier applications.

FRS: Fleet Replacement Squadron (used interchangeably with RAG)

FUR: Failure or Unsatisfactory Report

GCA: ground-controlled approach

Group I: physically qualified naval aviators less than forty-two years old

HERAP: Human Error Research and Analysis Program

HFACS: Human Factors Analysis and Classification System, promulgated by the DOD

Hydroaeroplane: early term for seaplane
IBTU: Instructors Basic Training Unit
IFLOLS: Improved Fresnel Lens Optical Landing System
JBD: jet-blast deflectors
JTTU: Jet Transition Training Unit
Link Trainer: now a generic term for many simulators but at first the simulator developed by Edwin Link
Low-frequency range: a nationwide navigation system based on low-frequency radio transmitters
LSO: Landing Signal Officer; an officer stationed at the stern of a ship or the landing end of a runway to monitor and advise, if necessary, the landing pilot. The LSO is positioned such that the pilot of a landing aircraft can see his/her signals, if any
MCAS: Marine Corps Air Station
Mirror: See Fresnel lens
Mishap: term preferred and used by all DOD in lieu of "accident"
NACA: National Advisory Committee on Aeronautics. Established in 1915, largely through the urging of then-Captain William Moffett, the longtime chief of the Navy Bureau of Aeronautics. The NACA was absorbed into NASA in 1958.
NAILC: Naval Air Integrated Logistics Support Center
NALCOMIS: Naval Aviation Logistics Information System
NAMP: Naval Air Maintenance Plan
NAS: Naval Air Station
NASA: National Aeronautics and Space Administration
NATOPS: Naval Air Training and Operating Procedures Standardization
NavAir: Naval Air Systems Command
NavAirNews: a colloquialism for *Naval Aviation News*
Naval aviation: the collective aviation elements of Navy, Marines, and Coast Guard, including fixed-wing, prop, jet, tilt-wing, and rotary-wing aircraft, whether they fly from ships, land, or the sea surface. The term includes officers and enlisted personnel and supporting government civilians
NavSup: Naval Supply Systems Command
NavWeps: Bureau of Naval Weapons
"Navy Hymn": hymn written by William Whiting in 1860, often played and sung at Navy and Marine church services and at funerals
NCLT: Night Carrier Landing Trainer
NDB: nondirectional beacon
Needle/Ball: See Turn and Bank indicator
NTSB: National Transportation Safety Board
OFT: Operational Flight Trainer

OP-05: office code for the Deputy Chief of Naval Operations (Air Warfare)
OPNAV: Office of the Chief of Naval Operations
ORM: Operational Risk Management
Paddles: colloquial term for either the handheld flags used by the LSO to signal the approaching aircraft or the LSO him/herself
PAR: Progressive Aircraft Rework
Part 121: shorthand for Title 14, Code of Federal Regulations, Part 121
PBL: performance-based logistics
Pitot-static: system found in almost all aircraft to sense airspeed, vertical speed, and altitude. It generally consists of a pitot tube mounted on the leading edge of the wing or fuselage away from turbulent airflow and a static port elsewhere on the aircraft. Named for Henri Pitot, an eighteenth-century French hydraulic engineer
PLAT: Pilot's Landing Aid Television
RAG: Replacement Air Group, often used as a substitute for FRS
SCB: Ships Characteristics Board–authorized changes, which in this book encompass several different major modifications to or conversions of seventeen World War II–era aircraft carriers and the three *Midway*s
SSC: Supply Support Center
Sea-based: referring to aircraft carriers and those other ships that operate aircraft of any type, as well as seaplanes
Self-cleared penetration: a descent through instrument flight conditions without clearance from a controlling authority, a totally illegal and inadvisable procedure whereby, for example, an aircraft caught on top of an overcast chooses an area where the pilot assumes there is no traffic in the clouds and descends to clear weather underneath
SHEL Model: human-factors model of Software, Hardware, Environment and Liveware (humans)
Stable element: a system of gyroscopes in the ship that generate electrical signals to radars, gun directors, and optical landing systems to compensate for ship's pitch, heave, and roll
Swiss-Cheese Model: A model likened to lining up holes in slices of Swiss cheese used to visualize a chain of failures leading to a mishap, an incident, or a procedural anomaly. See chapter 11
Systems safety: A risk-management strategy based on identification and analysis of hazards and application of design and remedial controls using a systems-based approach
TACAN: Tactical Air Navigation system; used for navigation in commercial airways and for location and approach to own ship
Tail chase: a single-file formation of aircraft; used in training
Truck lights: two steady, small, red lights atop a ship's mainmast

Turn and Bank (sometimes Turn and Slip) indicator: a flight attitude instrument consisting of either an air-driven or electric-driven gyroscope that indicates turn (a bank) from horizontal (level) flight, and also a curved level containing a ball damped by a fluid that will indicate whether flight is balanced or unbalanced

VHF: very high frequency

VOR: very-high-frequency omnidirectional radio

Vultures' Row: An open area on the after part of an aircraft carrier's island structure used for watching aircraft recoveries

Wheelbook: A small notebook, usually with a green cover, that fits in the maintenance chief's hip pocket. Everything worth knowing about the status and maintenance of squadron aircraft was recorded by the chief in this booklet.

WST: weapon-system trainer; a six-degree-of-motion simulator

YE/YG: An orientation and homing device that broadcasted a different Morse code letter in each thirty-degree sector around the ship. The sector letters were changed daily, sometimes more often

Bibliography

BOOKS

Alkov, Robert A. *Aviation Safety: The Human Factor.* Casper, Wyo.: Endeavor Books, 1989.
Allerton, D. J. *Principles of Flight Simulation.* John Wiley & Sons, 2009.
Anderson, John D., Jr. *Fundamentals of Aerodynamics.* New York: McGraw-Hill, 2011.
———. *A History of Aerodynamics: And Its Impact on Flying Machines.* New York: Cambridge University Press, 1997.
Bilstein, Roger E. *The Enterprise of Flight: The American Aviation and Aerospace Industry.* Washington, D.C.: Smithsonian Institution Scholarly, 2001.
Bolster, Calvin Mathews. *Assisted Take-Off of Aircraft.* Northfield, Vt.: Norwich University Press, 1950.
Boyne, Walter J. *Beyond the Wild Blue.* New York: St. Martin's, 1997.
Brown, Charles H. *Dark Sky, Black Sea: Aircraft Carrier Night and All-Weather Operations.* Annapolis, Md.: Naval Institute Press, 1999.
Brown, David F. *Tomcat Alley: A Photographic Roll Call of the Grumman F-14 Tomcat.* Atglen, Pa.: Schiffer Military History, 1998.
Brown, Eric Melrose. *Wings of the Weird and Wonderful.* Shrewsbury, U.K.: Airlife, 1983.
———. *Wings on My Sleeve.* Shrewsbury, U.K.: Airlife, 1961.
Cagle, Malcom W. *Naval Aviator's Guide: A Handbook for Navy Pilots.* Annapolis, Md.: Naval Institute Press, 1963.
Cobham 75: 1934–2009. Dorset, U.K.: Dovecote, 2009.
Cooper, Geoffrey G. J. *Farnborough and the Fleet Air Arm: A History of the Naval Aircraft Royal Aircraft Establishment.* Farnborough, U.K.: Midland, 1981.
Davis, Jeffrey R., Robert Johnson, Jan Stepanek, and Jennifer A. Fogarty, eds. *Fundamentals of Aerospace Medicine.* 3rd ed. Philadelphia: Lippincott, Williams and Wilkins, 2002.
Davis, Vincent. *The Admirals Lobby.* Chapel Hill: University of North Carolina Press, 1967.
Diehl, Alan E. *Silent Knights: Blowing the Whistle on Military Accidents and Their Cover-Ups.* Washington, D.C.: Potomac Books, 2003.
Edwards, David C. *Pilot Mental and Physical Performance.* Ames: Iowa State University Press, 1990.
Engen, Donald Davenport. *Wings and Warriors: My Life as a Naval Aviator.* Washington, D.C.: Smithsonian Institution, 1997.

Ewing, Steve. *Reaper Leader: The Life of Jimmy Flatley*. Annapolis, Md.: Naval Institute Press, 2002.
Faltum, Andrew. *The Essex Aircraft Carriers*. Baltimore, Md.: Nautical and Aviation, 1996.
Fishbein, Samuel B. *Flight Management Systems: The Evolution of Avionics and Navigation Technology*. Washington, D.C.: Smithsonian and Praeger, 1995.
Friedman, Norman. *British Carrier Aviation*. Annapolis, Md.: Naval Institute Press, 1988.
Friedman, Norman, and Arthur D. Baker III. *U.S. Aircraft Carriers: An Illustrated Design History*. Annapolis, Md.: Naval Institute Press, 1983.
Fulton, John F. *Aviation Medicine in Its Preventive Aspects: An Historical Survey*. London: Oxford University Press, 1948.
Hayward, John T., and C. W. Borklund. *Bluejacket Admiral: The Navy Career of Chick Hayward*. Annapolis, Md.: Naval Institute Press, 2000.
Heinemann, Edward H., and Rosario Rausa. *Ed Heinemann, Combat Aircraft Designer*. Annapolis, Md.: Naval Institute Press, 1980.
Holloway, James L., III. *Aircraft Carriers at War: A Personal Retrospective of Korea, Vietnam, and the Soviet Confrontation*. Annapolis, Md.: Naval Institute Press, 2007.
Hurst, Ronald. *Pilot Error: A Professional Study of Contributory Factors*. London: Crosby, Lockwood, Staples, 1976.
Kanki, Barbara G., Robert L. Helmreich, and Jose Anca, eds. *Crew Resource Management*. San Diego, Calif.: Academic, 2010.
Kelly, Lloyd L., as told to Robert B. Parke. *The Pilot Maker*. New York: Grosset & Dunlap, 1970.
Knott, Richard C., ed. *The Naval Aviation Guide*. Annapolis, Md.: Naval Institute Press, 1985.
Lawson, Robert L. *History of U.S. Naval Air Power*. London: Aerospace, 1985.
Love, Robert W., Jr. *History of the U.S. Navy*. Vol. 2, *1942–1991*. Harrisburg, Pa.: Stackpole Books, 1992.
Miller, Jerry. *Nuclear Weapons and Aircraft Carriers: How the Bomb Saved Naval Aviation*. Washington, D.C.: Smithsonian Institution, 2001.
Morgan, Mark, and Rick Morgan. *Intruder: The Operational History of Grumman's A-6*. Atglen, Pa.: Schiffer Military History, 2004.
Morrison, Tom. *Quest for All-Weather Flight*. Ramsbury, U.K.: Crowood, 2003.
Nelson, Derek, and Dave Parsons. *Danger: Life and Death Stories from the U.S. Navy's Approach Magazine*. Osceola, Wis.: Motorbooks International, 1991.
O'Rourke, Capt. Gerald G. "Korean Knights." In *Into the Jet Age: Conflict and Change in Naval Aviation 1945–1975*. Edited by E. T. Woolridge. Annapolis, Md.: Naval Institute Press, 1995.

———. "We Get Ours at Night." In *Into the Jet Age: Conflict and Change in Naval Aviation 1945-1975*. Edited by E. T. Woolridge. Annapolis, Md.: Naval Institute Press, 1995.

O'Rourke, Capt. G. G., with E. T. Woolridge. *Night Fighters over Korea*. Annapolis, Md.: Naval Institute Press, 1998.

Peattie, Mark. *Sunburst: The Rise of Japanese Naval Air Power, 1909-1941*. Annapolis, Md.: Naval Institute Press, 2001.

Polmar, Norman. *Aircraft Carriers: A History of Carrier Aviation and Its Influence on World Events*. Vol. 2, *1946-2006*. Washington, D.C.: Potomac Books, 2008.

Rae, John B. *Climb to Greatness: The American Aircraft Industry, 1920-1960*. Cambridge, Mass.: MIT Press, 1968.

Rausa, Rosario. *Skyraider: The Douglas A-1 Flying Dump Truck*. Baltimore, Md.: Nautical and Aviation, 1982.

Raven, Alan. *Essex Aircraft Carriers*. Annapolis, Md.: Naval Institute Press, 1998.

Reason, James. *Human Error*. Cambridge, U.K.: Cambridge University Press, 1990.

Reynolds, Clark G. *Admiral John H. Towers: The Struggle for Naval Air Supremacy*. Annapolis, Md.: Naval Institute Press, 1991.

Rolfe, J. M., and K. J. Staples, eds. *Flight Simulation*. Cambridge Aerospace Series. New York: Cambridge University Press, 1986.

Roscoe, Stanley N., Alexander C. Williams Jr., et al. *Aviation Psychology*. Ames: Iowa State University Press, 1980.

Schank, John F., Harry J. Thie, Clifford M. Graff II, Joseph Beel, and Jerry M. Sollinger. *Finding the Right Balance: Simulator and Live Training for Navy Units*. Santa Monica, Calif.: RAND, 2002.

Shepherd, Alan B. with Alan Bartlett. *Training by Simulation*. Washington, D.C.:Smithsonian Institution, 1965.

Smith, Maxwell. *Aviation Fuels*. Henley-on-Thames, U.K.: G. T. Foulis, 1970.

Smith, Richard K. *Seventy-Five Years of Inflight Refueling: Highlights, 1923-1998*. Ann Arbor: University of Michigan Press, 1998.

Swanborough, Gordon, and Peter M. Bowers. *United States Navy Aircraft since 1911*. Annapolis, Md.: Naval Institute Press, 1976.

Terzibaschitsch, Stefan. *Aircraft Carriers of the U.S. Navy*. London: Conway Maritime, 1980.

Thomasson, Tommy H. *Strike from the Sea: U.S. Navy Attack Aircraft from Skyraider to Super Hornet 1948-Present*. North Branch, Minn.: Specialty, 2009.

———. *U.S. Naval Air Superiority: Development of Shipborne Jet Fighters 1943-1962*. North Branch, Minn.: Specialty, 2007.

Trimble, William F. *Wings for the Navy: A History of the Naval Aircraft Factory, 1917–1956.* Annapolis, Md.: Naval Institute Press, 1990.
Trumbull, Archibald D., and Clifford L. Lord. *History of United States Naval Aviation.* New Haven, Conn.: Yale University Press, 1949.
Van Waarde, Jan. *US Military Aircraft Mishaps 1950–2004.* Amsterdam, Neth.: Scramble, 2004.
Weiner, Earl L., and David C. Nagel, eds. *Human Factors in Aviation.* San Diego: Academic, 1988.
Woolridge, E. T., ed. *Into the Jet Age: Conflict and Change in Naval Aviation 1945–1975.* Annapolis, Md.: Naval Institute Press, 1995.

Periodicals

Aero Safety World. [Flight Safety Foundation periodical]
Aerospace Medical Association Journal [Aerospace Medical Association, Alexandria, Va.; entire index and files on CD].
Aviation Week and Space Technology, 24 July 1950, 15.
Brown, Capt. Eric, RN. "Dawn of the Carrier Jet." *Air International* (January 1985): 31–36.
Buell, Cdr. Hal, USN (Ret.). "The Angled Deck Concept, Savior of the Tailhook Navy." *Hook* (Fall 1987).
"Crash Course." *USA Aviation Digest* (September 1963): 18–20. [Reprint of *USC Alumni Review,* November 1962]
Currier, Vice Adm. John P., USCG. "Risk Management for the Proficient Operator." U.S. Naval Institute *Proceedings* (August 2013): 18–21.
de Flores, Luis. "Synthetic Aircraft." *Aeronautical Engineering Review* (April 1949): 26–29.
Dose, Capt. Robert G., USN (Ret.). "The First Mirror Landing." *Hook* (Fall 1987): 27.
———. "The Replacement Air Group Concept." U.S. Naval Institute *Proceedings* (April 1960): 135–38.
Dunn, Robert F. "In-Flight Refueling." *Hook* (Fall 2010): 31–34.
———. "The Angle of Attack Indicator." *Approach* (January-February 2011): 9-10.
Gaskill, Rear Adm. Richard T. "Plane in the Water!" *Foundation* (Fall 2009): 20–29.
Hewes, Col. William T., USMC (Ret.). "The High Dive." *Hook* (Spring 2010): 96.
Hoover, Frederick J. "The Wright Brothers Flight Control System." *Scientific American* (November 1978): 132–40.
Lemmon, V. J., and W. A. Schroeder. "The Right Thing for Naval Aviation." U.S. Naval Institute *Proceedings* (January 1973): 23–27.
Morgan, Mark, and Rick Morgan. "Intruder: The Operational History of Grumman's A6." *Schiffer Military History* (2004).

———. "New Standards for Naval Air." *Approach* (August 1961): 6.
———. "The One Best Way," *Naval Aviation News* (August 1961): 6-7.
"A One-Stop Safety Shop for Sailors and Marines." *Hook* (Winter 2008): 33–38.
O'Rourke, Capt. Jerry. "Night Hookers, Part III." *Hook* (Fall 1988): 53.
Roemer, Capt. Charles E. "The Flatley Report: Which Saved Naval Aviation." *Foundation* (Spring 1985): 56–61.
Stobie, Cdr. Edwin F. "All Weather Landing System." U.S. Naval Institute *Proceedings* (July 1965): 156–59.
Strean, Vice Adm. Bernard M. "The Naval Aviation 3M Program: Success or Failure?" U.S. Naval Institute *Proceedings* (September 1970): 86–88.
Tissot, Rear Adm. E. E., USN (Ret.). "Prop Pilot Mentality." *Wings of Gold* (Fall 2012): 69.
Wheal, Lt. Cdr. C. A., RN. "Simulators in Flight Training: A Pilot's View." U.S. Naval Institute *Proceedings* (October 1976): 50–57.
Wiegmann, Douglas, and Scott A. Shappell. "Human Error and Crew Resource Management Failures in Naval Aviation Mishaps: A Review of U.S. Naval Safety Center Data, 1990–96." *Aviation, Space and Environmental Medicine* 70, no. 12 (December 1999): 1147–51.
———. "U.S. Naval Aviation Mishaps, 1972–1992: Differences between Single and Dual-Piloted Aircraft." *Air International* (January 1996).

GOVERNMENT PUBLICATIONS

"Aero Medical Men Study Flight Equipment." *Naval Aviation News*, 31 April 1955, 30–31.
"... And Then There Were None...." *Approach* (November 1955): 6–8.
Anonymous Air Force Exchange Pilot. "An Air Force Pilot Talks about Navy Operations." *Approach* (April 1977): 1–8.
"'Anymouse's' Anniversary." *Approach* (November–December 2005): 4–5.
"The AOA Indicator: Small Device, Huge Impact." *Approach* (January–February 2011): 9–10.
Approach (July 1955) [the first issue with sections covering flight operations, aeromedical issues, and maintenance].
Ault, Frank. "Safety and Command Responsibility." *Approach* (October 1961): 5–8.
Aviation Casualties from 1913–1931. Washington, D.C.: Navy Department, 1931.
Barlow, Jeffery G. *Revolt of the Admirals: The Fight for Naval Aviation, 1945–1950*. Washington, D.C.: Naval Historical Center, 1994.
Bauer, Maj. Richard A., USMC, and Lt. Leo L. Hamilton, USN. "Naval Aircraft Maintenance Program." *Naval Aviation News* (February 1961): 27–29.
"A Better Way to Do It." *Naval Aviation News* (July 1956): 7–11.

Bradford, Dave (comp.). "Mad about Safety: 70 Years of Grampaw Pettibone." *Naval Aviation News* (Winter 2013): 10–15.

Burch, Rear Adm. William O., and Capt. Gale E. Krouse. "Reporting Facts for the Naval Aviation Safety Program." *Judge Advocate Journal* (September 1959): 3.

Burlage, JOC John D. "From 'Pilot-Maker' to Multimillionaire."

———. "Some Call Him the 'Father of Training Devices.'" *Naval Aviation News* (September 1968): 7–11.

"Crash Program." *Approach* (August 1959): 16–19.

"Crusader College Carries On." *Naval Aviation News* (June 1958): 22–23.

Dalitsch, Cdr. Walter, MC, USN. "Blind Flying: What We Didn't Know Didn't Kill Us . . . Most of the Time." *Approach* (January–February 2011): 6–8.

Easler, Capt. Brett, and Cdr. Bruce Herman, "On Glide Path, on Course." *Naval Aviation News* (Summer 2014): 16–19.

Evans, Mark L., and Roy A. Grossnick. *United States Naval Aviation*. Vol. I and II, *1910—2010*. Washington, D.C.: Naval History and Heritage Command, 2015. Available at www.history.navy.mil/research/publications/recent-publications/1910.html.

Federal Tort Claims Act, 28 U.S. Code, 1346(b), 1988, pp. 2671–80, and predecessor legislation.

Fischl, Myron A., and Mark G. Pfeiffer. *Improvement of Flight Handbooks*, NAVTRADEVCEN Technical Report 748-1. Philadelphia: Courtney, 1961.

Furer, Julius Augustus. *Administration of the Navy Department in World War II*. Washington, D.C.: Navy Department, 1959.

Hess, Lt. Cdr. R. A. "System Safety and the Decision Maker." *Approach* (June 1973): 10–15.

Hone, Thomas C. *Power and Change: The Administrative History of the Office of the Chief of Naval Operations, 1946-1986*. Washington, D.C.: Naval Historical Center, 1989.

Hone, Thomas C., Norman Friedman, and Mark D. Mandeles. *Innovation in Carrier Aviation*. Newport Paper 37. Newport, R.I.: Naval War College Press, 2011.

Hurt, H. H., Jr. "Aerodynamics for Naval Aviators." *NAVWEPS*, 00-80T-80 (1960).

"Interview with Vice Adm. James B. Stockdale." *Approach* (April/May 1990): 31–33.

Krouse, Capt. Gale E. "Naval Supplement Investigation vs. The Aircraft Accident Report." *Judge Advocate Journal* (September 1959): 5. [Captain Krouse was the Judge Advocate General's director of the Investigations Division.]

"Maintenance Management." *Approach* (April 1971): 26–31.

McDaniel, Lt. Cdr. J. R. "NCLT, a Complete Approach." *Approach* (February 1972): 16–22.

"Mirror Landing System." *Approach* (April 1957): 6–19.

Mitchell, Robert E. *Aviation Medicine Research: A Historical Review.* NAMRL Special Report 92-3. 18 November 1992. Available at http://www.dtic.mil/get-tr-doc/pdf?AD=ADA258198.

"The 'New Approach' Continues." *Approach* (September 1972): 8–10.

Noland, David. "Panthers at Sea." *Air & Space* (June/July 2013).

Rausa, Rosario, ed. *Pistons to Jets.* Vol. 2. Washington, D.C.: Government Printing Office, 1986.

——. "Top Drawer." *Naval Aviation News* (June 1974): 8–12.

Rubel, Robert C. "The Navy's Transition to Jets." *Naval War College Review* (Spring 2010): 49–59.

Selmer, Capt. R. J. USN. "A Stan Man Speaks." *Approach* (October 1962): 1–4.

Shappell, Scott, and Dennis Wiegmann. *The Human Factors Analysis and Classification System: HFACS.* Report DOT/FAA/AM-00/7. Oklahoma City: FAA Civil Aeromedical Institute, February 2000.

"Supersonic Checkout." *Naval Aviation News* (April 1955): 1–5.

Tate, Rear Adm. J. R. "Moonlighters." *Naval Aviation News* (March 1972): 35–36.

U.S. Naval Aerospace Physiologist's Manual (NAVAIR 00–80T-99). Washington, D.C.: 1972.

U.S. Naval Flight Surgeon's Manual. Washington, D.C.: Bureau of Naval Medicine, 1969.

Van Wyn, Adrian O. "The 1956 Naval Aviation Review." *Naval Aviation News* (January 1957): 3, 5, 6, 8.

——. "The 1957 Naval Aviation Review." *Naval Aviation News* (January 1958): 2–7.

VNR-153 Accident Report 2-53, Naval Aviation Safety Activity letter NASA/P22/JHF/vc, serial 010, 3 September 1953, "Naval Aviation Accident Prevention Program, Discussion Of,"often known as "The Flatley Report."

Weisner, Vice Adm. M. F. "A New Approach." *Approach* (December 1971): 1.

West, Vita R., Martin G. Every, and James F. Parker Jr. *U.S. Naval Aerospace Physiologists' Manual,* NAVAIR 00-80T-99. Washington, D.C., 1972.

Wilkinson, Paul H. *Aircraft Engines of the World: 1950–1970.* Washington, D.C.: Navy Department, 1970.

Technical Reports

Malmin, O. Kirn, and Lyle A. Reibling. *The Contribution of Aircraft Simulators to the Training and Readiness of Operational Navy Aircraft Squadrons.* CRM 95-143. Arlington, Va.: Center for Naval Analyses, September 1995.

Marcus, Alan J., and Cdr. Lawrence E. Curran, USN. *The Use of Flight Simulators in Measuring and Improving Training Effectiveness.* CRM 86-27. Arlington, Va.: Center for Naval Analyses, February 1986.
Patrick, Pat, and Gregory N. Seuss. *Flying Hours, Simulators and Safety: A Look at Flight Safety Trends.* Report CIM 68.10. Arlington, Va.: Center for Naval Analyses, December 1999.
Wiegmann, Douglas, and Scott A. Shappell. *The Human Factors Analysis and Classification System: HFACS.* Oklahoma City, Okla.: FAA Civil Aeromedical Institute, 2000.

OFFICIAL DOD CORRESPONDENCE

Capt. James H. Flatley, Commander Naval Aviation Safety Activity letter to ComNavAirLant, 17 August 1953. Naval History and Heritage Command, Aviation Archives.
NAS Whiting Field Accident Report 2-53, R4Q 17 July 1953.
Naval Aviation Safety Center, Chronology of Highlights, Calendar Year 1960.
Naval Aviation Safety Center, Command Histories, 1966, 1967, 1968, 1975, and 1976.
Naval Aviation Safety Center, *U.S. Navy Safety Program,* Report RA 1-58 (Norfolk, Va., 2 February 1958), VI-6.
Navy Instructions. [These are periodically updated and current issues can be found at http://doni.daps.dla.mil/default.aspx. All remain pertinent to the basic text of this book, however.]
    OPNAV Instruction 1542.7 series, "Crew Resource Management Program."
    OPNAV Instruction 3500.39 series, "Operational Risk Management."
    OPNAV Instruction 3710.7 series, "NATOPS General Flight Instructions."
    OPNAV Instruction 3750.6 series, "Naval Aviation Safety Management Program."
    OPNAV Instruction 4790.2 series, "Naval Aviation Maintenance Program."
    OPNAV Instruction 5102.1 series, "Safety Investigation."
U.S. Naval Aviation Safety Activity Report, ser. 010, "The Flatley Report," 3 September 1953.
U.S. Naval Aviation Safety Activity Report, RA-1-57, "U.S. Navy Aviation Safety Program," 20 November 1956.
U.S. Naval Aviation Safety Activity Report, RA-1-58, "U.S. Navy Aviation Safety Program," 5 February 1958.
U.S. Naval Aviation Safety Activity Report 6061, "Readiness through Safety," August 1960.
VMR-153 Accident Report 2-53. Naval Aviation Safety Activity letter NASA/P22/JHF/vc, ser. 010, 3 September 1953, "Naval Aviation Accident Prevention Program, Discussion Of."

Personal Letters, Papers, and Addresses

Austin, Capt. Frank H., MC, USN. "Operational Aspects of Aviation Medicine." (Paper presented at the MIT Aerospace and Undersea Medicine Program Summer Session, 1969).

Ballentine, Vice Adm. John Jennings, personal letter to Rear Adm. Rico Botta, Naval Air Material Center, 30 June 1952. Box 13, J. J. Ballentine papers, Library of Congress Manuscript Division.

———, personal letter to Rear Adm. E. A. Cruise, March 11, 1954. Box 13, J. J. Ballentine papers, Library of Congress Manuscript Division.

———, ComNavAirLant training officer memorandum to Vice Adm. Ballentine, undated, box 13, J.J. Ballentine papers, Library of Congress Manuscript Division

Bohn, Roger H. Personal email to the author, March 2012.

de Florez, Rear Adm. Luis. "Synthetic Aircraft." (Address delivered at a 26 January 1949 luncheon session of the Institute of the Aeronautical Sciences, a forerunner of the American Institute of Aeronautics and Astronautics [AIAA]; later published in *Aeronautical Engineering Review,* April 1949.)

Mitchell, Robert E. Oral History, Naval Aviation Museum Foundation, 1990.

Moebus, Rear Adm. L. A., to Vice Adm. J. J. Ballentine and others, 17 July 1952. Box 13, J. J. Ballentine papers, Library of Congress Manuscript Division.

Outlaw, Rear Adm. Edward C. USN. "Design Safety and Material Reliability." (Remarks delivered before the International Air Safety Seminar in Athens, Greece, November 1963.)

Theses and Dissertations

Jones, Douglas W. *An Evaluation of the Effectiveness of U.S. Naval Aviation Crew Resource Management Training Programs: A Reassessment for the Twenty-First Century Operating Environment.* Thesis, Naval Postgraduate School, Monterey, Calif., 2009.

Roof, Robert S. *Naval Aviation's Use of Simulators in the Operational Training Environment: A Cost Analysis Perspective.* Thesis, Naval Postgraduate School, Monterey, Calif., 1996. Available at https://calhoun.nps.edu/10945/32118.

Schmidt, Cdr. John, et al. *Assessing Naval Aviation Maintenance Safety: Error Reporting, Data Management and Trend Analysis.* Thesis, Naval Postgraduate School, Monterey, Calif., 2001.

Web References

Air Force Safety Center History. www.af.mil/AboutUs/FactSheets/Display/tabid 224/Article/104488/air-force-safety-center.aspx. Last accessed 19 December 2015.

Ballentine Papers. http://memory.loc.gov/service/mss/eadxmlmss/eadpdfmss/1997/ms997013.pdf. Last accessed 12 December 2015.

"Flight Surgeon Requirements and Training." *Naval Medicine Operational Training Center.* http://www.med.navy.mil/sites/nmotc/nami/academics/Pages/FlightSurgeon.aspx. Last accessed June 2013.

History of GCA in the Navy. www.gca-atc.org/USN. Last accessed 2 August 2015.

National Center for Simulation. www.simulationinformation.com. Last accessed 21 August 2015.

Naval Air Warfare Training Systems Division. www.navair.navy.mil/nawctsd/. Last accessed 7 August 2015.

Naval Aviation HumanFactors Program. www.public.navy.mil/NAVSAFCEN/Pages/aviation/aeromedical/Human FactorsHFACS.aspx. Last accessed 10 August 2015.

Naval Safety Center. http://www.public.navy.mil/navsafecen. Last accessed 20 June 2016.

Naval Safety Center School of Aviation Safety. http://www.public.navy.mil/comnavsafecen/Pages/aviation/SAS/index.aspx. Last accessed 10 December 2015.

Index

accidents: AF Guardian squadron crashes, 13; Banshee crash, 2–4; Billingsley accident, 5; Capodichino Airport accident (Italy), 22, 164n8; Composite Squadron 4, 24–25; Cutlass squadron crashes, 13; deck crash, 3; Douglas A-4 Skyhawk, 159; F-14 Tomcats, 131; Fleet Aircraft Support Squadron 77, 9; Liftmaster accidents, 28, 43, 159; mountain crashes, 12, 51; San Francisco Bay crash, 12; shore-based accidents, 22; T2B mishaps, 110; TBM Avengers, 22, 153; transport accidents, 4, 23, 28, 43, 49–52, 155. *See also* investigations, accident

ACNO (Air Warfare), 162, 177n9

aerial refueling, 30–31, *31*, 154, 155, 157, 166n5; hydraulic reel system, 166n5

aerospace medicine, 70–83; Aviation Medical Acceleration Laboratory (AMAL), 154, 155; Bureau of Medicine and Surgery, 47; contributions of, 89, 112; importance of, 54, 69; influence of, 18; Naval Air Medical Center, 157; Naval School of Aviation Medicine, Pensacola, 154, 157. *See also* flight surgeons

Air Board, 79, 126, 132, 154, 171n11

Air Development Center, vendor cooperation, 15, 155

Air Force, Guardian squadron crashes, 13

Air Force, US: Air Force Chief of Safety, 169n7; Air Force Inspection and Safety Center, 169n7; Air Force Test Pilot School, US, 17; challenges to, 15; influence of, 19; mishap rates, 11, 15f.3.1, 17, 25, 49; post-WWII, 8; vendor cooperation, 15

air traffic control, 16, 24, 157

Air Traffic Control Centers, 24, 41, 158

aircraft advancements, 26; aircraft design, 44–45; effects of, 18; engine and systems design, 15, 24; instrumentation, 16, 26; navigation systems, 16, 26–27; and night flight, 21; and nuclear delivery, 18, 20; post-WWII progress in, 15. *See also* jet transition

aircrew: and aerospace medicine, 70, 72–77, 82–83; confidence, 28; and human error, 84, 90; and maintenance error, 91, 101; morale, 113; postwar deaths, 20, 21, 49; proficiency of, 23; rotation of, 63; and simulator time, 113, 120; training of, 13, 44, 54, 62, 106, 112. *See also* Aircrew Coordination Training (ACT); Crew Resource Management (CRM); ORM process model

Aircrew Coordination Training (ACT), 18f.3.3, 126. *See also* Crew Resource Management (CRM)

AirLant (Air Forces Atlantic), Commander, 11, 37, 46, 47, 154, 162, 168n3(Ch.8), 171n11

195

AirPac (Air Forces Pacific), Commander, 11, 46, 47, 60, 154, 155, 168n3(Ch.8), 171n11
all-weather flight: *All Weather Flight Manual*, 65; All Weather Flight School, 25; F3D Skyknights, 29; FAWTUPAC/FAWTU-LANT, 25, 166nn11,12; and GCA adoption, 27–28; increase of, 18; and instrumentation, 26, 27; and jet transition, 44; and mishap rates, 21, 35; and modifications, 42, 76; training for, 20, 60. *See also* weather conditions, bad
angled decks: on *Antietam*, 155, 167n5; conversions to, 18, 86, 155, 156, 157, 159, 167n6; and jet transition, 38, 134; and landing patterns, 151; and landing safety, 33–36, 35t.6.1, 44–45; and mirror landing systems, 157; and mishap rates, 18f.3.3, 69, 112, 134; proposals for, 154; SCB Alterations, 149; trials of, 155
anonymous reports, 7, 13, 110
Antietam, 34, 41, 155, 157, 158, 167nn5,6
antisubmarine aircraft carriers (CVSs), 37, 167n6
antisubmarine warfare (ASW) aircraft, 9, 20; helicopter use in, 22, *22*; and Lockheed P2V Neptune, 105; and mishap rates, 13; and simulations, 120, 176n22; and Soviet threat, 21, 44
Anymouse concept, 54, 108, 110, 169n17; cartoons, 6, 7, 153, 155; periodic summary, 147
Approach (periodical), 147, 153, 165n1; and Anymouse, 7; first edition, 156; forerunners of, 6, 46, 153; importance of, 53; NATOPS summary, 67;

shared lessons in, 85; T2B mishaps, 110
approaches: and angled deck, 34, 151; and angle-of-attack indicators, 31–32; automatic approach, 41; carrier approach, 151–52; ground-controlled approach (GCA), 17, 153; jet penetration, 27; and jet transition, 24, 27–29; low angle approach, 37–38; and mirror use, 38–39; and radar, 17
arresting gear: angled decks and, 35, 154; bolter landing, 34, 179; conversions and, 155, 167n6; conversions to, 29; and mishaps, 30, 31, 152
Atlantic Fleet: carrier-based ASW, 21; and FAGU, 156; and innovations, 165n5(Ch.4); and NATOPS, 66; night flights, 165n5(Ch.4); and RAG (FRS) Concept, 63; and Soviet threat, 21. *See also* AirLant (Air Forces Atlantic)
Austin, Frank, 79–80, *80*, 157, 171n13
automatic direction finder (ADF), 26–27, *26*
aviation industry, 107–8
aviation safety boards, 6, 46, 153. *See also* Naval Aviation Safety Activity; Naval Aviation Safety Center

beacons, nondirectional and marker, 26–27
blind flying, 26, 117
Bohn, Roger, 5, 6
bombers, 8, 18, 20, 49, 65
budgetary issues: 1950s, 8, 9, 20; and commonality in design, 107; funding, 10, 98–100, 121; and Grinstead, 95; and military procurement, 111; and mishap rates, 47; and NAMP, 96; and simulators, 113

Bureau of Aeronautics (BuAer), 63, 79, 85–87; and automatic landings, 41; on catapult malfunctions, 37; cooperation, 15; and First Air Board, 154; and flight surgeons, 110; and maintenance systems, 92–94; merger of, 158; modifications, 173n3; and Naval Aviation Safety Activity, 52–53; publications of, 6, 7, 46, 78, 153; safety efforts, 46–48; staff responsibilities of, 10; vendor cooperation, 15

bureaus: Bureau of Aviation Safety, 164n4; Bureau of Medicine and Surgery, 47, 48; Bureau of Naval Personnel (BuPers), 11, 13, 43, 63; Bureau of Naval Weapons (BuWeps), 96, 158; Bureau of Supplies and Accounts (BuSandA), 92, 173n3. *See also* Bureau of Aeronautics (BuAer)

carrier-controlled approach (CCA), 17, 27–28, 179

carriers: carrier launches, *22*; carrier mishaps, 1–4, 25, 35t.6.1; changes and modifications, 33–42, 166n6; escort carriers (CVEs), 8; *Essex*-class carriers, 166n6; HU-a carrier launch, *22*; Korean War, 9; light carriers (CVLs), 8. *See also* carriers nuclear delivery capability, 9, 18; post-WWII reductions, 8; squadron aircraft loss, 21

cartoons, safety program, 6–8, 47, 153, 155, 162

catapults: electromagnetic, 36, 167n12; and jet transition, 29; and mishaps, 36–37; mishaps associated with, 81; slotted-cylinder, 153

civil aviation: Civil Aeronautics Administration, 26; cooperation, 15; navigation systems, 16; pre-WWII, 16

clouds, flying through, 16; accidents, 12; and instrumentation, 26–27; and pilot error, 51; pilots opinion of, 23–24; self-cleared penetration, 182; *Sense* series, 6, 8

commanding officers (COs): board screening of, 13, 43, 86; *Cockpit Crossfeed*, 147; and culture workshops, 132; leadership of, 47–49, 63, 134; and maintenance systems, 91; and night flight, 24; and Safety Survey, 56; and SOPs, 65; and standardization, 11–12

commercial aviation: aviation industry and, 107, 108; challenges to, 15; and CRM, 126; human factors, 80–81, 89; improvements in, 25; influence of, 19, 45; innovations, 16; instrumentation developments, 16; and jet transition, 30; mishap rates, 16, 16f.3.2, 25, 133; regulations, 164n1; and simulators, 114, 120, 176n28; TACAN, 182

commonality: in design, 107; in improvements, 16, 16f.3.2; and maintenance systems, 96; in mishap rates, 15–16, 15f.3.1, 16f.3.2

comparisons: to 1950s, 44, 57; to Air Force, 61; in aircraft maintenance, 93; of aviation sectors, xi; carrier mishap comparison, 35t.6.1; ORM/traditional approach, 130, 130t.15.2; and RPOW study, 81, 82

Congress, US, 17, 111, 164n4

cooperation: across sectors, 15–16, 45; with flight surgeons, 110; international, 16; and NATOPS, 68

Crew Resource Management (CRM): and Anymouse program, 169n17; CRM skills, 127t.15.1; implementation of, 131; and mishap rates, 18f.3.3; and safety efforts, 14, 132, 134; term usage, 176n1; use of, 125–28. *See also* Operational Risk Management (ORM)

cruise boxes, 12, 44, 92–93

Culture Workshops, 14, 57, 101, 124, 131–32, 134

Davis, William V., Jr., 61, 164n14

demobilization, 8, 10, 20

Deputy Chief of Naval Operations, Air (DCNO), 11, 153, 154, 171n11, 173n11

Douglas aircraft: A-3 Skywarrior, 36, 37, 58; A-4 Skyhawk, 30, 60, 66, 86, 139, 159, 166n3; AD Skyraider, 58, 59, 86, 105–6; F3D Skyknights, 29, 41, 105, 158, 166n2, 174n13

ejection seats, 4, 32, 75–76, *76*, 106, 158

elevators, 106, 115, 149, 155

engine design, 13, 15, 18, 29, 44, 104–7, 109, 149

FAA Part 121, 16f.3.2, 164n1

Fairchild R4Q Flying Boxcar, 4, 23, *23*, 43, 49, 155. *See also* Flatley Report

Flatley, James H., 50, 60. *See also* Flatley Report

Flatley Report, 23, 49–53, 156, 169n9

Fleet Air Gunnery Unit (FAGU), 60, 155

Fleet Air Support Squadrons (FASRONs), 59, 92–94, 158, 173n2, 180

Fleet All Weather Training Unit Atlantic (FAWTU-LANT), 25, 166n12

Fleet All Weather Training Unit Pacific (FAWTUPAC), 25, 166n11

Flight Replacement Squadron (FRS), and RAG (FRS) Concept, 170n16

Flight Safety Bulletins, Number One, 153

Flight Safety Council, establishment of, 153

Flight Safety Foundation, 17

Flight Safety Section, establishment of, 153

flight surgeons: and air-craft designers, 89; Austin, Frank, 80; aviators' attitude towards, 71–72, 73; and BuAer, 110; career patterns, 70–71; contributions of, 14, 81, 82–83; Flight Safety Branch, 47–48; flight surgeon wings, *83*; Flight Surgeon's Newsletter (periodical), 147; and human error, 78; and investigations, 5, 6, 14, 71; and mishap rates, 77, 165n5(Ch.4); Mitchell, Robert, 82; and personal equipment, 76–77; and personnel health, 77–78; physical exams, flight, *72*; and pilot training, 76; responsibilities of, 72–73; training of, 71, 73; WWII, 48

Florez, Luis de, 116–17, *116*, 175nn15, 16

Foss, Joe, *82*

Franklin D. Roosevelt, 157

Fresnel Lens Optical Landing System (FLOS), 34, 180, 181. *See also* mirror landing systems

Gerald Ford, 167n12

Goben, Howard, 173n11

Graybiel, Ashton, *75*

Grinstead, Eugene, *95*

ground-controlled approach (GCA), 17, 27–28, 154

Grumman aircraft: F9F Panthers, 12, 29, 36, 59, 105, 106, 154, 155, 174n13; F-14 Tomcats, 19, 98, 131; TBM Avengers, 22, 58, 105, 106, 153, 163n8
guidance systems: airborne guidance, 174n12; and CNO, 171; glide-slope guidance, 38; HFACS, 173; LSO guidance, 39; and OSD, 111
gyro compass/scopes, 25, 26, 167n13, 182, 183

Hamilton, Leo, 173n11
helicopters, 9, 19, 22, 35, 43, 44, 62, 67, 98, 105–6, 107, 122, 162
Holl, Trgve A., 6, 153
homing devices, 27, 28, 166n13, 183
Human Error Research and Analysis Program (HERAP), 172n14; description of, 79; and design process, 110; establishment of, 87; and mishap analysis, 101
human factors: and Austin, 79–80, 171n13; beyond pilot error, 79; discovery of, 84–91; and flight surgeons, 14; personnel factors, 10, 11–12, 172n2; Reason, James, 80, 87, 172n15. *See also* pilot error

improvements: commonality in, 16, 16f.3.2; and Naval Safety Center, 46–57; in navigation, 27
indicators: airspeed indicators, 114; angle-of-attack indicator, *32*; angle-of-attack indicators, 31–32, *32*; electrical attitude indicator, 16, 26; Ground Position Indicator, 27; horizontal situation indicator, 16; rate-of-climb indicators, 26; turn-and-bank indicators, 114, 115, 181, 183; vertical gyro attitude indicators, 26; vertical speed indicators, 24, 182
innovations: AN/ASN-6 Ground Position Indicator, 27; distance-measuring equipment (DME), 16; and flight safety, 30; and mishap rates, 22, 44, 165n5(Ch.4); Reduced Oxygen Breathing Device, 171n8; TACAN navigation aid, 27, 28. *See also* aerial refueling; instrumentation; navigation systems
instrument flight, 24–25; Instrument Flight Standardization Board, 25, 154; landing systems, 16; pilot proficiency, 154
instrumentation: advancements, 16; cockpit instruments, 24; commercial aviation, 16; development of, 5, 26; instrument ratings, 25; magnetic compasses, 25, 26; pitot-static system, 25, 182; post-WWII progress in, 15; turn needle/needle ball, 24–25, 181. *See also* indicators; navigation systems
investigations, accident, 5; Air Commerce Act of 1926, 164n4; investigators, 13, *52*; Naval Aviation Safety Center, 53–54; Safety Survey, 56

jet transition, 15, 20, 24, 29–32; carrier-suitable, 9; instrumentation, 24, 26; problems of, 21; and Reserves, 22
Johnson, Louis, 8, 177n10
Jordan, crisis response, 21, 177n3 (Ch. 16)

Korean War, 154, 177n1; close air support, *10*, *11*, 20; crisis response, 21; demands of, 21; effects of, 24; "first generation" jet aircraft, 29,

174n13; onset of, 9; and pilot training rate, 22

Lake Champlain, 166n6
land-based naval aviation, 25, 26
landing patterns: carrier-controlled approach (CCA), 27–28; flat pattern, 151–52, 166nn5,6; straight-deck, 151–52, 151f.A6.1
leadership: Chief Naval Officer (CNO), 10, 154, 171n11; Commander, Naval Air Forces (CNAF), 127, 132, 177n9, 179; ComNavAirLant/ComNavAirPac, 154, 168n3(Ch.8), 171n11; and culture workshops, 132; and design problems, 86; effects of, 12, 18; executive leadership philosophy, 10–11, 49; favoritism, 11–12; improvements in, 18; and information flow, 52; and jet transition, 65; and maintenance systems, 91–92; and mishap rates, 4, 6, 9, 19, 45, 51, 68, 78; and ORM/CRM adoption, 126, 128; participatory, 125; and pilot proficiency, 25; and politics, 15, 43; professionalism of, 12; squadrons, 59, 63; and success, 133–34; and training, 58
learning curve, 112, 119
legislation: Air Commerce Act of 1926, 164n4; Defense Reorganization Acts, 158, 161
Link Trainers, 25, 114, 115, *115*, 117, 176n18, 181
Lockheed P2V Neptune, 20, *21*, 43, 105–7
low-frequency navigation range, 24, 26–28, 27, 117, 181
LSO, *2*, 32

maintenance and supply, 91–102; Aviation Maintenance and Management Office, 173n11; Aviation Maintenance Duty Officers, 173n11; effects of, 18; first generation jet aircraft, 19; Korean War, 9; local repair, 167n10; maintenance errors, 91, 101, 173n5; Naval Aviation Maintenance Program, 18f.3.3; pre-1950s, 12; and problem forecasting, 172n17; problem forecasting, 172n17
maintenance officers, and quality assurance, 14
major mishaps rates, 103f.13.1, 141–43, 166n8, 168n6
Marine Corps: Commandant of, 171n11; marine aviation, 139; mishap rates, 11, 15f.3.1; post-WWII, 8; use of helicopters, 22
McDonnell aircraft: F2H Phantoms, *1*; F2H-2 Banshees, 1–4, *2–4*, 29–30, 36–37, 105–6, 155, 174nn12,13; F-4 Phantoms, 30, 58, 139; FH-1 Phantoms, 19, 36, 58, 104–5
McDonnell Douglas, F/A-18 Hornet, 4, 30, 99
media, 17, 48, 52–57, 101; aviation safety magazine, 153; aviation-oriented safety center publications, 147; *Crossfeed* (periodical), 147; *Emergency Airborne Escape Summary* (periodical), 147; *Flight Deck Awareness* (periodical), 147; Flight Surgeon's Newsletter (periodical), 147; *Foundation* (journal), 168n1(Ch.8), 171n1; handbooks, 164n14; *Hook* (journal), 24; *Mech* (periodical), 85, 147; Media and Statistics Divisions, 56, 101; *Naval Aviation News* (periodical), 7, 28, 168n2(Ch.8), 168n5; posters, 8;

Sense series, 6; *Sense* series pamphlets, 6, 8; training movies, 8; *U.S. Navy/Marine Corps Aircraft Accident Statistical Summary* (periodical), 147; *Weekly Summary* (periodical), 56, 147
Midway, 154, 155
Miller, Jerry, 173n11
Minas Gerais (Brazil), 166n3
mirror landing systems: and angled-deck carriers, 167; *Antietam*'s lack of, 167nn5,6; on *Bennington*, 156–57; and Fresnel Lens, 41, 180; introduction of, 33, 34, 37–40, 157; and jet transition, 32; and mishap rates, 69; phasing in of, 44; use of, 39, 154, 155. *See also* Fresnel Lens Optical Landing System (FLOS)
mishap investigation: and maintenance errors, 173n5; pre-1950s, 12; pre-WWII, 5
mishap rates, 4, 167n10; in 1950s, xi, 4, 166n8; Air Force, 15f.3.1; annual major mishaps, 141–43, 166n8; FAA Part 121, 16f.3.2; mishap curves, 15f.3.1, 16–18, 16f.3.2, 18f.3.3, 25, 30; Naval aviation Class A, 18f.3.3; Navy, 15f.3.1, 141–43, 166n8; Navy/Marine, 10; post-WWII, 8, 21; pre-WWI, 5; rate calculations, 168n6; and weather, 5; WWI, 5; WWII, 6
Mitchell, Robert, 82, *82*
Moffett, William, 164n3

NASA (National Aeronautics and Space Administration), 54, 80, 81, 164n3
National Advisory Committee on Aeronautics (NACA), 17, 164n3
National Transportation Safety Board (NTSB), 17, 164n4

Naval Air Medical Center, 157
Naval Air Stations: Barber's Point, 166n11; Key West, 166n12; Miramar, 61, 158, 166n11; Moffett Field, 165n5(Ch.4), 166n11, 166n12; Oceana, 166n12; Pensacola, 154; Quonset Point, 153
Naval Air Training and Operating Procedures Standardization (NATOPS), 18f.3.3, 46, 54, 58, 64–69, 87, 91, 94, 112, 119, 120, 122, 128, 134, 139, 159, 170n12; standardization, 13
Naval Air Training Command, 4; Chief of, 171n11; instrument flying requirements, 24; mishap rates, 22; night flight requirements, 24; training standardization, 60
Naval Aircraft Factory, Philadelphia, 6, 153
naval aviation: capability of, xi; defined, 163n1(preface); flight hour accural, 18; improvements in, 19; policy, 171n11
Naval Aviation Safety Activity: authority of, 48; establishment of, 8, 23, 155; Flatley Report, 23, 49–53, 156, 169n9; Medical Safety Division, 78
Naval Aviation Safety Center, 7, 18f.3.3, 44, 46, 53, 54, 57, 79, 87, 156, 159, 164n16, 168n1(Ch.8); Commander, 170n19; and HERAP, 172n14
Naval Aviation Safety Program, 155
Naval Safety Center, Chapter 8 note 21, 17, 18f.3.3, 168n1(Ch.8); as catalyst for improvement, 46–57; effects of, 18; establishment of, 164n16; motorcycle mishaps, 4, 101; motto, 170n21; Naval Submarine Safety Center, 164n16

navigation systems: air-driven artificial horizon, 26; compasses, 25–26, 114; gyro horizon, 24; horizontal situation indicator, 16; inertial navigation systems, 26, 27; and jet transition, 24; Lear remote-reference pictorial vertical gyro attitude indicator, 26; long-range, 17; post-WWII, 21; ultra high-frequency (UHF) radio, 26; VOR (VHF omni-directional radio range), 16, 183. *See also* instrumentation

night flights: Atlantic Fleet, 21, 165n5(Ch.4); and helicopters, 9; and instrumentation, 5, 16; night mishaps, 1–4, 5; overcoming common problems in, 16; Pacific Fleet, 165n5(Ch.4); pilot attitude towards, 25; pilots' aversion to, 23–24; post-WWII, 21; proficiency in, 25; training requirements, 24; WWII, 20

North American aircraft: AJ Savage, 20, 30–31, *31*, 105–6, 155; FJ-1 Fury, 104–5

nuclear delivery capability, 9, 20, 25, 174n11

Operational Risk Management (ORM), 14, 125–32; and Anymouse program, 169n17; comparisons to, 130t.15.2; Johnson on, 177n10; ORM process model, 18f.3.3, 131f.15.1; training curriculum, 177n7

OPNAV Instructions, 155, 169n14

O'Rourke, Jerry, 24, 34–35

Pacific Fleet, 21, 60, 63, 66, 165n5(Ch.4)

patterns, straight-deck landing pattern, 151–52

Perseus, 154, 155

Persian Gulf wars, xi, 177n1

Peters, M. A., 155

Philippine Sea, 27

pilot error: Flatley Report, 23, 49–53, 156, 169n9; as mishap cause, 12–14, 78–79, 84–86, 89, 91, 101, 132. *See also* human factors

pilots: and Air Board, 171n11; exchange programs, 17; FARs grading system, 171n7; Group I aviators, 25, 47, 154, 168n4(Ch.8), 180; Group II/III aviators, 168n4(Ch.8); instrument qualification of, 9; Korean War, 9; NCLT pilot view, *118*; pilot training rate, 21, 22; post-WWII reductions, 8; prerequisites, 171n6; training of, 20, 21, 22, 164n14. *See also* pilot error; schools

Pirie, Robert B., 67

Poppin, J. R., 154

propeller patrol planes (P2Vs), 20, 21, *21*

radar: commercial aviation, 16–17; and landing patterns, 151; and maintenance mishaps, 92; and mishap avoidance, 17, 27–28; and night fighter trainers, 117; RATTC at Miramar, 158; and stable element system, 182; in TBM Avengers, 106

radios: limitations of, 24–25; radio altimeters, 25, 26; UHF radios, 26; VHF radios, 26; VOR (VHF omni-directional radio range), 16, 183

RAG (FRS) Concept, 18f.3.3, 58–69, 170n16

Rausa, Rosario, 13, 174n1

Reason, James, 80, 87, 172n15

reconnaissance attack aircraft, 20, 62, 98

reports: accident reporting classifications, 145–46; anonymous, 13; mishap damage, 167n10; pre-WWII, 5
reservists, 9, 21, 22; Naval Reserves, Chief of, 171n11

schools: Air Force Test Pilot School, US, 17; All Weather Flight School, 25; aviation safety schools, 13, 18; flight instruction schools, 6, 171n7; naval aviation safety schools, 13; Naval School of Aviation Medicine, Pensacola, 154, 157; Navy Test Pilot School, 17
search and rescue, 22, 25
self-cleared penetration, 24, 25, 165n4(Ch.4), 182
Shappell, Scott, 80, 88, 126, 172n16
Ships Characteristic Board (SCB) alterations, 34, 35, 149, 154, 157, 159, 167nn5,6, 182
shore-based operations, 19, 22, 164n16
simulations/simulators, 113–24; and commerical pilots, 176n28; Link Trainers, 6, 25, 114, 115, 117, 181; Schank on, 176n22
Soviet Union: challenges of, 174n; submarine fleet, 20, 21, 24; threats from, 18, 20, 21, 24, 177n3 (Ch. 16)
spare parts, 12, 44, 59, 92–93, 98–100
squadrons: AF Guardian squadron crashes, 13; CASUs (Carrier Aircraft Support Units), 173n2; Composite Squadron 4 (VC-4), 24, 25, 165n5(Ch.4); Cutlass squadron crashes, 13; Fleet All Weather Training Unit Atlantic (FAW-TU-LANT), 25; Fleet All Weather Training Unit Pacific (FAW-TUPAC), 25; patrol squadrons mishaps, 4; squadron safety officers, 12; Squadron Safety Program, 18f.3.3; VA-44 squadron, 166n12; VCN-1/VCN-2 squadrons, 25, 166n12; VF-21 squadron, 166n12
stable element system, 41, 182
standardization: and Air Force, 11, 68; and FAGU, 60, 156; of flight operations, 12; of flight schools. *See also* Naval Air Training and Operating Procedures Standardization (NATOPS)and innovations, 85; Instrument Flight Standardization Board, 154; lack of, 59, 104; and maintenance systems, 94, 98; NATOPS, 13; and RAG (FRS) Concept, 64; in Training Command, 64–65
statistics: and problem forecasting, 172n17; yearly major mishaps, 141–43
steam catapult: *Antietam*'s lack of, 166nn5,6; British development of, 33, 153, 154, 155; British sea trials of, 154; on *Hancock*, 156; and jet transition, 18; reliability of, 45; USN adoption of, 34, 36–37, 149, 155
strike-fighters, 139, 178chron9/30
Suez crisis response, 21, 177n3 (Ch. 16)
Supply Systems Command, 14, 173n3
Swiss-cheese model, 80, 87–88, 88f.11.1, 90, 174n17, 182
synthetic trainers, 114–15, 117

Tactical Air Navigation (TACAN), 27–28, 154, 182
training: aircrew, 54; and aviation medicine, 54; and aviation safety boards, 6; Aviation Safety Officer's Course, 169n14; and commerical pilots, 176n28; development of, 20, 24; FAGU, 60; and FAWTUP/

FAWTU-LANT, 25; first generation jet aircraft, 19; improvements, 45; instrument training, 47, 59, 62; and jet transition, 20, 22, 24; Korean War, 10; and leadership philosophy, 10, 13; Level Readiness, 58; maintenance and supply, 54, 59, 62; mandatory, 25; and mishap rates, 5, 19, 51; movies for, 8; NAS Miramar, 61; NATOPS, 46, 58; Naval Air Training Command, 4, 22, 24, 46, 46–47, 58, 60; proficiency/readiness distinction, 176n21; RAG (FRS) Concept, 46, 58, 61–64; replacement training squadrons, 13, 58–59, 61; and safety, 12; and Soviet threat, 44; squadron training, 60; standardization, 64

transports mishaps, 4, 22, 23, 28, 43, 49, 155

Triumph (Britain), 9, 154, 155

United States, 8, 33, 36, 154

Valley Forge, 9, 154, 163n5
Vietnam War, 19, 82, 139, 177n1
visibility, poor, 16, 17, 25, 27–28

visual conditions air-control systems, 27–28
visual flight rules (VFR), 8, 24, 51, 64, 129, 164n8
Vought F7U Cutlasses: air-refueling, *31*; first flown, 104; launching on a steam cat, *38*; and mishap rates, 13, 29–31, 174n4; and NATOPS, 66; and steam catapult, 156; training with, 60

weapons delivery, 4, 9, 18, 20, 105, 121, 174n2
weather conditions, bad, 165n1; challenges of, 15; and in-flight refueling, 30; forecasting improvements, 6; and GCA adoption, 27–28; and helicopters, 9, 22; and mishap rates, 5, 18; pilot attitude towards, 25; self-cleared penetration, 182; and Soviet threat, 21; WWII, 20. *See also* all-weather flight; clouds, flying through
wheelbook system, 12, 13–14, 92–93, 183
Wiegmann, Douglas, 80, 88, 126, 172n16

About the Author

Vice Adm. Robert F. Dunn, USN (Ret.), was a naval aviator who commanded a jet squadron in combat, the aircraft carrier USS *Saratoga*, and the Naval Safety Center. His last Navy assignment was as Deputy Chief of Naval Operations for Air Warfare. In retirement he served as deputy chairman of the NASA Aerospace Advisory Panel and chairman of a GSA Blue Ribbon Panel to examine non-DOD government aircraft safety.

The **Naval Institute Press** is the book-publishing arm of the U.S. Naval Institute, a private, nonprofit, membership society for sea service professionals and others who share an interest in naval and maritime affairs. Established in 1873 at the U.S. Naval Academy in Annapolis, Maryland, where its offices remain today, the Naval Institute has members worldwide.

Members of the Naval Institute support the education programs of the society and receive the influential monthly magazine *Proceedings* or the colorful bimonthly magazine *Naval History* and discounts on fine nautical prints and on ship and aircraft photos. They also have access to the transcripts of the Institute's Oral History Program and get discounted admission to any of the Institute-sponsored seminars offered around the country.

The Naval Institute's book-publishing program, begun in 1898 with basic guides to naval practices, has broadened its scope to include books of more general interest. Now the Naval Institute Press publishes about seventy titles each year, ranging from how-to books on boating and navigation to battle histories, biographies, ship and aircraft guides, and novels. Institute members receive significant discounts on the Press' more than eight hundred books in print.

Full-time students are eligible for special half-price membership rates. Life memberships are also available.

For more information about Naval Institute Press books that are currently available, visit www.usni.org/press/books. To learn about joining the U.S. Naval Institute, please write to:

> Member Services
> **U.S. Naval Institute**
> 291 Wood Road
> Annapolis, MD 21402-5034
> Telephone: (800) 233-8764
> Fax: (410) 571-1703
> Web address: www.usni.org

www.ingramcontent.com/pod-product-compliance
Ingram Content Group UK Ltd.
Pitfield, Milton Keynes, MK11 3LW, UK
UKHW041918140426
5217IPUK00013B/214